New Directions
in Mission
and Evangelization 3

New Directions in Mission and Evangelization
Edited by
James A. Scherer
Stephen B. Bevans, S.V.D.

New Directions in Mission and Evangelization is an Orbis Series that offers collections of important articles and papers, all previously published but not easily available to students and scholars of mission. Selections included in each volume represent examples of mission theology and theological reflection that deal creatively with issues affecting the church's mission and the postmodern world.

Volumes in the series will appear periodically and will include Roman Catholic, Orthodox, Conciliar Protestant, Evangelical, Pentecostal, and other points of view. Each volume focuses on a theme such as
- Theological Foundations of Mission
- Contextualization of Theology
- Mission Spirituality
- Theology of Religion and Dialogue between Persons of Living Faiths
- Ecology and Mission
- Social Justice and Mission

NEW DIRECTIONS IN MISSION AND EVANGELIZATION 3

Faith and Culture

Edited by
James A. Scherer
Stephen B. Bevans

ORBIS BOOKS

Maryknoll, New York 10545

The Catholic Foreign Mission Society of America (Maryknoll) recruits and trains people for overseas missionary service. Through Orbis Books, Maryknoll aims to foster the international dialogue that is essential to mission. The books published, however, reflect the opinions of their authors and are not meant to represent the official position of the society. To obtain more information about Maryknoll and Orbis Books, please visit our website at www.maryknoll.org.

Copyright © 1999 by James A. Scherer and Stephen B. Bevans.
Published by Orbis Books, Maryknoll, New York, U.S.A.
All rights reserved. No part of this publication may be reproduced or transmitted in any form or by any means, electronic or mechanical, including photocopying, recording, or any information storage or retrieval system, without prior permission in writing from Orbis Books, P.O. Box 308, Maryknoll, NY 10545-0308, U.S.A.
Manufactured in the United States of America.

Cataloging-in-Publication Data is available from the Library of Congress, Washington, D.C.

ISBN 1-57075-258-3

*To
Louis J. Luzbetak, S.V.D.
On his eightieth birthday, 19 September 1998,
in gratitude for his pioneering work
in understanding the relationship of
Gospel and Culture.*

Contents

A Word on Style ... ix

Acknowledgments ... x

Introduction: Faith and Culture in Perspective ... 1
James A. Scherer and Stephen B. Bevans

Part I
Perspectives on Inculturation

1. The Gospel as Prisoner and Liberator of Culture ... 17
   Andrew F. Walls

2. The Incarnation of the Gospel in Cultures: A Missionary Event ... 29
   Aram I

3. Contextualization: The Theory, the Gap, the Challenge ... 42
   Darrell L. Whiteman

4. Inculturation: Win or Lose the Future? ... 54
   Aylward Shorter

5. Inculturation of Faith or Identification with Culture? ... 68
   Robert J. Schreiter

6. Hearing and Talking: Oral Hermeneutics of Asian Women ... 76
   Kwok Pui-lan

7. Theses on Inculturation ... 91
   Theological Advisory Commission of the Federation of Asian Bishops' Conferences

8. Cultural Barriers to the Understanding of the Church and Its Public Role ... 104
   Robert N. Bellah

9. Doing Theology as Inculturation in the Asian Context ... 117
   José M. de Mesa

10. Called to One Hope: The Gospel in Diverse Cultures 134
    Musimbi R. A. Kanyoro

11. Translatability and the Cultural Incarnations of the Faith 146
    Kwame Bediako

12. Evangelization and Inculturation: Concepts, Options, Perspectives 159
    Paulo Suess

Part II
Documentation

13. Nairobi Statement on Worship and Culture 177
    Lutheran World Federation
        Introduction by S. Anita Stauffer 177
        The Statement 180

14. On Intercultural Hermeneutics 185
    World Council of Churches

15. Report from the Ecumenical Conference on World Mission
    and Evangelization, Salvador de Bahia, Brazil 196
    World Council of Churches

Index 235

A Word on Style

The articles and papers that make up *New Directions 3* come from a variety of sources. Together they say a great deal about the plurality of voices and points of view that comprise World Christianity. They also testify to the immense variety of usages of English worldwide. While we have corrected typographical errors and actual "mistakes" that we have found in materials selected for this volume, we have made no attempt to standardize such things as reference styles, spelling, and punctuation. While this will no doubt annoy purists, it has the advantage of retaining the linguistic and stylistic varieties of the original sources.

Acknowledgments

The editors and Orbis Books gratefully acknowledge the holders of copyright and original publishers of the materials in this volume for permission to reprint the articles contained in *New Directions 3*. Persons wishing permission to reproduce any of these materials should apply to the original publisher for this permission, not to Orbis Books.

Introduction

Faith and Culture in Perspective

James A. Scherer and Stephen B. Bevans

Since about 1970, two sets of missiological issues have surpassed others in the attention they have received from theologians, church leaders, and missiologists. These are: (1) the relationship between the gospel and other living faiths, and (2) the relationship between the gospel and culture/cultures. Noted cultural anthropologist Louis Luzbetak, S.V.D., speaks of the relationship between faith and local cultures as "the burning missiological issue of our times" (Luzbetak 1993: 43). The essays in Volume 3 of *New Directions in Mission and Evangelization* deal with aspects of the relationship between Christian faith (or the gospel) and culture in general, or between the faith/gospel and particular local cultures. "Gospel and culture/s" and "faith and culture/s" are here used almost without distinction, even though the emphasis in the first lies on the *message* of proclamation, while in the second it lies on the faithful *response* of the believing community. Although we distinguish between "inter-cultural" and "inter-religious" relations, it is well to recognize that the two cannot be neatly separated, since "religion is the soul of culture" (Tillich).

Why the special concern with faith and culture (or gospel and culture) at this time? What accounts for the multiplication of books, articles and reports on the subject? After all, it can easily be shown that contact and conflict between revealed religion as we know it in the Bible, and the indigenous customs, cultures and religions of various peoples we encounter in the Scriptures, belongs to the warp and woof of the history of the Chosen People. In the Jewish scriptures, the People of the Covenant are commanded to "have no other gods" before Yahweh, to remove idolatrous cults and offensive pagan practices, and generally to keep themselves separate from heathen abominations. Only in the eschatological prophecies of the later post-exilic prophets is there a hint that the gifts and cultures of gentile nations can be redeemed and made acceptable to God and find their place in a restored messianic kingdom (a "new Jerusalem"). On the whole, condemnation of existing customs and cultures is the norm in the Hebrew scriptures.

The New Testament, particularly the book of Acts, presents us with a picture of a nascent Christian church made up exclusively of Jewish believers in Christ along with some gentile proselyte converts who have conformed to requirements of the Jewish Law. At first, there is no break between these earliest Christians and the Jewish community in Jerusalem. Christians worship in the temple, keep the sabbath, and observe the ordinances of the Law. Then suddenly, as a result of Peter's "conversion" (Acts 10), the launching of Paul's mission to the gentiles from the Antioch church (Acts 13), and the holding of the first "apostolic council" (Acts 15), a totally new situation emerges for the church. The first essay in this volume, by Andrew F. Walls, engagingly recreates this transition from an exclusively Jewish to a mainly gentile church. Of course, the four gospels and the Pauline and pastoral epistles were all written at a time when the original Jewish church had virtually disappeared and a newer gentile Christianity was already the dominant reality. These documents picture Jesus as a messianic figure friendly toward the gentiles, affirmative toward their faith and liberated from the narrow religious and cultural exclusivism of his Jewish contemporaries. Jesus models the inclusive cultural attitudes which were to shape the church in the Hellenistic era.

With the hindsight of nearly twenty centuries of church and mission history we now know that the "apostolic council" (Acts 15) marked the first, but only the first, of many cultural transitions and border crossings of the gospel into new cultural territory. With the intensification of Bible translation and distribution efforts in the past three centuries, the Bible has been translated into thousands of vernacular languages and dialects of the human race. Drawing on the preexisting religious vocabulary of unevangelized peoples in new scripture translations, evangelists have preached the gospel in the vernacular tongues of all nations, tribes and ethnic groups. People have made their professions of faith in Christ in words of their own language. The gospel has proved to be infinitely "translatable," and the church as a local community of faith and worship has been endlessly replicated in local cultures and social structures. Enroute to becoming a universal community, the church has experienced the power of the gospel to set itself free from both Jewish and western cultures, and so to unite with the cultures and customs of all people.

What is different about the contemporary understanding of faith and culture? Our thesis is that recognition of *cultural pluralism* as a theological expression of God's good creation is the decisive new element shaping our ecumenical perspective on gospel or faith and culture. With it has come a far profounder understanding of the meaning and function of culture in human society. Cultural pluralism does not mean that a plurality of cultures did not exist from the beginning of creation. On the contrary, an incredibly rich variety of cultures and languages has existed from the beginning. But in missiological terms, culture was not—with few exceptions—taken seriously, valued, or reflected upon as part of the process of gospel transmission. Up to the recent past, the cultural transition of the gospel simply "happened," most often linked to colonial penetration of third world societies by western commerce, conquest and education. In the religious as in other spheres, existing structures were simply displaced or forced to "accommodate" to the superior culture of the west. Terms like "indigenization" and "adaptation" were used by earlier missiologists to describe the manner in which western missions adapted the gospel and the life of the church to local cultures and societies, or conversely, those societies adapted their customs and cultures to imported religious values and norms from the west. At its best, this approach—in both Catholic and Protestant forms—amounted to little more than *faithful translation* of western creeds, cultures and customs into the languages, symbols, and religious practices of the people being evangelized. What was lacking was any kind of serious concern for the input of receptor cultures into the process.

From the standpoint of western mission groups in the colonial period, the notion of a God-given cultural pluralism, in which each existing local culture reflected in some way the *imago Dei*, simply did not exist. In various national and confessional forms—Catholic, Protestant, Orthodox, Evangelical, Spanish, Portuguese, British, Continental, American—the missionary gospel came as part of a monolithic western cultural package embedded in one of the competing forms of western civilization, and seldom apart from this total package. Today's missiology likes to lift up Mateo Ricci's, Roberto de Nobili's, or Alexandre de Rhodes' unique Jesuit experiments in inculturation as exemplary, or to recall Count Zinzendorf's enlightened warning to early Moravian missionaries not to export the customs and confessional labels of Christendom to the mission field. In actual fact, however, western mission practice until well into the twentieth century was marked by a prevailing ignorance of, and a general indifference to, the role of receptor cultures in the transmission of the gospel. Even so exalted a figure as Francis Xavier, S.J., seems never to have given much thought to the role of receptor cultures until he encountered the stubborn and resistant religious culture of Japan. It was only after his Japan mission experiences that Xavier began to develop some notion of inculturation.

A typical expression of western cultural exclusivism is found in the instructions given by early American Puritan divines to the first missionaries to work among Native Americans. They were advised to "make them English in their language, civilized in their habits, and Christian in their religion" (Scherer 1964: 32, cited from Rufus Anderson). Missionaries of the Protestant American Board (ABCFM) sent to the Hawaiian Islands were encouraged to replicate New England culture and "to aim at nothing short of covering those islands with fruitful fields and pleasant dwellings and schools and churches, and raising the whole people to an elevated state of Christian civilization" (Scherer 1964: 32). Whether in Asia, Africa, Latin America or Oceania, "culture" in the European sense was considered not to exist outside the West, apart from certain ancient civilizations. Evangelization was viewed as the dual task of christianizing and civilizing, the gospel being bracketed with western culture. Ironically, while the first century "apostolic council" set the gospel and the gentile mission free from Jewish legalism, colonialism enslaved these once again by making them culturally subservient to western culture. Historically, this cultural captivity of the gospel to eurocentric culture corresponded to the high water mark of western imperialism, the period of unchallenged belief in the superiority of western civilization and religion.

The gradual liberation of western mission from its own bondage to a monolithic, anti-pluralist cultural viewpoint came about through revolutionary changes which shook the foundations of western life in the twentieth century. Two horrifying world wars undermined western assumptions about the superiority and validity of western civilization. Decolonization in the third world and the collapse of western colonial empires touched off movements for cultural authenticity in newly independent nations, including numerous declarations of independence from subservience to European cultures. Many formerly important mission fields were suddenly for political reasons closed to missionaries from the west, the largest of these being China. Previously quiescent world religions—above all Hinduism, Buddhism and Islam—suddenly assumed missionary vigor and carried their claims to the west. Meanwhile, atheistic communism made vast inroads into the former Christian heartlands of Eastern Europe, while churches in the west suffered from secularization, attrition, membership loss and declining missionary commitment. Yet the myth of western cultural superiority persisted generally without challenge.

Few Christians in the west seemed aware that the demographic balance of Christian population had already shifted southward to the newly evangelized lands of the third world. Western Christianity would in time become a minority religious tradition. Meanwhile, such academic disciplines as history of religions and cultural anthropology were bringing their critical perspectives to bear on Christian relations with other faiths and cultures. With the invasion of eastern religions and cults into urban centers, rural monasteries and college campuses, and the genesis of new religious movements, religious pluralism was quickly becoming an everyday phenomenon. Cultural pluralism also became an established fact with the migration of peoples, especially from Latin America and Southeast Asia, to larger metropolitan centers in North America, some of them refugees seeking freedom from persecution, others in search of job opportunities. Churches in the west were tested by formidable new challenges. Overseas mission agencies, grieving over lost mission fields and troubled by proposals for a moratorium on mission sending, felt the loss of a sense of clear direction about the future. Many sought to devise new strategies for changing times.

Fortunately, several new developments brought healing and a sense of renewal to beleaguered western mission bodies. The first was the gradual emergence of local (national, or indigenous) churches in third world lands, in large part due to the earlier faithful efforts of western missionaries. This network of emerging young churches on all six continents constituted, in Anglican Archbishop William Temple's phrase, "the great new fact of our time." These new local churches and their progress toward selfhood and autonomy were a presupposition for the second development: the rise of the *ecumenical movement* in its various forms (Protestant, Catholic, Orthodox, and Evangelical), and the formation of regional church councils (e.g., AACC, CCA) and bishops' councils (FABC, CELAM) in major regions and continents. The ecumenical movement as expressed in the International Missionary Council (1921), the World Council of Churches (1948), the Second Vatican Council (1962-65), periodic conferences of the WCC's Commission on World Mission and Evangelism (CWME) and regional conferences of Catholic bishops in Latin America, Asia, and Africa became an important catalyst which helped to rescue western missions from isolation and stagnation. Global and regional ecumenical networks fostered cross-cultural dialogue on changing issues of mission and evangelization. Independent organizations of third world theologians such as EATWOT (1976) played an important role, as did professional missiological associations such as the International Association of Mission Studies (IAMS, 1970), the American Society of Missiology (ASM, 1973) and journals such as the *International Bulletin of Mission Studies* (OMSC), *Missiology* (ASM) and *Mission Studies* (IAMS). The newer grass-roots theologies of Latin America, Asia and Africa all gave prominence to local cultures.

Significantly, the two newest and now preferred terms for defining the proper faith (or gospel) and culture relationship both came into use in the 1970's out of the third world (rather than western) context. These are *contextualization* (1971) and *inculturation* (1974) (see article by Darrell Whiteman in this volume). A third widely used term, *incarnation*, is considered to be synonymous with the other two (Luzbetak 1993: 49, footnote, and the essay by Paulo Suess in this volume). The decade of the 70s, with the coining of new missiological language and the holding of several key missiological conferences focused on the faith and culture issue, marks a definitive turning point. From that time we observe the abandonment of the older monolithic thesis of western cultural dominance and its replacement by a newer thesis of cultural and religious pluralism.

"Inculturation," as defined by a Catholic cultural anthropologist, is "the expression of one's faith through one's own culture . . . The goal of every community of disciples is none other than to make the mind and heart of Christ their own and that of the world . . . This goal must be achieved without compromise or manipulation but with the zeal and courage of a prophet and at no small price. Inculturation means that faith must somehow become an integral part of the cultural community's cognitional, emotional and motivational way of life. Christ must become an integral and fully functioning part of the local culture and hopefully, its very heart and center" (Luzbetak 1993: 44-45). "Contextualization," as defined by a Protestant evangelical mission faculty, is "the dynamic reflection carried out by the particular church upon its own life in light of the Word of God and historic Christian truth. Guided by the Holy Spirit, the church continually challenges, incorporates and transforms elements of the cultural milieu, bringing these under the Lordship of Christ. As members of the Body of Christ interpret the Word, using their own thoughts and employing their own cultural gifts, they are better able to understand the gospel as incarnation" (Gilliland 1989:12-13).

Human culture is now understood as an essential characteristic of human existence. It can be helpfully analyzed with reference to its diverse parts, and it is capable of an endless variety of combinations and possibilities. Moreover, the culture of receptor communities in evangelization now assumes a decisive importance. Use of biased terms such as "high" or "primitive" to describe a particular culture reflects a value orientation on the part of the observer that should normally be avoided. Culture is a system that gives meaning to life in all its dimensions, that is learned and realized in a particular social group. All cultures are subject to continuous change, rapid or slow; therefore every culture must be understood from a dynamic perspective. Moreover, all cultures are in some sense in contact, conflict, and exchange with other cultures, either in a positive or negative sense. Today it can be said that all cultures find themselves in a "more or less marked crisis situation," encountering a global culture shaped by world commerce, technology and the information age (Nunnemacher 1997: 94-95). The fact that all cultures are in a state of change and crisis quite obviously also applies to western culture.

In order to achieve a deeper level of contextualization or inculturation, missiology must recognize the important role of three fundamental aspects of culture: (1) the *nature* of culture (culture as a symbolic system of knowledge, attitudes and goals); (2) the *structure* of culture (how components of a particular culture are organized into an integrated whole); and (3) the *dynamics* of culture (how cultures operate, and how and why they change). Inculturation takes place in all three areas and presupposes a knowledge and appreciation of the context, i.e., the culture and society, in such a way that faith becomes incarnated through the culture (Luzbetak 1993: 44-45). Inculturation is essentially the gracious work of the Holy Spirit, but the community of Christ's disciples are its principal human agents. Inculturation is meant for all churches, east or west, old or young. Nevertheless, local churches need more than local symbols; they must also retain the symbols of the universal church to retain their identity as both local and universal. As the document on "worship and culture" in this volume points out, Christian faith is "contextual" but also "transcultural." "Unity in diversity" remains the goal, and thus local churches must remain in communion with the church universal. The goal is the penetration of the gospel message into the local community's culture in such a way that the message becomes one with the culture. It goes without saying that inculturation must penetrate below the surface level of a culture to its deeper level of meanings, motives and emotions (Luzbetak 1993: 46-48).

Catholic missiological statements beginning with the Second Vatican Council reflect an increasingly high view of human culture, and generally point toward the goal of inculturation. In the Pastoral Constitution on "The Church in the Modern World" (1965) we read that "the human person . . . can achieve true and full humanity only by means of culture" (GS 53; see Flannery 1975). "There are many links between the message of salvation and culture. In his self-revelation to his people culminating in the fullness of manifestation in his incarnate Son, God spoke according to the culture proper to each age" (GS 58). Similarly, the "Decree on the Church's Missionary Activity" (1965), speaking of the missionary activity carried out through the preaching of the gospel and the celebration of the sacraments, observes that "whatever goodness is found in the minds and hearts of men, or in the particular cultures and customs of peoples, far from being lost is purified, is raised to a higher level and reaches its perfection for the glory of God, the confusion of the demon and the happiness of men" (AG 9).

This newer approach to faith and culture comes to climactic expression in Pope Paul VI's Apostolic Exhortation, *Evangelii Nuntiandi* (1975). Speaking of the method of evangelization in the modern world, Paul VI says: "What matters is to evangelize man's culture and cultures (not in a purely decorative way as it were by applying a thin veneer, but in a vital way, in depth and to their very roots) . . . The Gospel, and therefore evangelization, are certainly not identical with culture, and they are independent in regard to all cultures. Nevertheless, the Kingdom which the Gospel proclaims is lived by men who are profoundly linked to a culture, and the building up of the Kingdom cannot avoid borrowing the elements of human culture or cultures" (EN 29). In *Redemptoris Missio*, Pope John Paul II's Encyclical Letter on the "Permanent Validity of the Church's Missionary Mandate" (1991), the pope unhesitatingly endorses the process of inculturation as the normal and expected method of missionary activity. "As she carries out missionary activity among the nations, the Church encounters different cultures and becomes involved in the process of inculturation. The need for such involvement has marked the Church's pilgrimage throughout her history, but today it is particularly urgent. The process of the Church's insertion into peoples' cultures is a lengthy one. It is not a matter of purely external adaptation, for inculturation 'means the intimate transformation of authentic cultural values through their integration in Christianity and the insertion of Christianity in the various human cultures.' The process is thus a profound and all-embracing one which involves the Christian message and also the Church's reflection and practice. But at the same time it is a difficult process, for it must in no way compromise the distinctiveness and integrity of Christian faith. Through inculturation the Church makes the Gospel incarnate in various cultures and at the same time introduces peoples, together with their cultures, into her own community" (RM 52; Burrows 1993: 33-34). The pope is aware of the blessing which comes to the universal church through the inculturation process. "Thanks to this action within the local churches, the universal Church herself is enriched with forms of expression and values in the various sectors of Christian life, such as evangelization, worship, theology and charitable works. She comes to know and express better the mystery of Christ, all the while being motivated to continual renewal" (RM 52). Expatriate missionaries have a special obligation to immerse themselves in local cultures and languages (RM 53). Other important Catholic statements are found in the 1987 statement of the International Theological Commission, "Faith and Inculturation," and the 1991 joint statement of the Pontifical Council for Interreligious Dialogue and the Congregation for the Evangelization of Peoples, "Dialogue and Proclamation" (Scherer-Bevans 1992: 154-61, 177-200).

In evangelical missionary circles, a major re-evaluation of the place of culture in mission was also taking place, led by contributions of missionary anthropologists, Bible translators, and communications specialists. The publication *Practical Anthropology*, later incorporated into the ASM publication *Missiology*, played a leading role in this change. In the earlier Word-oriented tradition of Protestant evangelicalism, especially in its Reformed variety, culture had been viewed as more of an obstacle than an aid to evangelism. Dutch missiologist Hendrik Kraemer had argued that a "discontinuity" existed between the revealed Word of God and human cultures and religions, ruling out any real evangelistic point of contact. This negative attitude toward culture, still widely held as late as the 1939 Tambaram CWME Conference, now began to give way to a more positive, though still ambiguous, view of culture. A modified reinterpretation of the traditional viewpoint was put forward at the 1974 Lausanne International Congress on World Evangelization. The *Lausanne Covenant* called for the development of imaginative new strategies for world evangelization. "Under God, the result will be the rise of churches deeply rooted in Christ and closely related to their culture. Culture must always be tested and judged by Scripture (Mk. 7: 8, 9, 13). Because men and women are God's creatures (Gen. 4: 21, 22), some of their culture is rich in beauty and goodness. Because they are fallen, all of it is tainted with sin and some of it is demonic. The gospel does not presuppose the superiority of any culture to another, but evaluates all cultures according to its own criteria of truth and righteousness, and insists on moral absolutes in every culture (I Cor. 9: 19-23). Missions have all too frequently exported with the gospel an alien culture and churches have sometimes been in bondage to culture rather than to Scripture . . . churches must seek to transform and enrich culture, all for the glory of God" (LC 10; Scherer-Bevans 1992: 257). In 1978 the Lausanne Committee convened a special "Consultation on Gospel and Culture" (Willowbank, 1978) which declared: "In the process of church formation, as in the communication and reception of the gospel, the question of culture is vital. If the gospel must be contextualized, so must the church. Indeed, the sub-title of our consultation has been 'the contextualization of Word and Church in a missionary situation'" (Scherer-Bevans 1992: 263). Willowbank deplored the unimaginative export of western models of church structure, worship, administration, and architecture to the mission field. Using a contextual methodology, the Lausanne Committee convened an international Consultation on World Evangelization (Pattaya, 1980) which surveyed in detail fifteen distinct sub-cultures as fields for evangelization (Scherer-Bevans 1992: 274-75). When the faculty of the School of World Mission at Fuller Seminary in Pasadena, California published a group of analytical studies written from the perspective of "contextual theology as incarnational mission" (Gilliland 1989), it appeared to mark the ascendancy of a biblically based understanding of contextualization as the new norm for evangelical missions. It should not be assumed, however, that all evangelical missionaries were in agreement on the subject.

In conciliar ecumenical circles, reflecting major Protestant denominations and many Orthodox churches, intense engagement with the gospel and culture relationship begins with the Bangkok CWME Conference (1973) and continues through the Salvador de Bahia CWME Conference (1996) (see Scherer 1995: 225-29). Bangkok, giving powerful voice to indignant feelings of third world church leaders, declared that cultural identify was "a matter of life and death," involving the relationship of Christ as bringer of salvation with the person or group receiving it. It deplored white racism as a betrayal of the gospel and condemned missionary alienation. The report of Bangkok Section I stated: "The problem of personal identity is closely related to the problem of cultural identity. 'Culture shapes the human voice that answers the voice of Christ.' Many Christians who have received the gospel through western agents ask the question: 'Is it really I who answer Christ? Is it not another person instead of me?' This points to the problem of so-called missionary alienation. Too often, in the history of western missions, the culture of those who received the gospel was either ignored or condemned . . . How can we responsibly answer the voice of Christ instead of copying foreign models of conversion— imposed, not truly accepted? We refuse to be raw materials used by other people to achieve their own salvation. The one faith must be at home in every context and yet it can never be completely identical with it." "Christ has to be responded to in a particular context." At Bangkok, the word "contextual" entered the ecumenical vocabulary. "Proper theology is a reflection on the experience of the Christian community in a particular place, at a particular time. Thus it will necessarily be a contextual theology; it will be a relevant and living theology which refuses to be easily universalized because it speaks to and out of a particular situation" (for the above quotes, see WCC-CWME 1973; cf. IRM, April 1973, pp. 188-90).

The following WCC Assembly (Nairobi, 1975) went beyond Bangkok in adding a fresh new note to the discussion of contextuality. It maintained that the cultural context can disclose something *new* and *original* about the confession of Jesus Christ in particular confessional contexts. "In our sharing with one another we have discovered that the Christ who meets us in our own cultural contexts is revealed to us in a new way as we confess him . . . We affirm the necessity of confessing Christ as specifically as possible with regard to our cultural settings . . . we can say that Jesus Christ does not make copies; he makes originals. We have found this confession of Christ out of our various cultural contexts to be not only a mutually inspiring, but also a mutually corrective change. We need each other to regain the lost dimensions of confessing Christ and even to discover dimensions unknown to us before. Sharing in this way we are all changed and our cultures are transformed" (WCC 1976: 22-23).

The Melbourne CWME meeting (1980), while concentrating on "good news to the poor," repeated the recommendation of Bangkok 1973 urging local churches to formulate their own responses to God's calling by creating liturgies and forms of outreach and community rooted in their own cultures. Conceding the risk of syncretism, Melbourne encouraged churches to seek liberation from imprisonment in inherited forms and structures. "Too many churches are still imprisoned by forms and structures inherited from other countries and are thus not free to establish such signs of the kingdom of God as to make use of their own cultural context . . . The churches must live with the tensions between the Gospel and their local cultures. There is the risk of syncretism for all churches in relation to their own context, but that must not prevent the churches from struggling with the necessity of relating the local cultures to the Kingdom of God" (WCC-CWME 1980: 182-83).

The next WCC Assembly at Vancouver (1983), seemingly dissatisfied with the result of the discussion, demanded a fundamental rethinking of the faith-culture relationship. It hoped to gain a deeper understanding of the meaning and function of culture and cultural plurality; a better understanding of ways in which the gospel has interacted with cultures; and a clearer realization of the problems caused by "ignoring or denigrating the receptor cultures during the missionary era" (WCC 1983: 32). Reflecting on the complex relationships between the gospel and receptor cultures in past cultural transitions—sometimes accepting them while at other times transforming or partly rejecting them—Vancouver observed that "not all aspects of every culture are necessarily good"; there are aspects which "deny life and oppress people" and even demonic forms which project life-denying world views. Tying together the missionary agenda with a parallel faith and order concern, Vancouver called for a deeper theological understanding of culture as part of a "new ecumenical agenda": "The Gospel message becomes a transforming power within the life of a community when it is expressed in the cultural forms in which the community understands it. Therefore, in the search for a theological understanding of culture we are working toward a new ecumenical agenda in which various cultural expressions of the Christian faith may be in conversation with each other" (WCC 1991: 32-33; Scherer-Bevans 1992: 54-55). The WCC also called for a reassessment of the "new global culture" based on modernization and technology, and the role of secular and religious ideologies, etc. This new ecumenical agenda, which would demand a careful balance between cultural diversity and the christological center and trinitarian source of that diversity, became the starting point for planning the most recent CWME Conference (Salvador, 1996), "Called to One Hope: The Gospel in Diverse Cultures."

The CWME San Antonio Conference (WCC-CWME 1989) made passing reference to the transformation of cultures and drew attention to instances where the majority culture had been used to oppress minority peoples. But it did not deal with the previously mentioned Vancouver ecumenical agenda calling for the development of a theological understanding of culture, and initiating a conversation between churches on the subject. Meanwhile, the WCC Canberra Assembly (WCC 1991) kept the Vancouver agenda alive by placing it in the context of "a reconciled and renewed creation as the goal of the church's mission." Canberra said: "The gospel of Jesus Christ must become incarnate in every culture. When Christianity enters any culture, there is a mutual encounter, involving both the critique of culture and the possibility of the culture questioning our understanding of the gospel. Some of the ways in which the gospel has been imposed on particular cultures call for repentance and healing. In each case we need to ask: Is the church creating tension or promoting reconciliation?" (WCC 1991: 272). Indeed, the gospel-culture issue as it developed in the Canberra assembly proceedings, later erupting in a heated discussion, nearly produced a rupture of fellowship within the WCC when several protesting Eastern Orthodox Churches threatened to suspend their membership in the WCC. Some church delegates at Canberra were scandalized by a multimedia presentation, making use of song and dance, which invoked the spirit of Korean ancestors as an illustration of the Holy Spirit's work. The final report of Canberra Sec. IV included a statement that "the Holy Spirit cannot be understood apart from the life of the Holy Trinity" and called for a "careful discernment of spirits in dealing with the often profound spirituality of other religions" (WCC 1991: 273, 275). Canberra will be remembered for underscoring the potential dangers to Christian unity of cultural diversity, and pointing to the ecumenical urgency of renewing the search for [theological] unity in [cultural] diversity.

The Salvador de Bahia Conference (24 November–3 December 1996) on "Called to One Hope: The Gospel in Diverse Cultures" (WCC-CWME 1998: 2-17) was the eleventh in the series of CWME conferences on mission and evangelism beginning with Edinburgh 1910, and probably the last such major conference that will be held in the twentieth century. Nearly 500 participants from 98 nations and WCC member churches in all major regions of the world (including 29 Roman Catholic observers) came to the Brazilian city. It was the earliest colonial capital of the Portuguese empire in the Americas, and a major entry point for the forced importation of slaves from West Africa. With its unique concentration of Afro-Brazilian culture and diverse spiritualities, Salvador was a challenging venue for the engagement with gospel and culture issues. Many participants had already taken part in a four-year faith and cultures study process resulting in sixty local reports. Lively contextual worship, Bible studies based on passages from the first seventeen chapters of Acts, and a "rainbow" festival of cultural symbols and encounters provided a spiritual undergirding for the conference. Plenary addresses explored the main theme, and panel discussions treated evangelism and Bible reading in cross-cultural contexts. The main work of the conference was carried out in four sections dealing with specific aspects of the theme. A concluding section called "Acts of Commitment," with reminders of follow-up tasks, sought to extend the impact of Salvador into the post-conference period. In words from the conference prayer, the entire event was planned so that "through it God's people may be strengthened in their cultural identity, renewed in their Christian life and equipped for authentic witness in each context" and led to "discern and celebrate the wondrous variety of expression of the Christian faith and the unity that binds them together" (WCC-CWME 1998: 17).

The scope of issues dealt with in the four sections was broad, complex and all-encompassing. The section reports succeeded in maintaining a delicate balance between viewpoints, sometimes simply articulating crucial issues but leaving them unresolved. A few emerging issues of the late twentieth century were tackled, e.g. the impact of global culture on local cultures. In the Conference Message, the conference sought to recall delegates from over-concentration on details and diverse challenges, and possible loss of the "big picture," by reminding them of the dominant theme, *Called to One Hope—The Gospel in Diverse Cultures.* "The gospel to be most fruitful needs to be both true to itself, and incarnated or rooted in the culture of a people. . . . the church must hold on to two realities: its distinctiveness from, and its commitment to, the culture in which it is set . . . the gospel becomes neither captive to a culture nor alienated from it, but each challenges and illuminates the other" (WCC-CWME 1998: 21-22, 24). Section I, "Authentic Witness Within Each Culture," explored the theological understanding of culture; examined religion, culture and gospel in scriptural perspective; and carefully considered the dynamic interaction between gospel and culture. It concluded with criteria for authentic witness to eschatological hope in Jesus Christ. Section II, "Gospel and Identity in Community," touched on the "crushed identities" of marginal and oppressed peoples, and indigenous populations; it called for the empowerment of youth and women and spoke of the devastating consequences of ethnicity, identity politics, and national pride for uprooted peoples. This section included an incisive critique of the destructive effects of globalization and of the global market economy on local communities, noting the growing gap between rich and poor, the dominance of western information technology, and environmental degradation. Section III, "Local Congregations in Pluralist Societies," concerned itself with ways of inculturating faith in the church's worship life and local symbols, how the church might become a sign of God's inclusive love in a world of racial, ethnic, and language divisions and learning to witness in religiously plural societies, including the practice of dialogue. Section IV, "One Gospel—Diverse Expressions," called for an authentic understanding of the gospel as both "contextual" and "catholic"; it urged the cross-cultural sharing of diverse expressions of the one gospel and examined "syncretism" in relation to authentic gospel witness. This section also restated principles of missionary partnership, touching on responsible relationships, mission in unity, common witness, and the avoidance of proselytism. "We actively seek a new era of 'mission in Christ's way' at the dawn of the third millennium, enriched by one another's gifts and bound together in the Holy Spirit, to the glory of the triune God" (WCC-CWME 1998: 29-75).

The question of faith/gospel and cultures has certainly been one of the most significant questions for missiology over the last three decades. Salvador de Bahia showed that we have come a long way in our reflection, but it also raised a number of new issues and revealed that Christians are still in disagreement on a number of points. Among the points on which there appears to be growing consensus are these. Culture is now recognized as an indispensable component in evangelization and in the life of each local church. God's word reaches people through culture, and the human response to God's word is through culture. Proclamation, worship, personal discipleship, and Christian community life are all unthinkable apart from local culture. We now agree that the uninformed and heedless equation of the gospel with eurocentric culture in the period of colonial missions was a serious aberration. Missiology condemns attitudes and practices which were commonplace during the Vasco da Gama and Columbian eras. Contextualization, or inculturation, is recognized as the proper way of implanting the church in an unevangelized area. Salvador de Bahia emphasizes that the church must hold on to two realities: its *distinctiveness from*, and its *commitment to*, the culture in which it is set. The gospel must be neither *captive* to the local culture nor *alienated* from it. This implies a tension between gospel and culture and calls for a self-critical and prophetic stance on the part of the local Christian community. This is true for all churches, not least for churches in the west, which are in danger of falling prey to cultural captivity. Indeed, re-evangelization in the west depends to a large degree on the ability of western churches to cut the Gordian knot between the gospel, or Christian faith, and western civilization. Finally, the horrendous practices of identity politics and ethnic genocide, tragically misguided abuses of gospel and culture in our time, have been soundly condemned.

Nonetheless, much remains to be done before a truly satisfactory relationship between gospel, or faith, and culture, allowing for "authentic witness within each culture," can be said to exist. Much progress has been made in the *theory* of inculturation, yet the gap between theory and *practice* looms large. We lack adequate scientific evidence on how the understanding of the gospel and the practice of Christian faith are transformed by receptor cultures. But we must now encourage local Christian congregations, as they discern the Holy Spirit and allow the life of Christ and the words of Scripture to indwell them, to learn to contextualize the gospel in their own worship, religious symbols, behavior and thought patterns, and community life. In keeping with the Conference Message—"both true to itself, and incarnated or rooted in the culture of a people," and "distinctive from, yet committed to the culture"—the church must continue its task of evangelization, to the ends of the earth and the end of time. Just here arises the ecumenical urgency of sharing many diverse expressions of the one gospel cross-culturally among local churches, old and young, north and south. For only so can the church universal maintain the tension between "contextual" and "catholic," upholding unity in diversity. Salvador de Bahia promoted this process, but it must proceed much further both within and between continents and regions, and across the divides of north and south, rich and poor. In our six-continent mission era, where mission takes place "from everywhere to everywhere," the priority task for Faith and Order has now changed from one of comparing doctrinal differences between western confessions to one of facilitating global dialogue between churches about how to maintain oneness in Christ amid cultural diversity. Closely related to this is the challenge of transforming each local embodiment of the Body of Christ into a universal sign of peace and reconciliation in a world fractured by racial, ethnic and religious divisions. Scarcely less important is the ecumenical Life and Work responsibility of dealing with the devastating effects of globalization, especially as caused by the world market economy and western media influence, on religious values and local cultures everywhere. Some already observable offshoots of the globalization process are the intensification of third world poverty, the degradation of the human environment, and the provoking of violent fundamentalist religious reactions. These endanger the churches' ability to witness to "one hope" in Jesus Christ. They will remain as important unfinished tasks for the third millennium. Yet the ultimate goal remains to inculturate the gospel everywhere by overcoming obstacles to "authentic witness [to Christ] in each culture," so as to prepare for the eschatological entry of Christ into all the world's societies and cultures. That is also the hope shared by the editors in preparing this volume and in selecting the essays and reports which follow.

REFERENCES CITED

WORLD COUNCIL OF CHURCHES (WCC) ASSEMBLIES

Gill, David, ed.
- 1983 "VI Assembly World Council of Church, July-August 1983" *Gathered for Life*. Geneva: WCC; Grand Rapids: Eerdmans.
- 1991 "WCC Canberra Report," *Ecumenical Review* April.

Paton, David M., ed.
- 1976 "The Official Report of the World Council of Churches, Nairobi, Nov.-Dec. 1975," *Breaking Barriers: Nairobi 1975*. London: SPCK; Grand Rapids: Eerdmans.

WORLD COUNCIL OF CHURCHES COMMISSION ON WORLD MISSION AND EVANGELISM (WCC-CWME) CONFERENCES

- 1973 "Bangkok Report," *International Review of Mission* April.

Duraisingh, Christopher, ed.
- 1998 "Salvador, Brazil, Nov.-Dec. 1996," *Called to One Hope: The Gospel in Diverse Cultures*. Geneva: WCC.

Wilson, Frederick R., ed.
- 1990 "Your Will Be Done: Mission in Christ's Way, May 1989," *The San Antonio Report*. Geneva: WCC.
- 1980 "Report on the World Conference on Mission and Evangelism, Melbourne, Australia, May 1980," *Your Kingdom Come: Mission Perspectives*. Geneva: WCC.

OTHER REFERENCES

Burrows, William R., ed.
- 1993 *Redemption and Dialogue: Reading Redemptoris Missio and Dialogue and Proclamation*. Maryknoll, NY: Orbis Books.

Flannery, Austin P., ed.
- 1975 *Documents of Vatican II*. Grand Rapids: Eerdmans.

Gilliland, Dean S., ed.
1989 *The World Among Us: Contextualizing Theology for Mission Today*. Dallas: Word Publishing.

Luzbetak, Louis J., S.V.D.
1993 "'Inculturation': A Call for Greater Precision," in *Verbi Praecones: Festschrift fuer P. Karl Mueller, SVD: zum 75 Geburtstag,* eds. K. Piskaty and H. Rzepowski. Nettetal: Steyler Verlag, 43-50.

Nunnenmacher, Eugen, S.V.D.
1997 "Culture," in *Dictionary Of Mission: Theology, History, Perspectives*, eds. Mueller, Sundermeier, Bevans, and Bliese. Maryknoll, New York: Orbis Books, 94-98.

Scherer, James A.
1964 *Missionary, Go Home!* Englewood Cliffs: Prentice-Hall.
1995 "Salvador, Bahia 1996: What Will It Mean?," *International Review of Mission* July: 223–35.

Scherer, James A. and Stephen B. Bevans, S.V.D., eds.
1992 *New Directions in Mission and Evangelization 1: Basic Statements, 1974-1991*. Maryknoll, New York: Orbis Books.

Part I

PERSPECTIVES ON INCULTURATION

1

The Gospel as Prisoner and Liberator of Culture

*Andrew F. Walls**

Christian history, says Andrew F. Walls, contains within it two dynamics that work together both dialectically and complementarily. The first is the "indigenizing" principle, by which Christianity takes into itself the values and world views of particular cultures and historical situations. The second is the "pilgrim" principle, by which Christianity calls for personal and societal transformation. While the former makes Christian faith "a place to feel at home" for people of every time and place, the latter whispers that there is no abiding city, and warns that faithfulness to Christ is ultimately to be out of step with society. While Third World Theologies will certainly differ from Western theology—and even be disturbing at times for Western Christians—their validity will nonetheless be based on their rootedness in the Bible, and in the Christian tradition of prophetic challenge to cultural and historical bias and blindness. As First and Third World Christians read the scriptures and wrestle with tradition together, new possibilities will emerge for both mutual enrichment and critique.

IS THERE A "HISTORIC CHRISTIAN FAITH?"

Let us imagine a long-living, scholarly space visitor—a Professor of Comparative Inter-Planetary Religions perhaps—who is able to get periodic space-grants which enable him to visit Earth for field study every few centuries. Let us further assume that he wishes to pursue the study of the earth-religion Christianity on

---

* Taken from Chapter 1 of *The Missionary Movement in Christian History* (Maryknoll, NY: Orbis Books, 1996). First published in *Faith and Thought*, 108, 1 & 2 (1982); a slightly revised form appeared in *Missionalia*, 10, 3 (1982). Andrew F. Walls is a former missionary to Sierra Leone and Professor Emeritus of the Study of Christianity in the Non-Western World at the University of Edinburgh, Scotland.

principles of Baconian induction, observing the practices, habits, and concerns of a representative sample of Christians, and that he exploits the advantage he has over any earthbound scholar by taking his sample across the centuries.

Let us assume his first visit to be to a group of the original Jerusalem Christians, about 37 CE. He notes that they are all Jews; indeed, they are meeting in the Temple, where only Jews can enter. They offer animal sacrifices. They keep the seventh day punctiliously free from work. They circumcise their male children. They carefully follow a succession of rituals, and delight in the reading of old law books. They appear, in fact, to be one of several "denominations" of Judaism. What distinguishes them from the others is simply that they identify the figures of Messiah, Son of Man, and Suffering Servant (figures all described in those law books) with the recent prophet-teacher Jesus of Nazareth, whom they believe to have inaugurated the last days. They live normal family lives, with a penchant for large, close families; and they have a tightly knit social organization, with many common meals taken in each other's houses. Law and joyful observance strike our spaceman observer as key notes of the religion of these early Christians.

His next visit to Earth is made about 325 CE. He attends a great meeting of Church leaders—perhaps even the Council of Nicea. The company come from all over the Mediterranean world and beyond it, but hardly one of them is Jewish; indeed on the whole they are rather hostile to Jews. They are horrified at the thought of animal sacrifices; when they talk about offering sacrifices they mean bread and wine used rather as it was in the house meals our observer noticed in Jerusalem. They do not have children themselves, since Church leaders are not expected to marry, and indeed most of them regard marriage as an inferior, morally compromised state; but they would regard a parent who circumcised his children as having betrayed his faith. They treat the seventh day as an ordinary working day: they have special religious observances on the first day, but do not necessarily abstain from work or other activities. They use the law books that the Jerusalem Christians used, in translation, and thus know the titles Messiah, Son of Man, and Suffering Servant; but "Messiah" has now become almost the surname of Jesus, and the other titles are hardly used at all. They give equal value to another set of writings, not even composed when the Jerusalem Christians met, and tend to use other titles, "Son of God," "Lord," to designate Jesus.

Their present preoccupation, however, is with the application of another set of words to Jesus—words not to be found in either set of writings. The debate (and they believe it of absolutely fundamental importance) is over whether the Son is *homo-ousios* with the Father, or only *homoi-ousios* with Him.

The dominant factors which the outsider notices as characteristic of these Christians are the concern with metaphysics and theology, an intense intellectual scrutiny, an attempt to find precise significance for precise terms. He thinks of the Jewish Christians in the Temple nearly three centuries back, and wonders.

The best cure for his wonderment is the still greater wonder of a journey to Ireland some three centuries later still.

A number of monks are gathered on a rocky coastline. Several are standing in ice-cold water up to their necks, reciting the psalms. Some are standing immobile, praying—with their arms outstretched in the form of a cross. One is receiving six strokes of the lash because he did not answer "Amen" when the grace was said at the last meal of brown bread and dulse. Others are going off in a small boat in doubtful weather with a box of beautiful manuscripts and not much else to distribute themselves on islands in the Firth of Clyde, calling the astonished inhabitants to give up their worship of nature divinities and seek for joy in a future heavenly kingdom. Others are sitting quite alone in dark caves by the seashore, seeking no intercourse with men.

He ascertains from these curious beings that their beautiful manuscripts include versions of the same holy writings that the Greek fathers used. He notices that the Irish use the same formula that he heard being hammered out in Nicea in 325 CE; somewhat to his surprise, because they do not in general seem very interested in theology or very good at metaphysics. They attach great importance to the date on which they celebrate their main festival, Easter; an outsider is most likely to notice their desire for holiness and their heroic austerity in quest of it.

Our spaceman delays his next visit until the 1840s, when he comes to London and finds in Exeter Hall a large and visibly excited assembly hearing speeches about the desirability of promoting Christianity, commerce, and civilization in Africa. They are proposing that missionaries armed with Bibles and cotton seeds be sent a distance of four thousand miles to effect the process. They are also proposing a deputation to the British Government about the necessity of putting down the slave trade, raising a subscription to promote the education of Black mechanics, agreeing that letters be written, pamphlets and articles published. The meeting has begun with a reading from the same book (in English translation) that the other Christians used, and there have been many other quotations from the book; indeed, a large number of people in the meeting seem to be carrying it. On enquiry, the observer finds that most also accept without question the creed of Nicea. Like the Irish, they also use the world "holy" quite a lot; but they are aghast at the suggestion that holiness could be connected with standing in cold water, and utterly opposed to the idea of spending life praying in an isolated cave. Whereas the Irish monks were seeking to live on as little as possible, most of this group look remarkably well fed. What impresses the outsider is their activism and the involvement of their religion in all processes of life and society.

In 1980 he comes to Earth again, this time to Lagos, Nigeria. A white-robed group is dancing and chanting through the streets on their way to their church. They are informing the world at large that they are Cherubim and Seraphim; they are inviting people to come and experience the power of God in their services. They claim that God has messages for particular individuals and that his power can be demonstrated in healing. They carry and quote from the same book as the Exeter Hall gentlemen. They say (on being shown the document in a prayer book) that they accept the creed of Nicea, but they display little interest in it: they appear somewhat vague about the relationship of the Divine Son and the Holy Spirit. They are not politically active and the way of life pursued by the Exeter Hall gentlemen is quite foreign to them; they fast like the Irish, but only on fixed occasions and for fixed purposes. The characteristic which springs most readily to the spaceman's mind is their concern with power, as revealed in preaching, healing, and personal vision.

Back in his planetary home, how does our scholar correlate the phenomena he has observed? It is not simply that these five groups of humans, all claiming to be Christians, appear to be concerned about different things; the concerns of one group appear suspect or even repellent to another.

Now in no case has he chosen freakish examples of Christians. He has gone to groups which may, as far as such statements can be permissible at all, be said to reflect representative concerns of Christians of those times and places, and in each case the place is in the Christian heartlands of that period. In 37 CE most Christians were Jews. Not only was Jerusalem the Christian center; Jerusalem Christians laid down the norms and standards for other people. By 325 CE few Christians were Jews, the main Christian centers lay in the Eastern Mediterranean and the key language for Christians was Greek. By 600 CE, the balance had shifted westward, and the growing edge of Christianity was among the northern and western tribal and semi-tribal peoples—and Ireland was a power center. In the 1840s Great Britain would certainly be among the outstanding Christian nations, and certainly the one most notably associated with the expansion of the Christian faith. By 1980, the balance had shifted again, southwards; Africa is now the continent most notable for those that profess and call themselves Christians.[1]

So will our visitor conclude that there *is* no coherence? That the use of the name Christian by such diverse groups is fortuitous, or at least misleading? Or does he catch among the spheres some trace of Gilbert Murray's remark that representative Christians of the third, thirteenth, and twentieth centuries would have less in common than would a Catholic, Methodist, and Free-thinker, or even (glancing round the College Common Room and noting the presence of Sir Sarvepalli Radhakrishnan) "a well-educated Buddhist or Brahmin at the present day?"[2] Is shared religion in the end simply a function of shared culture?

Our spaceman may, however, note that among the five groups he has visited there is a historical connection. It was Christians scattered from Jerusalem who first preached to Greeks and founded that vast Greek edifice he observed in 325; it is in Eastern Christianity that we must seek some of the important features and some of the power of Celtic Christian religion. That Celtic religion played a vital part in the gradual emergence of the religion of Exeter Hall. And the Cherubim and Seraphim now in Lagos are ultimately a result of the very sort of operations which were under discussion at the Exeter Hall meeting.

But besides this historical connection, closer examination reveals that there are other definite signs of continuity. There is, in all the wild profusion of the varying statements of these differing groups, one theme which is as unvarying as the language which expresses it is various: that the person of Jesus called the Christ has ultimate significance. In the institutional sphere, too, all use the same sacred writings; and all use bread and wine and water in a special way. Still more remarkable is the continuity of consciousness. Each group thinks of itself as having some community with the others, so different in time and place, and despite being so obviously out of sympathy with many of their principal concerns. Still more remarkable, each thinks of itself as in some respect continuous with ancient Israel, even though only the first have any conceivable ethnic reason to do so, and though some of the groups must have found it extremely hard to form any concept of ancient Israel, or any clear idea of what a Jew might be or look like.

Our observer is therefore led to recognize an essential continuity in Christianity: continuity of thought about the final significance of Jesus, continuity of a certain consciousness about history, continuity in the use of the Scriptures, of bread and wine, of water. But he recognizes that these continuities are cloaked with such heavy veils belonging to their environment that Christians of different times and places must often be unrecognizable to others, or indeed even to themselves, as manifestations of a single phenomenon.

THE "INDIGENIZING" PRINCIPLE

Church history has always been a battleground for two opposing tendencies; and the reason is that each of the tendencies has its origin in the Gospel itself. On the one hand it is of the essence of the Gospel that God accepts us as we are, on the ground of Christ's work alone, not on the ground of what we have become or are trying to become. But, if He accepts us "as we are" that implies He does not take us as isolated, self-governing units, because we are not. We are conditioned by a particular time and place, by our family and group and society, by "culture" in fact. In Christ God accepts us together with our group relations; with that cultural conditioning that makes us feel at home in one part of human society and less at home in another. But if He takes us with our group relations, then surely it follows that He takes us with our "dis-relations" also; those predispositions, prejudices, suspicions, and hostilities, whether justified or not, which mark the group to which we belong. He does not wait to tidy up our ideas any more than He waits to tidy up our behavior before He accepts us sinners into His family.

The impossibility of separating an individual from his social relationships and thus from his society leads to one unvarying feature in Christian history: the desire to "indigenize," to live as a Christian and yet as a member of one's own society, to make the Church (to use the memorable title of a book written in 1967 by F.B. Welbourn and B.A. Ogot about Independent churches in Africa) *A Place to Feel at Home*.

This fact has led to more than one crisis in Christian history, including the first and most important of all. When the elders at Jerusalem in the council of Acts 15 came to their decision that Gentiles could enter Israel without becoming Jews, had they any idea how close the time would be when *most* Christians would be Gentiles? And would they have been so happy with their decision had they realized it? Throughout the early years the Jerusalem Church was in a position to set the standards and to make the decisions, because of its direct connection with the Savior, and its incomparably greater knowledge of the Scriptures. And when its historic decision opened the door wide for Gentile believers in the Jewish Messiah, there must have been many who assumed that nevertheless Gentile Christians, as they matured, would come to look as much like Jerusalem Christians as was possible for such benighted heathen. At least Acts 21:20 suggests that, while being decently glad of the "mission field" conversions recounted by Paul, they continued to think of Jerusalem as the regulative center of God's saving word. What were the thoughts of those who fled from Jerusalem as the Roman armies moved in to cast down the Temple? Did they realize that the future of Messiah's proclamation now lay with people who were uncircumcised, defective in their knowledge of Law and Prophets, still confused by hangovers from paganism, and able to eat pork without turning a hair? Yet this—and the fact that there were still many left to speak of Jesus as Messiah—was the direct result of the decision of the Jerusalem Council to allow Gentile converts "a place to feel at home." So also was the acceptance of Paul's emphatic teaching that since God accepts the heathen as they are, circumcision, food avoidances, and ritual washings are not for them. Christ has so made Himself at home in Corinthian society that a pagan is consecrated through his or her Christian marriage partner (1 Cor. 7:14). No group of Christians has therefore any right to impose in the name of Christ upon another group of Christians a set of assumptions about life determined by another time and place.

The fact, then, that "if any man is in Christ he is a new creation" does not mean that he starts or continues his life in a vacuum, or that his mind is a blank table. It has been formed by his own culture and history, and since God has accepted him as he is, his Christian mind will continue to be influenced by what was in it before. And this is as true for groups as for persons. All churches are culture churches— including our own.

THE "PILGRIM" PRINCIPLE

But throughout Church history there has been another force in tension with this indigenizing principle, and this also is equally of the Gospel. Not only does God in Christ take people as they are: He takes them in order to transform them into what He wants them to be. Along with the indigenizing principle which makes his faith a place to feel at home, the Christian inherits the pilgrim principle, which whispers to him that he has no abiding city and warns him that to be faithful to Christ will put him out of step with his society; for that society never existed, in East or West, ancient time or modern, which could absorb the word of Christ painlessly into its system. Jesus within Jewish culture, Paul within Hellenistic culture, take it for granted that there will be rubs and frictions—not from the adoption of a new culture, but from the transformation of the mind towards that of Christ.

Just as the indigenizing principle, itself rooted in the Gospel, associates Christians with the *particulars* of their culture and group, the pilgrim principle, in tension with the indigenizing and equally of the Gospel, by associating them with things and people outside the culture and group, is in some respects a *universalizing* factor. The Christian has all the relationships in which he was brought up, and has them sanctified by Christ who is living in them. But he has also an entirely new set of relationships, with other members of the family of faith into which he has come, and whom he must accept, with all their group relations (and "disrelations") on them, just as God has accepted him with his. Every Christian has dual nationality, and has a loyalty to the faith family which links him to those in interest groups opposed to that to which he belongs by nature.

In addition—as we observed to be the case in all the spaceman's varied groups of representative Christians—the Christian is given an adoptive past. He is linked to the people of God in all generations (like him, members of the faith family), and most strangely of all, to the whole history of Israel, the curious continuity of the race of the faithful from Abraham. By this means, the history of Israel is part of Church history,[3] and all Christians of whatever nationality, are landed by adoption with several millennia of someone else's history, with a whole set of ideas, concepts, and assumptions which do not necessarily square with the rest of their cultural inheritance; and the Church in every land, of whatever race and type of society, has this same adoptive past by which it needs to interpret the fundamentals of the faith. The adoption into Israel becomes a "universalizing" factor, bringing Christians of all cultures and ages together through a common inheritance, lest any of us make the Christian faith such a place to feel at home that no one else can live there; and bringing into everyone's society some sort of outside reference.

THE FUTURE OF CHRISTIAN THEOLOGY AND ITS CULTURAL CONDITIONING

In the remainder of this paper I would like to suggest something of the relevance of the tension between the indigenizing and the pilgrim principles for the future of Christian theology.

First, let us recall that within the last century there has been a massive southward shift of the center of gravity of the Christian world, so that the representative Christian lands now appear to be in Latin America, Sub-Saharan Africa, and other parts of the southern continents. This means that Third World theology is now likely to be the representative Christian theology. On present trends (and I recognize that these may not be permanent) the theology of European Christians, while important for them and their continued existence, may become a matter of specialist interest to historians (rather as the theology of the Syriac Edessene Church is specialist matter for early Church historians of today, not a topic for the ordinary student and general reader, whose eyes are turned to the Greco-Roman world when he studies the history of doctrine). The future general reader of Church history is more likely to be concerned with Latin American and African, and perhaps some Asian, theology. It is perhaps significant that in the last few years we have seen for the first time works of theology composed in the Third World (the works of Latin American theologians of liberation, such as Gutiérrez, Segundo, and Míguez Bonino) becoming regular reading in the West—not just for missiologists, but for the general theological reader. The fact that particular Third World works of theology appear on the Western market is not, however, a necessary measure of their intrinsic importance. It simply means that publishers think them sufficiently relevant to the West to sell there. Theology is addressed to the setting in which it is produced.

This is perhaps the first important point to remember about theology: that since it springs out of practical situations, it is therefore *occasional* and *local* in character. Since we have mentioned Gutiérrez, some words of his may be quoted here. Theology, he says, arises spontaneously and inevitably in the believer, in all who have accepted the gift of the word of God. There is therefore in every believer, and every community of believers, at least a rough outline of a theology. This conviction leads to another: whatever else theology is, it is what Gutiérrez calls "critical reflection on Christian praxis in the light of the word."[4] That is, theology is about testing your actions by Scripture.

In this, of course, we are hearing the typical modern Latin American theologian, who is stung by the fact that it has taken Marxists to point out things that Amos and Isaiah said long ago, while Christians have found good theological reasons to justify the position of Jeroboam, Manasseh, and Dives, and is nagged by the remark of Bernanos that "God does not choose the same men to keep his word as to fulfil it." But it is likely to be the way of things also in Africa. The domestic tasks of Third World theology are going to be so basic, so vital, that there will be little time for the barren, sterile, time-wasting by-paths into which so much Western theology and theological research has gone in recent years. Theology in the Third World will be, as theology at all creative times has always been, about *doing* things, about things that deeply affect the lives of numbers of people. We see something of this already in South African Black Theology, which is literally about life and death matters (as one South African Black theologian put it to me, "Black Theology is about how to stay Christian when you're a Black in South Africa, and you're hanging on by the skin of your teeth"). There is no need to go back to wars of religion when men shed blood for their theologies: but at least there is something to be said for having a theology about things which are worth shedding blood for. And that, Third World Theology is likely to be.

Because of this relation of theology to action, theology arises out of situations that actually happen, not from broad general principles. Even the Greek Church, with centuries of intellectual and rhetorical tradition, took almost 200 years to produce a book of theology written for its own sake, Origen's *De Principiis*. In those two centuries innumerable theological books were written, but not for the sake of producing theologies. The theology was for a purpose: to *explain* the faith to outsiders, or to point out where the writer thought someone else had misrepresented what Christians meant.

It is therefore important, when thinking of African theology, to remember that it will act on an African agenda. It is useless for us to determine what we think an African theology ought to be doing: it will concern itself with questions that worry Africans, and will leave blandly alone all sorts of questions which we think absolutely vital. We all do the same. How many Christians belonging to churches which accept the Chalcedonian Definition of the Faith could explain with any conviction to an intelligent non-Christian why it is important not to be a Nestorian or a Monophysite? Yet once men not only excommunicated each other, they shed their own and others' blood to get the right answer on that question. The things which we think are vital points of principle will seem as far away and negligible to African theologians as those theological prize fights among the Egyptian monks now seem to us. Conversely, the things that concern African theologians may seem to us at best peripheral. Remembering the emergence of theology at a popular level, it is noteworthy how African Independent churches sometimes seem to pick on a point which strikes us by its oddity or irrelevance, like rules about worship during the menstrual period. But this is usually because the topic, or the sort of topic, is a major one for certain African Christians, just as it apparently was for the old Hebrews, and it needs an answer, and an answer related to Christ. There often turns out to be a sort of coherence in the way in which these churches deal with it, linking Scripture, old traditions, and the Church as the new Levitical community—and giving an answer to something that had been worrying people. In short, it is safe for a European to make only one prediction about the valid, authentic African Biblical theology we all talk about: that it is likely either to puzzle us or to disturb us.

But is not the sourcebook of all valid theology the canonical Scriptures? Yes, and in that, as the spaceman found, lies the continuity of the Christian faith. But, as he also found, the Scriptures are read with different eyes by people in different times and places; and in practice, each age and community makes its own selection of the Scriptures, giving prominence to those which seem to speak most clearly to the community's time and place and leaving aside others which do not appear to yield up their gold so readily. How many of us, while firm as a rock as to its canonicity, seriously look to the book of Leviticus for sustenance? Yet many an African Independent church has found it abundantly relevant. (Interestingly, Samuel Ajayi Crowther, the great nineteenth-century Yoruba missionary bishop, thought it should be among the first books of the Bible to be translated.)

The indigenizing principle ensures that each community recognizes in Scripture that God is speaking to its own situation. But it also means that we all approach Scripture wearing cultural blinkers, with assumptions determined by our time and place. It astonishes us when we read second-century Christian writers who all venerated Paul, and to whom we owe the preservation of his writings, that they never seem to understand what we are sure he means by justification by faith. It is perhaps only in our own day, when we do not read Plato so much, that Western Christians have begun to believe that the resurrection of the body is not the immortality of the soul, or to recognize the solidly material content of biblical salvation. Africans will have their cultural blinkers, too, which will prevent, or at least render it difficult for them to see some things. But they will doubtless be different things from those hidden in our own blind spots, so they should be able to see some things much better than we do.

That wise old owl, *Henry Venn* of the Church Missionary Society, reflecting on the Great Commission in 1868, argued that the fullness of the Church would only come with the fullness of the national manifestations of different national churches:

> Inasmuch as all native churches grow up into the fullness of the stature of Christ, distinctions and defects will vanish.... But it may be doubted whether, to the last, the Church of Christ will not exhibit marked national characteristics which, in the overruling grace of God, will tend to its perfection and glory.[5]

Perhaps it is not only that different ages and nations see different things in Scripture—it is that they *need* to see different things.

The major theological debate in independent Africa[6] just now—Item 1 on the African theological agenda—would appear to be the nature of the African past. Almost every major work by an African scholar in the field of religions—Harry Sawyerr,[7] Bolaji Idowu,[8] J. S. Mbiti,[9] Vincent Mulago[10]—is in some way dealing with it. Now each of the authors named was trained in theology on a Western model; but each has moved into an area for which no Western syllabus prepared him, for each has been forced to study and lecture on African traditional religion—and each has found himself writing on it. It seems to me, however, that they all approach this topic, not as historians of religions do, nor as anthropologists do. They are still, in fact, Christian theologians. All are wrestling with a theological question, the prime one on the African Christian's intellectual agenda: who am I? What is my relation as an African Christian to Africa's past?

Thus, when Idowu concludes with such passion that the *orišas* are only manifestations of Olódùmare, and that it is a Western misrepresentation to call Yoruba religion polytheistic, the urgency in his voice arises from the fact that he is not making a clinical observation of the sort one might make about Babylonian religion: he is handling dynamite, his own past, his people's present. One can see why a non-Christian African writer like Okot p'Bitek, who glories in pre-Christian Africa, accuses John Mbiti and others so bitterly of continuing the Western missionary misrepresentation of the past.[11] It is as though he were saying "They are taking from us our own decent paganism, and plastering it over with interpretations from alien sources." Here speaks the authentic voice of Celsus.

The mention of Celsus reminds us perhaps that African Christians are not the first people to have a religious identity crisis. Gentile Christians had precisely the same issue to face—an issue that never faced the Jewish missionaries, Paul, Peter, Barnabas. They knew who they were ("circumcised the eighth day, of the tribe of Benjamin . . ."), just as Western missionaries for more than 150 confident years knew who *they* were. It is our past which tells us who we are; without our past we are lost. The man with amnesia is lost, unsure of relationships, incapable of crucial decisions, precisely because all the time he has amnesia he is without his past. Only when his memory returns, when he is sure of his past, is he able to relate confidently to his wife, his parents, or know his place in a society.

Early Gentile Christianity went through a period of amnesia. It was not so critical for first-generation converts: they responded to a clear choice, turned from idols to serve the living God, accepted the assurance that they had been grafted into Israel. It was the second and third generations of Christians who felt the strain more. What was their relation to the Greek past? Some of them (some indeed in the first generation, as the New Testament indicates) solved the problem by pretending their Greek past did not exist, by pretending they were Jews, adopting Jewish customs, even to circumcision. Paul saw this coming and roundly condemned it. You are *not* Jews, he argues in Romans 9-11; you *are* Israel, but grafted into it. And, defying all the realities of horticulture, he talks about a wild plant being grafted into a cultivated one. But one thing he is saying is that Gentile Christianity is part of the *wild* olive. It is different in character from the plant into which it is grafted. Such is the necessity of the indigenizing principle.

Later Gentile Christians, by then the majority in the Church, and in no danger of confusing themselves with Jews, had a major problem. Yes, they were grafted into Israel. The sacred history of Israel was part of their history. Yes, the idolatry and immorality of their own society, past and present, must have nothing to do with them. But what was God doing in the Greek world all those centuries while he was revealing himself in judgment and mercy to Israel? Not all the Greek past was graven images and temple prostitution. What of those who testified for righteousness—and even died for it? Had God nothing to do with their righteousness? What of those who taught things that are true—that are according to reason, *logos*, opposed to the Great Lies taught and practiced by others? Had their *logos* nothing to do with The Logos, the light that lighteth every man coming into the world? Is there any truth which is not God's truth? Was God not active in the Greek past, not just the Jewish? So Justin Martyr and Clement of Alexandria came up with their own solutions, that there were Christians before Christ, that philosophy was—and is—the schoolmaster to bring the Greeks to Christ, just as was the Law for Jews.

This is no place to renew the old debate about continuity or discontinuity of Christianity with pre-Christian religion, nor to discuss the theology of Justin and Clement, nor to consider the correctness of Idowu and Mbiti. My point is simply that the two latter are wrestling with essentially the same problem as the two former, and that it seems to be the most urgent problem facing African Christians today, on their agenda. Until it is thought through, amnesia could make African Christianity tentative and unsure of its relationships, and unable to recognize important tasks. More than one answer may emerge; the early centuries, after all, saw the answer of Tertullian as well as of Clement. And there may be little that outsiders can do to assist. Once again Paul saw what was coming. "Is He not," he asks his Jewish interlocutor, and on the most thoroughly Jewish grounds, "the God of the Gentiles also?" (Rom. 3:29f.).

The debate will certainly reflect the continuing tension between the indigenizing and the pilgrim principles of the Gospel. Paul, Justin, and Clement all knew people who followed one without the other. Just as there were "pilgrims" who sought to follow, or to impose upon others the modes of thought and life, concerns and preconceptions which belonged to someone else, so there were Greek-educated "indigenizers" who sought to eliminate what they considered "barbarian" elements from Christianity such as the Resurrection and the Last Judgment. But these things were part of a framework which ultimately derived from the Christian faith, and thus they played down, or ignored, or explicitly rejected, the Old Testament, the Christian adoptive past. Perhaps the most important thing to remember about the opponents of these Gnostics is that they were just as Greek as the Gnostics themselves, with many of the same instincts and difficulties; but they knew instinctively that they must hold to their adoptive past, and in doing so saved the Scriptures for the Church. Perhaps the real test of theological authenticity is the capacity to incorporate the history of Israel and God's people and to treat it as one's own.

When the Scriptures are read in some enclosed Zulu Zion, the hearers may catch the voice of God speaking out of a different Zion, and speaking to the whole world. When a comfortable bourgeois congregation meets in some Western suburbia, they, almost alone of all the comfortable bourgeois of the suburbs, are regularly exposed to the reading of a non-bourgeois book questioning fundamental assumptions of their society. But since none of us can read the Scriptures without cultural blinkers of some sort, the great advantage, the crowning excitement which our own era of Church history has over all others, is the possibility that we may be able to read them together. Never before has the Church looked so much like the great multitude whom no man can number out of every nation and tribe and people and tongue. Never before, therefore, has there been so much potentiality for mutual enrichment and self-criticism, as God causes yet more light and truth to break forth from his word.[12]

NOTES

1. See David B. Barrett, "A.D. 2000: 350 Million Christians in Africa," *International Review of Mission* 59 (1970): 39-54; A.F. Walls, "Towards Understanding Africa's Place in Christian History," in J.S. Pobee, ed., *Religion in a Pluralistic Society: Essays Presented to Professor C.G. Baëta* (Leiden, 1976), pp. 180-89.

2. Gilbert Murray, *Five Stages of Greek Religion* (1935), p. 174.

3. ". . . the first fact of the Church [is] that we are Gentiles who worship the God of the Jews"—with *their* psalms, in Gentile languages but their concepts (Paul van Buren, "The Mystery and Salvation and Prayer," *Ecumenical Institute for Advanced Theological Studies Yearbook* [Jerusalem, 1977-78], pp. 37-52).

4. Gustavo Gutiérrez, *A Theology of Liberation* (Maryknoll, N.Y.: Orbis Books; London: SCM, 1973; rev. ed., with new introduction, 1988), pp. 6-15.

5. Instructions of the Committee of the Church Missionary Society to Departing Missionaries, June 30, 1868, reproduced in W. Knight, *The Missionary Secretariat of Henry Venn* (1880), p. 284.

6. "Independent Africa" is here distinguished from South Africa, where different conditions have produced different priorities and a different debate.

7. See Harry Sawyerr, *God—Ancestor or Creator*? (1970).

8. See Bolaji Idowu, *Olódùmare: God in Yoruba Belief* (1962) and *African Traditional Religion: A Definition* (1973).

9. See John S. Mbiti, *New Testament Eschatology in an African Background* (Oxford, 1971); *African Religions and Philosophy* (1969); and *Concepts of God in Africa* (1970).

10. See Vincent Mulago, "Christianisme et culture africaine," in C.G. Baèta, ed., *Christianity in Tropical Africa* (1968), pp. 308-28.

11. See Okot p'Bitek, *African Religions in Western Scholarship* (Kampala, 1971).

12. I have quoted here sentences from my paper "African and Christian Identity," which first appeared in the Mennonite journal *Mission Focus* and was later reprinted in W.R. Shenk, ed., *Mission Focus—Current Issues* (Scottdale, Penna.: Herald Press, 1980).

2

The Incarnation of the Gospel in Cultures: A Missionary Event

Geneva, 1995

Aram I*

This essay originally appeared as part of the 1995 Moderator's Report of Aram (Keshishian) I, moderator of the WCC's central committee. Because contemporary global society is marked by pluralism, secularism, and cultural divisions and tensions, the question of the relationship of faith and culture is no longer "how to relate gospel to culture but how gospel can liberate, transform and reorient cultures." While "alienating from culture is alienating from the gospel," "the gospel is affirmed through cultures, not in cultures." Like Andrew Walls in the first article of this collection, Aram I believes that "the gospel helps us to be genuinely indigenous yet critically open to other cultures."

The question of gospel and culture is an old ecumenical concern. Practically all the major ecumenical gatherings have, in different contexts and from different perspectives, touched the issue. This complex question has re-emerged in a new context and framework, and has acquired a focal attention in the life and witness of our churches and the ecumenical movement. With this concern in mind, the central committee in Johannesburg called the Council and its member churches "to explore afresh the relations between the gospel and cultures" and its implications for the pluralistic societies of today. As you know, this study process will lead us to the conference on world mission and evangelism in November/December 1996. The theme of this conference is "*Called to One Hope: The Gospel in Diverse Cultures.*" Gospel and culture will then become one of the major foci of the eighth assembly in 1998.

---

* Originally published in *The Ecumenical Review*, 48, 1 (1996). Besides being moderator of the central committee of the World Council of Churches, Aram I is primate of the Armenian Apostolic Church in Lebanon.

Since the Council has already embarked on a dynamic process of intense theological reflection, discussion and exploration on local, regional and global levels, it is appropriate at this point that we, as the central committee, make our own contribution to the process.

Three features of modern society deserve our attention. First, what we call pluralism has become an existential and global reality. It has penetrated all spheres of life, introducing new fears, hopes and challenges. Second, due to close interaction between culture, religion and ethnicity, cultures have become sources of social, political, economic, religious and ethnic divisions and tensions. Third, Western society has considerably changed its identity, having become a technological society which breeds secularism and spreads a mono-culture.

The churches' close identification with cultures raises critical missiological questions for the ecumenical movement. The encounter between the gospel and cultures in pluralist societies poses a major challenge to the churches *to develop a new vision of missio Dei*. For many years, the question was how to relate the gospel to cultures. Now the question is *how to liberate*, transform and *reorient* the cultures. Let me try to point out some significant aspects of this challenge and identify, in the perspective of gospel-culture interaction, a few vital dimensions of the emerging new vision of mission.

CULTURES IN CRISIS

Contemporary cultures are in deep crisis. They have become the arena for new powers of evil, destruction, dehumanization and death. What then are the symptoms of the growing cultural crisis?

1. Culture is the self-expression of a group of people in time and space. It is an expression of life, a mode of becoming oneself, a way of relating to one another and to nature. Culture thus embraces the wholeness of language, tradition, beliefs, institutions and customs that hold a community together. Culture is a complex reality that includes spiritual, material, intellectual and emotional features. The ethos, the self-identity of people, is manifested through culture. Culture, then, is a dynamic reality, and as such is subject to change. Culture and religion are intimately interrelated, and in many societies they express themselves through each other, conditioning each other. While for religions such as Judaism, Islam and Hinduism, the founding culture is the sacred model for encountering the ultimate reality, for Christianity culture has instrumental and transitory value.[1]

2. The world is moving towards one dominant culture. The emergence of this new global mono-culture seriously threatens humanity and all of creation. Produced by modern advanced technology and the market economy, the new global culture is based on profit, quantitative growth and exploitation. It denies participation, sharing and equal rights. It dehumanizes and disintegrates local cultures and alienates people from their cultural roots. This new and dominant culture is a product of Western culture which is overwhelmed by norms and patterns of relationships that call into question its own quality, integrity and credibility. In fact, Western culture is dominated by an economic materialism that reduces value-judgment to the cal-

culation of costs and benefits. It is sustained by a growth-oriented value that disregards the dignity of the human person and the integrity of creation. It is guided by an uncritical secularization that affirms the human at the expense of the Divine.

Canberra spoke of *hidden ideologies*[2] that are deeply rooted in our cultures, ideologies that introduce new cultural norms, paradigms, and value systems. These *hidden ideologies*, embodied in Pizza Huts, McDonalds, Coca-Cola, etc., now infuse the entire globe. By transmitting these hidden ideologies, electronic global communication has transformed the whole ethos of culture: marginalized Christian values, elaborated ethics which are more and more counter to the gospel and are moving humanity and the whole of creation from theocentrism to anthropocentrism. In its pride, humanity has forgotten its finite nature. The growing perception of self-sufficiency of the people has made cultures lose the sense of dependence on, and accountability to, an ultimate reality. Sacred and mystical dimensions of cultures have become secularized. The horizontal has established its predominance. In other words, secularism,[3] materialism and technology have made cultures exclusively human-oriented, yet less humane.

3. While this human-oriented culture is penetrating the globe through communication and technology, local indigenous cultures are struggling to affirm their identity through their own structures, value systems and through their own experiences of responding to the call of the gospel.

The encounter between the local and the global has created several responses. Some people and communities are searching for meaning through counter-culture paradigms such as neo-fascism, religious fundamentalism, the esoteric, the occult. Others believe in ethical relativism. For these people, ethical relativism ensures tolerance and mutual respect between people; however, for others, it destroys the ethical foundations of societies and leads these societies to total disintegration[4] and self destruction. Amidst this gloomy picture, there are also efforts to seek alternative paradigms to communicate the meaning and value of human life across cultures. The question is not one of the *relationship* between gospel and culture. but one of the very *presence* of the gospel itself, particularly in those cultures that used to be referred to as "Christian cultures." In the midst of cultures of fear, hopelessness, violence and death, how do we proclaim the gospel? How could the gospel by its life-generating action become a source of liberation, renewal and transformation? The gospel is Jesus Christ, not written book. It is the living encounter between God and humanity. Hence, the gospel is the beginning of a new humanity and a new world. It is with such an understanding of the nature of the gospel that I would like now to outline some of the significant aspects pertaining to the role of the gospel in contemporary cultures.

FROM INDIGENIZATION TO CONTEXTUALIZATION

The gospel becomes relevant and reliable when it is communicated to people through their own culture. The word was incarnated in a given cultural context. He must be reincarnated in a specific culture and find appropriate human response through it. Therefore the gospel is received, experienced, affirmed and proclaimed through a culture. Culture plays a crucial role in the God/humanity dialogue. In this regard, one should keep in mind the following points:

1. The gospel is experienced and expressed in different ways at different times. While God's self-revelation took place in Judaic culture, Pentecost was the manifestation of God's impartial action in all cultures. Since Pentecost, the gospel has taken root in several cultures. Church history reveals that any authentic response to the gospel has always been contextual. In fact, the gospel is contextual by its very nature. The Christ-event is the saving event of God and, as such, pertains to all of humanity and creation. The uniqueness and universality of the gospel is experienced and continuously affirmed in the diversity of cultures. This is its strength. The gospel makes the church a confessing community of one faith in many cultures.

But how can the various cultural expressions of Christian faith enter into dialogue with each other? The church suffered enormously for not having been able to develop a creative dialogue among the various expressions of the one gospel. Diversities of expression and interpretation led the church to polarization and division. I believe that it is the task of the ecumenical movement to develop an ecumenical hermeneutic which will establish mutual understanding among the churches as they confess and proclaim one gospel in diverse cultural contexts.

2. The gospel should not simply be transmitted from one culture to the other; it must be reincarnated. Being God's saving act in the life of human beings, the gospel must be fully re-owned by people in and through their own cultural forms, patterns, norms and values. The gospel deals with God/humanity relations; therefore it cannot be isolated from the concrete world. It has to become incarnate in the life of human beings and the community.

The Orthodox churches have the rich experience of rooting the gospel in their cultures. There, the gospel has permeated all aspects and dimensions of community life. In an Orthodox context one cannot speak in terms of gospel/culture relations—only of gospel/culture identification. This is particularly true in my own church. The penetration of the gospel into Armenian life was described by our historians as the process of *Armenianization* of the Christian faith. The gospel loses its authenticity and relevance without a dynamic process of genuine inculturation which is not merely an adoption or an adaptation, but a conscious response and a faithful commitment to Christ in a concrete place and through a specific culture. In our missionary involvement we may use all the technological facilities of communication we have; we may develop new missionary strategies and methodologies. But the issue is not efficient communication, it is not strategies or methodologies. The issue is how to incarnate the gospel in a cultural context and make it a transforming reality; the issue is how to bring different cultures in dialogue to express the universality of Christian faith.

3. The gospel should cross all human frontiers and be taken to all people, cultures and lands. The gospel is not only a reality to be lived out (in-reach), but a reality to be taken out (out-reach). It is a missionary event which calls for missionary engagement. However, crossing frontiers must be accompanied by respect and sensitivity to the cultural values and norms of the other. Mission must proclaim the gospel through the receiving culture; missionaries must not seek to impose their own culture. When the gospel imposes a new culture, it destroys the existing one.

In many places, Western missions have introduced cultural norms and values that alienated local Christians from their own cultures. Missionary outreach meant cultural outreach. Thus to become Christian meant being "Westernized." There were also cases—very few, indeed—where the gospel was taken to people through a process of contextualization. I can give you here the example of Danish missionaries in the Armenian church. They did not bring with them the Danish culture; they did not bring the Lutheran confession. They learned Armenian and accommodated to the Armenian way of life, solely in order to serve the spiritual needs of the Armenian people. The ecumenical movement challenged the assumption that the Western culture is *the* Christian culture, and that any Christian culture must follow its example. It is time now to go back to the authentic roots of cultures.

Some of our churches which were formed by colonial rule still carry much of its symbolism. However, they are now rediscovering their cultural identity. They realize that, in order for the church to survive in Africa, it has to become African; the church in Latin America must become Latin American; the church in the Middle East must become Middle Eastern. In other words, the "new" churches are seeking to become self-nourishing, self-governing, self-ministering in their own cultures in openness and dialogical interaction with other churches and cultures. Alienating from culture is alienating from the gospel. The gospel distorts its own nature and vocation when it aims to change the identity of indigenous culture and subjugate the people to a supra-culture. This old model of mission that marked a certain period of history is now reappearing in the countries of the former USSR. Western sects are not only bringing with them a distorted gospel but also the Western culture. The ecumenical movement must remain constantly alert to this threat.

4. The gospel cannot exist without some form of inculturation, but it is never exhausted by any particular culture. It transcends every culture; it is trans-cultural. God assumed humanity in a particular culture to restore it to its authenticity. The blind identification of the gospel with a particular culture is the negation of the very nature of the gospel. Christ meets us in our own cultural contexts. He is confessed through specific cultural patterns and forms. The gospel is affirmed *through* cultures, not *in* cultures. Culture is only an instrument, framework and context to embody and articulate the gospel. During the colonial era, mission emphasized the text and ignored the context, while during the post-colonial era, mission focused on context to the extent of losing sight of the text. How can we go beyond the Jesus of history who is so deeply rooted in our cultures, and identify ourselves with the Christ of faith? In fact, the identification of gospel and culture is so close in many churches that it may result in endangering the universality of the gospel by substituting the one for the other. Incarnating the gospel in a culture is one thing, but making a culture a source and criterion of revealed truth is something else. The gospel helps us to be genuinely indigenous yet critically open to other cultures.

The fear that churches were substituting culture for the gospel was expressed sharply in Canberra. Should we limit ourselves to our specific context? Can we transcend our specific understanding and expressions of the gospel? How can the universal gospel become particular, and how can we express the universality of the gospel in the midst of particularities? Is there a transcultural identity that must be given due consideration by the churches and the ecumenical movement? Answers to these questions provide the alternative vision being sought by the ecumenical movement in the gospel and culture reflection process. This vision affirms that the gospel creates a dynamic dialogue of cultures and finally leads people to one Christ through cultural diversities. Therefore we have to take care that the growing global ecumenical culture does not dominate the cultures of particular churches. We must have a contextual approach to mission which avoids both total indigenization and globalization, and which conceives mission as the reincarnation of the gospel in a context that is open to interaction between cultures.

PLURALISM: A FEAR OR A HOPE?

As the world becomes more and more pluralistic, the question of how to proclaim the gospel in a multi-cultural context acquires critical urgency and priority. Growing cultural interaction often resulting from uncritical use of non-Christian cultural elements and categories in the Christian church raises some controversial questions. For some this is a threat to mission. For others it provides a greater possibility to Christian mission for an efficient outreach. Canberra challenged the churches to move beyond formal encounters to a "culture of dialogue."[5] On this point it is important to make the following observations:

1. Cultures are no longer self-contained; they constantly dialogue and interact. Population movements have virtually made every part of the globe multi-cultural. The old boundaries between Christian West and Muslim East, white North and black South, have disappeared. I wonder whether Hendrik Kraemer would have given the same title to his well-known book, *The Christian Message in a Non-Christian World*, had he written it today. In fact there is no Christian world or non-Christian world today. The world has become one place, one community, where cultures cannot maintain themselves apart from each other. They inter-relate and interpenetrate. Is multi-culturalism a threat or a challenge, a weakness or a strength? The inter-relatedness of all cultures is affirmed by the gospel. A dialogue of cultures is integral to the nature of the gospel. The ethos of the gospel encourages cultural pluralism. It affirms inclusiveness in culture. Cultures are mutually inspired, corrected, challenged and enriched through creative dialogical relations.

We find a cultural rigidity among minorities. They maintain their specificity through their culture. Culture is a safe refuge for survival. Hence, any threat to culture is a serious threat to the very existence of these ethnic groups. But this growing search for ethnic roots in today's societies, manifested most concretely through cultures, may become a destructive force by generating exclusiveness; it may also become a source of reaffirming one's authenticity. In fact, the survival of the Armenian people in a diaspora situation after the genocide is due to the Armenian culture.

2. The whole gospel for the whole world! This is the missionary calling of the church. Dialogue is not an alternative to mission; dialogue should not compromise our faith. We have again and again reminded ourselves of this basic missiological stand. We have made a clear distinction between witness and dialogue, at the same time affirming their inter-relatedness. We are now much more open to people of

other cultures and faiths, willing to learn more from them and to share with them our concerns and perspectives. We are coming to a better understanding of the ways in which gospel and cultures interact. Therefore we have to be bold in our proclamation of the gospel and, at the same time, humble in our interfaith dialogue. In other words, I believe that responsible dialogue with other faiths and firm attachment to the uniqueness of the gospel are not contradictory. The inclusiveness of the gospel helps it to establish dialogue and remove the barriers of a given culture.

But what does it mean to have a missionary calling in a world of many faiths? What are the missionary challenges of living in close interdependence with other faiths? The fear of syncretism will always be with us as we try to relate the gospel to other cultures. But such a legitimate concern should lead the church in its missionary calling to take with renewed awareness and vision the uniqueness and universality of the gospel and the enduring validity and urgency of its call to make disciples of all nations. This is not an aggressive evangelism; it simply means that the church in pluralistic societies must take more seriously and responsibly the message of the gospel.

San Antonio referred to the need for a holistic understanding of mission. What does this mean? We cannot accept the so-called "larger ecumenism" that advocates the kind of dialogical interaction with religions that may relativize the basic foundations of Christian faith. For Christian mission, Jesus Christ is the centre of all inclusiveness and absoluteness. In him all particularities merge. Mission is a faithful witness to Christ; it rejects unfaithful compromise. Yet, "Christian theology cannot give adequate expression to the missiological thrust of the Christian vision unless it is thoroughly dialogical in its stance and style."[6] San Antonio stated: "Witness does not preclude dialogue but invites it, and that dialogue does not preclude witness but extends and deepens it."[7] Since our existence is a missionary one, our very existence as God's people must be dialogical.

A CRITERION FOR JUDGING CULTURE

It is a basic missiological conviction that the gospel has a prophetic role vis-à-vis cultures.[8] In fact, Christ shared a specific culture; he affirmed and at the same time judged it. God's assuming humanity through a particular culture was intended to be a sign that every human culture is under the same promise and judgment of God. The death and resurrection of Jesus Christ put an end to all cultural claims. The gospel is related to every culture—critically, creatively and redemptively. A culture is under judgment from beyond culture. But what is the criterion for judging a culture? The ecumenical movement has not been able to spell out clearly such a "gospel criterion." Is it not the time for us to work together for an ecumenical ethics that clearly outlines the demands and imperatives of the gospel? Is it not the time to re-emphasize the interconnectedness that exists between mission and ethics? At this point, let me offer the following remarks:

1. The gospel is the self-revelation of God. Cultures are devoid of meaning without God's revealing presence which transcends all cultural patterns, norms and values. Only the gospel can give a real value to cultures by introducing transcendental,

spiritual and eschatological dimensions.[9] Therefore the gospel should challenge secularist, consumerist and militarist "values" that have become norms in many cultures.

2. Technological progress has given cultures the impression that their power is indestructible. The gospel must challenge this arrogance of cultures. God's powerlessness challenges human power. The encounter of gospel and culture is the encounter of God's humility and human pride, God's faithfulness and human unfaithfulness, God's love and human rejection. The gospel is a reminder of cultural limitation and human finiteness. The power struggle is not between the gospel and cultures, but between the gospel and the "powers" within any culture which dehumanize and enslave people.

3. The gospel should reject cultural superiority and any hierarchy of cultures. All cultures are equal and full of inherent ambiguities that make them susceptible to both false and true prophecy. Hence, the gospel should reorient cultures so that they may overcome this power of evil and death.

4. Cultures have broken the human community. They have bred injustice and oppression manifested through sexism, racism, classism and poverty. Many cultures are still patriarchal, discriminatory and exclusive. This is a root cause of many conflicts. How can the gospel help to eliminate the mutual exclusiveness of cultures? How can the gospel challenge injustice and exploitation and struggle against oppressive and life-destructive structures and values? The prophetic judgment "must begin at the house of God" (1 Pet. 4:17).

5. The gospel in its turn is challenged by the cultures in which it finds itself. The gospel itself is marked by peculiarities of specific cultures. In gospel/culture interrelations, culture may question particular understandings of the gospel which are alien to its norms and perceptions. A culture cannot become a criterion to judge gospel. Yet a culture cannot accept any cultural patterns and norms pertaining to gospel that are not compatible with its own.

THE GOSPEL: GOD'S LIBERATING PRESENCE

We have already stated that cultures are in crisis. They are in need of transformation. In gospel/culture relations, the gospel not only challenges and judges cultures, but also shapes, purifies and transforms them, giving them a new identity. This process of transformation implies liberation and renewal.

1. Today more than ever, humanity is exposed to a great variety of evil and destructive forces that are manifested through cultures. Cultures today offer fear, confusion and disorientation. Violence is the most characteristic feature of contemporary cultures. Militarism, consumerism and socio-economic injustice have produced the kind of violence that threatens human life and the whole creation. Humanity is directly and constantly exposed to the "culture of death." How can we transform this "culture of death" to a "culture of life?" How can we enhance life-promoting cultures? The gospel is a gospel of life. Whatever is opposed to life is the rejection of the gospel. The gospel of life is a reality made manifest in Jesus Christ. In him the gospel of life was fully and concretely given to humanity both as a gift and as a task. Through the life-affirming message of the gospel, the churches should

challenge the cultures of violence and death, and proclaim and celebrate the gospel of life over against the "culture of death."

The world convocation on Justice, Peace and the Integrity of Creation in Seoul, Korea (1990), called for a culture of active non-violence. In Johannesburg we established, within the WCC structure, a new "Programme to Overcome Violence." Violence is caused by a lack of justice and meaning. To combat violence we must eradicate these root causes, reaffirm the sacredness of life, promote justice and respect for human rights and restore human dignity. To overcome violence through "active non-violent action" is now a clear ecumenical strategy. This strategy should undergird all ecumenical actions. Its aim ought to be to develop "a just peace culture" where conflicts are resolved through non-violent action.

2. Cultures are deeply affected by human sin. Exploitation, domination and inhumanity generate violence, poverty and unemployment. According to estimates in the USA, a crime is committed every minute. You cannot stop crime by collecting weapons from the streets or putting murderers in jail; you stop crime by transforming cultures, by liberating them from their inherent evil forces and providing them with the power to struggle against social injustice, moral degeneration and economic exploitation.

3. The gospel should become incarnate in a given culture so that it liberates those whom it holds and does not make them captives of culture. The gospel is a liberating event—it liberates cultures from their self-imprisonment. Any culture that generates alienation and exclusiveness negates the gospel. In some situations the gospel itself has become a captive of culture, while in others, the gospel has alienated people from their own cultures. In some of our churches the indigenization of the gospel has produced parochialism. The ecumenical movement should help the churches to assert both their identity in culture and their identity in Christ which is beyond every culture. The first without the second is a source of imprisonment.

4. The gospel renews cultures; it promises a new life: "*Behold, I make everything new*" (Rev. 21:5). Christ did not bring a new culture; he did not destroy the Jewish culture; he renewed and transformed it. In his missionary activities St. Paul did not seek to replace cultures with a "Christian culture." Rather, he called for the liberation of what is authentically human within the culture (Acts 17). In the gospel/culture encounter, the vertical and the horizontal engage in existential dialogue. The gospel is the breaking in of the vertical and transformation of the horizontal from within. Many of our churches have gone through similar enriching and transforming experiences. I refer again to the experience of the Armenian church: with the coming of the gospel to heathen Armenia, the Armenian culture underwent a dynamic process of inner transformation. Many of the heathen cultural patterns and elements, customs and traditions remained the same, but they were "Christianized" by changing their meaning and identity.

5. The gospel restores wholeness and integrity to cultures. God's saving act in Christ is to restore wholeness to his creation (2 Cor. 5:19). Salvation includes the cultures; it also embraces the totality of the life of societies, i.e., humanity/God/creation relationships. In drawing persons around him, Jesus recreated humanity by making it a community of shared life, and by giving it a common identity. In the gospel, cultures are healed and their integrity is recovered and affirmed.

THE GOSPEL: A RECONCILING OR A DIVIDING FACTOR?

The gospel is a unifying factor in the midst of cultural diversities. It may also become a divisive factor. In other words, a culture provides a basis for bringing people together as well as a basis for excluding others. Let me elaborate on this point.

1. In cultures, particularities have become walls of division. They have also become forces of defence, self-protection and survival. In the gospel, the local and the global interact. The gospel makes people affirm their cultural identity, and at the same time it enables them to transcend their cultures, to become part of a global community. But can the gospel really play a unitive role in those cultures which are producing so many polarizations and confrontations? We should not forget the religious and confessional dimensions of some of the prevailing conflicts. I believe that the gospel as a unitive factor must acquire a crucial importance in the societies torn apart by so many tensions and contradictions.

2. In the gospel there is a creative interdependence and complementarity between the one and the many. The gospel is a concrete manifestation of what we call in ecumenism "unity in diversity" and "diversity in unity." The one gospel is received, experienced and proclaimed within the diversity of cultures. And cultures are reconciled and come together through the gospel. Belonging to one gospel does not preclude belonging to different cultures. Missions alienated people from their own cultures: the gospel became a divisive factor. Such a missionary methodology and practice belong now, I hope, to the past. Any missionary initiative that brings division and tension is simply proselytism and must be rejected. Western missionaries who are currently carrying on activities in Eastern Europe, the Middle East and Africa must constantly be reminded of this basic concern.

3. The gospel is also a healing reality. The gospel is not taken to others only through teaching and preaching, but also through healing. The English words "healed" in Acts 4:9 and "salvation" in Acts 4:12 both come from the same Greek root—*sothenai*, meaning "to be made whole." This dimension of wholeness is almost forgotten in our missiology. Healing as being made whole is, in fact, reconciliation. It brings together those who were separated. The gospel is God's healing presence. In the midst of cultures that create tensions and separation, the gospel is called to promote reconciliation. The gospel is a call for *metanoia*, a renewed relation with God and creation. It is a message of divine reconciliation in Jesus Christ addressed to the whole world. In the world where there are so many wounds, we badly need the healing presence of the gospel.

CHRISTIAN MISSION FACING NEW CHALLENGES

What new perspectives and tasks are opening up for Christian mission in a world where geographical and cultural boundaries are removed, distances are shortened and humanity is moving towards one interdependent community?

1. Recently in one of my readings I came across the following question: "Does the church have a mission in the contemporary world?" In our missionary thinking and engagement, we have reached the irreversible convictions that, first, mis-

sion is not the church's "mandate" but God's "initiative"—it belongs to God, it is *missio Dei*. And, second, mission is not one of the functions of the church—it is the *esse*, the raison d'etre, and *the* action of the church by which the church becomes fully and authentically itself.

Hence, mission pertains to the whole people of God. The concepts of "missions" and "missionary agencies" which still prevail in some of our churches must be revised. We have to think and act in terms of one mission of the one and the whole church. Mission has become multi-dimensional; it is no longer merely a matter of sharing the good news among people. The church's mission is to promote koinonia in a world where cultures have brought divisions; it is to judge, heal, liberate and transform the cultures which generate injustice and violence. And mission has become multi-directional: it is no longer from West to East and from North to South —it takes place in each and in all places, from and to all directions. Mission has also become multi-cultural: it is no longer a Western or a Northern enterprise— it is essentially a cross-cultural venture. Therefore we need the kind of mission that is not dominated by the peculiarities of one locality and one culture. The mission of the church is not just to proclaim the gospel but to live it, articulate its demands and be a sign of the kingdom. A reincarnation of the gospel in the cultures of today remains a basic missionary concern. We must develop an incarnational missiology.

2. The church has been a major factor in preserving cultural identity and cultural values. It has also been an efficient instrument for imposing culture on an unwitting group. Many of our churches are closely identified with their cultures. In a world where small nations and ethnic minorities are struggling to reaffirm their ethnic and cultural identities, how can the ecumenical movement help the churches to break out of their cultural captivity and transcend their cultural boundaries while at the same time remaining faithful to their cultural heritage and identity? The gospel affirms cultural identity and promotes a dialogue of cultures. A holistic approach to mission which has become a new ecumenical strategy must take this dimension seriously.

The ecumenical movement must develop an ecumenical hermeneutic to enable churches to understand each other across cultural boundaries. This has become, in fact, a growing concern in the past few years. The koinonia that the gospel proclaims is inclusive community, open community, a community for others. Canberra appealed for a "wholeness" of the mission of the church.[10] The aim of the gospel is not to convert people to a specific culture but to proclaim Jesus Christ. Mission is by its very nature and aim a cross-cultural and multi-ethnic outreach that embraces all cultures, the whole of humanity and of creation. The church is called to become an inclusive community; it should not aim at an "inclusive culture." The churches and the ecumenical movement must give due consideration to this challenge.

3. The church is a reality "in each place" and "in all places," as is mission. Taking the gospel to the ends of the earth is the unequivocal mission of the church. But mission is primarily the *in-reach* of the church, not simply an "overseas" or "foreign" enterprise. In the past we have perceived mission as being exclusively the outgoing of the church. We organized mission to six continents. The growing globalization has considerably marginalized our missionary concern for "all in each place." Without losing this global dimension and vision, the churches should now engage in serious missionary work at home. The global missionary outreach

of the church becomes more credible and efficient if it is authenticated by a local missionary engagement.[11] In other words, the supra-national, supra-cultural and ecumenical character of mission acquires real validity when it emerges from a concrete missionary situation. Therefore a renewed dynamism ought to be given to the contextual dimension of mission.

4. Mission should enhance and orient the dialogue of cultures. But the question is how to "speak the truth in love" (Eph. 4:15) in cultures which have different criteria for truth. The tension between the gospel and culture will never be resolved. The gospel will always challenge those aspects of culture that are not compatible with the gospel. God took the path of humility and dialogue in order to make himself known. Should this not also be the way of Christian mission? Let us not forget the call and challenge of San Antonio to carry on our mission "in Christ's way." The dialogue between gospel and culture is the encounter between divine love and human pride. Human pride destroys; divine love builds, liberates, transforms, reconciles.

The role of the ecumenical movement, which is called to speak and act in the name of the gospel, is to reorient cultures towards the kind of humanity/creation/God relationship that is portrayed in the gospel and given as a gift and call of God. "One world—one culture" is a dangerous illusion. The ecumenical movement itself—being a concrete manifestation of the creative dialogue of cultures—will never accept such an agenda offered by the world. The ecumenical vision remains more than ever *towards one gospel in many cultures, towards one humanity in a reconciled diversity*.

Therefore, in obedience to the gospel message, the role of the ecumenical movement is, first, to call the cultures to quality of life that is manifested in its fullness and authenticity through the gospel; second, to give wholeness, integrity and authenticity to cultures and converge them towards the crucified and risen Christ; and, third, to help the churches speak and act together in the common language of the gospel by affirming *life* in the midst of cultures of death, *peace* in the midst of cultures of violence, *justice* in the midst of cultures of injustice and koinonia in the midst of cultures of conflict and division.

The coming millennium brings with it a new way of being a missionary church in a new world.

NOTES

1. Because of the crucial importance of culture for Christian faith and mission, the ecumenical movement should develop a theological understanding of culture. The Vancouver and Canberra assemblies did make a limited attempt in this respect.
2. M. Kinnamon, ed., *Signs of the Spirit*, official report of the WCC's seventh assembly, Canberra, Geneva, WCC, and Grand Rapids, MI. Eerdmans, 1991, p. 106.
3. It is a fact that Western cultures are vehicles of secularist trends. That is why one of the basic reasons for the resurgence of Muslim fundamentalism is the growing penetration of Western values into Muslim culture.
4. *Evangelium Vitae*, John Paul II, 1995, Vatican, p. 100.
5. *Signs of the Spirit*, p. 104.
6. E.J. Lott, "On Being Religiously Theological and Theologically Religious." *Bangalore Theological Forum*, Jan.-June 1988, p. 75.

7. F.R. Wilson, ed., *The San Antonio Report*, Geneva, WCC, 1990.

8. D. Gill, ed., *Gathered for Life*, official report of the WCC's sixth assembly, Vancouver, Geneva, WCC, and Grand Rapids, MI, Eerdmans, 1983, p. 33.

9. This point is strongly emphasized in E. Brunner's *Christianity and Civilization* and R. Niebuhr's *Christ and Culture*.

10. *Signs of the Spirit*, p. 187.

11. This point is stressed in *Ecumenical Affirmation on Mission and Evangelism*, Geneva, WCC, 1982. In spite of the particular importance of this ecumenical document, in my view we need a renewed "ecumenical affirmation" vis-a-vis the changing missionary realities and perspectives.

3

Contextualization

The Theory, the Gap, the Challenge

Darrell L. Whiteman*

> *In this essay Darrell Whiteman first discusses three functions of contextualization in mission today: to communicate the gospel in an adequate manner, to ensure that the inevitable offense of the gospel is given for the* right *reasons, and to expand the church's understanding of the gospel. Whiteman then goes on to speak of the gap between the theory and the practice of contextualization. Progress is notable, however, in some places, particularly those in which foreign missionaries are no longer in control of the local church. After outlining two points of resistance to contextualization—from missionaries who do not think missiologically enough and from local leaders who do not think courageously enough—the essay concludes by proposing that contextualization lays down three challenges: prophetic, hermeneutical and personal.*

Contextualization may be one of the most important issues in mission today. Unlike the "Death of God" movement in theology, contextualization is no mere missiological fad that will fade when another "hot topic" catches our attention. Concern over issues of contextualization has been a part of the Christian church from its inception, even though the vocabulary of contextualization dates back only to the early 1970s. It is a perennial challenge—one that Christians have faced every time they have communicated the Gospel across language and cultural boundaries. The church has struggled with this problem through the ages as it has evolved from one era to another. Essentially, contextualization is concerned with how the Gospel and culture relate to one another across geographic space and down through time.

Contextualization captures in method and perspective the challenge of relating the Gospel to culture. In this sense the concern of contextualization is ancient—

---

* Originally published in *International Bulletin of Missionary Research*, 21, 1 (January 1997). Darrell L. Whiteman is Professor of Cultural Anthropology in the E. Stanley Jones School of World Mission and Evangelization at Asbury Theological Seminary, Wilmore, KY. He is editor of *Missiology: An International Review*.

going back to the early church as it struggled to break loose from its Jewish cultural trappings and enter the Greco-Roman world of the Gentiles. At the same time, it is something new. Ever since the word emerged in the 1970s, there has been almost an explosion of writing, thinking, and talking about contextualization.[1]

Contextualization is part of an evolving stream of thought that relates the Gospel and church to a local context. In the past we have used words such as "adaptation," "accommodation," and "indigenization" to describe this relationship between Gospel, church, and culture, but "contextualization," introduced in 1971, and a companion term "inculturation" that emerged in the literature in 1974, are deeper, more dynamic, and more adequate terms to describe what we are about in mission today.[2] So I believe we are making some progress in our understanding of the relationship between Gospel, church, and culture, but we have a long way to go in everyday practice.

Contextualization is not something we pursue motivated by an agenda of pragmatic efficiency.[3] Rather, it must be followed because of our faithfulness to God, who sent God's son as a servant to die so that we all may live. As Peter Schineller says, "We have the obligation to search continually for ways in which the good news can be more deeply lived, celebrated and shared."[4]

In this essay I will discuss three functions of contextualization in mission today. I will then look at the gap that exists between the theory and the practice of contextualization, and then I will discuss two areas of resistance to contextualization.

Last year one of our students at Asbury Seminary, studying with us from Thailand, said to me, "Now that I have been studying contextualization and have discovered how the Gospel relates to culture, I am realizing that I can be both Christian and Thai." On a recent sabbatical in Southeast Asia, I probed the question of how the Gospel was being proclaimed and lived out in a contextualized manner, and, frankly, I was disappointed. In Thailand I heard over and over again. "To be Thai is to be Buddhist." The notion that one could be both Thai and Christian was an oxymoron to many. My student at Asbury went on to confide, "It always seemed strange to me that after I converted to Christianity out of Buddhism, I became so aggressive and felt forced to turn my back on my Buddhist family and denounce my culture. Now I realize through the insights of contextualization that I can practice a cherished value of meekness, affirm much of my Thai culture, and follow Jesus in the Thai way." Contextualization was the key that unlocked the door in her understanding that had kept Christianity bound up in a Westernized room. But now, with this new insight, a burst of sunshine has come into her room that affirmed Buddhist teaching on meekness and reinforced her love and respect for her family, while at the same time strengthening her love for God as revealed in Jesus Christ. She is now working on a dissertation entitled "The Way of Meekness: Being Christian and Thai in the Thai Way."

THREE FUNCTIONS OF CONTEXTUALIZATION

This story of my Thai student sets the stage for discussing the first function of contextualization in mission. Contextualization attempts *to communicate the Gospel in word and deed and to establish the church in ways that make sense to people within their local cultural context, presenting Christianity in such a way that it meets people's deepest needs and penetrates their worldview, thus allowing them to follow Christ and remain within their own culture.*

This function seems at first to be self-evident, but it is clear we have not always done mission in this mode. Why, then, this sudden burst of energy and excitement, at least in the academy, about this notion of contextualization? I believe the answer lies partly in the postcolonial discovery that much of our understanding and practice of faith has been shaped by our own culture and context, and yet we often assumed that our culturally conditioned interpretation of the Gospel *was* the Gospel. We are now beginning to realize that we have often confused the two and have inadvertently equated our culturally conditioned versions of the Gospel with the kingdom of God.

As we have become more critical in a postmodern world, we have discovered how urgent the task of contextualization is everywhere in the world, including—or should I say especially—in North America. An example of contextualization is the Willow Creek Community Church in suburban Chicago, Illinois, which discovered the need to contextualize the Gospel and the church in order to reach a particular subculture of American society in this location.[5]

My concern over why the mission of the church so often required people to abandon their culture is the main reason I trained as an anthropologist in preparation for cross-cultural ministry. I initially expected my research and ministry in Melanesia to help primarily expatriate missionaries figure out the complex and diverse Melanesian cultural context. But it did not take me long to discover that when I talked about contextualization with Melanesians, they became very excited about the possibility of being Christian *and* Melanesian without first having to become Australian, German, American, or whatever the cultural origin was of the missionaries with whom they identified.

On a furlough assignment I remember sharing with churches in the United States about my mission work in Melanesia and driving home the idea that my work was not to encourage Melanesian Christians to become like Americans but rather to enable Melanesians to become better Melanesians by becoming Christian. This was a brand new idea for many congregations with whom I spoke. I remember the enthusiasm of one elderly parishioner when she asked, "Did you invent this way of missionary work? I've never heard anyone talk like this." "No," I replied, "I can't take credit for it. It's not my invention." Being a good Methodist, she figured this must have been John Wesley's invention. And although he was certainly on target, credit for this approach to mission must go back to the early church as it broke free from its Jewish cultural trappings and made the important decision at the Jerusalem Council that one could follow Christ without first becoming culturally a Jew (Acts 15).

Present-day discussions of contextualization are getting us back in touch with this principle, for at nearly every era of the church's history, Christians have had to relearn this important principle. Contextualization is a fine balancing act between necessary involvement in the culture, being in the situation, and also maintaining an outside, critical perspective that is also needed. In anthropology, we would call this holding in tension emic and etic perspectives—the insider's deep understanding with the outsider's critique.

GOOD CONTEXTUALIZATION OFFENDS

Another function of contextualization in mission is *to offend—but only for the right reasons, not the wrong ones*. Good contextualization offends people for the right reasons. Bad contextualization, or the lack of it altogether, offends them for the wrong reasons. When the Gospel is presented in word and deed, and the fellowship of believers we call the church is organized along appropriate cultural patterns, then people will more likely be confronted with the offense of the Gospel, exposing their own sinfulness and the tendency toward evil, oppressive structures and behavior patterns within their culture. It could certainly be argued that the genius of the Wesleyan revival in eighteenth-century England was precisely that through preaching, music, and social organization in a society undergoing rapid and significant social and economic change, John and Charles Wesley contextualized Christianity so well that the power of the Gospel transformed personal lives and reformed a nation.[6]

Andrew Walls said it so clearly years ago in contrasting the indigenizing and the pilgrim principles, which we must always strive to hold in balance. He notes:

> Along with the indigenising principle which makes his faith a place to feel at home, the Christian inherits the pilgrim principle, which whispers to him that he has no abiding city and warns him that to be faithful to Christ will put him out of step with his society; for that society never existed, in East or West, ancient time or modern, which could absorb the word of Christ painlessly into its system. Jesus within Jewish culture, Paul within Hellenistic culture, take it for granted that there will be rubs and friction—not from the adoption of a new culture, but from the transformation of the mind towards that of Christ.[7]

Unfortunately, when Christianity is not contextualized or is contextualized poorly, then people are culturally offended, turned off to inquiring more about who Jesus is, or view missionaries and their small band of converts with suspicion as cultural misfits and aliens. When people are offended for the wrong reason, the garment of Christianity gets stamped with the label "Made in America and Proud of It," and so it is easily dismissed as a "foreign religion" and hence irrelevant to their culture. When this happens, potential converts never experience the offense of the Gospel because they have first encountered the cultural offense of the missionary or Westernized Christians.

Contextualization need not prohibit the prophetic role in mission as some fear it will. Paul Hiebert's landmark article "Critical Contextualization" is a wonderful tool for applying this prophetic dimension and critiquing function of contextualization.[8]

A third function of contextualization in mission is to *develop contextualized expressions of the Gospel so that the Gospel itself will be understood in ways the universal church has neither experienced nor understood before, thus expanding our understanding of the kingdom of God*. In this sense contextualization is a form of mission in reverse, where we will learn from other cultures how to be more Christian in our own context.

This is an important function of contextualization in mission because it connects the particular with the universal. The challenge is creating a community that is both Christian and true to its own cultural heritage. Peter Schineller points out in addition that "every local Christian community must maintain its links with other communities in the present around the world, and with communities of the past, through an understanding of Christian tradition."[9]

I have experienced this connection many times where two Christians from very different cultures have much more in common than do their respective cultures. This is because the common bond that unites them and bridges the chasm created by language and cultural differences is the Holy Spirit, who knows no boundaries of race, class, gender, or social location.

Encounters with Christians from other cultural contexts expand our understanding of God, for no longer are we satisfied with our own limited perception and experience. For example, I learned very little about the church functioning as a community and body of believers growing up in the United States, where faith is so privatized and individual. I had to learn this important biblical principle of the community nature of the church from living with Christians in a Melanesian village. Contextualization, therefore, forces us to have a wider loyalty that "corresponds to an enlarged and more adequate view of God as the God of all persons, male and female, and as a God who especially hears the cry of the poor. God can no longer simply be the god of myself, my family, my community, my nation; such a god is ultimately an idol or false god, one made according to my narrow and limited image and perspective."[10]

In this sense the anthropologists are correct—human beings have a tendency to create God in their own image, but we must always counter this observation with the biblical view that God has created all human beings in God's image. Stretching our understanding of God through contextualization will enable us to gain insights from around the world, which we need to inform each other and certainly the church in North America. From Asia we can learn more about the mystery and transcendence of God; from Oceania we can recover the notion of the body of Christ as community; from Africa we can discover the nature of celebration and the healing power of the church; and from Latin America we are learning about the role of the church in the work for justice.

In his well-known book *The Primal Vision* (1963), which reflects on his study of the growth of the church in Buganda, John V. Taylor helps us realize the value of learning from and listening to other voices of Christian faith. He notes:

> The question is, rather, whether in Buganda, and elsewhere in Africa, the Church will be enabled by God's grace to discover a new synthesis between a saving Gospel and a total, unbroken unity of society. For there are many who feel that the spiritual sickness of the West, which reveals itself in the divorce of the sacred from the secular, of the cerebral from the instinctive, and in the loneliness and homelessness of individualism, may be healed through a recovery of the wisdom which Africa has not yet thrown away.

The world church awaits something new out of Africa. The church in Buganda, and in many other parts of the continent, by obedient response to God's calling, for all its sinfulness and bewilderment, may yet become the agent through whom the Holy Spirit will teach his people everywhere how to be in Christ without ceasing to be involved in mankind.[11]

When I think about this function of contextualization in expanding the universal church's understanding of God, I am reminded of the picture we are given in Revelation 7:9 of people from every ethnolinguistic group surrounding the throne of God, not worshiping God in English, or even English as a second language, but in their own language shaped by their own worldview and culture. We can count on hearing about 6,280 languages. The view we get of the kingdom is a multicultural view, not one of ethnic uniformity. One of the things we admire most about the Gospel is its ability to speak within the worldview of every culture. To me, this feature is the empirical proof of the Gospel's authenticity.

Perhaps one of the most important functions of contextualization in mission is to remind us that we do not have a privileged position when it comes to understanding and practicing Christianity. It cannot be the exclusive property of any one culture, for it refuses to be culture bound; it continually bursts free from the chains of bondage to cultural tradition. Kosuke Koyama reminded us that there is "no handle" on the cross,[12] and Lamin Sanneh has persuasively argued that Christianity demands to be "translated" from one cultural context to another.[13]

THE GAP BETWEEN OUR TALK AND OUR PRACTICE

Recently I had breakfast with the president of a large Protestant denominational mission board in the United States. In our conversation he said, "I have come to realize that the cutting edge of missiology and our most urgent need in mission today is contextualization. Unless we present the Gospel locally in ways that connect to peoples' language, culture, and worldview, we will fail in our efforts at world evangelization." I nodded my head in hearty agreement, cheered him on, and affirmed his insight. I said that this approach to cross-cultural ministry represented the best thinking in missiology today and was clearly anchored in the biblical model of our Lord in his incarnation. But then this mission executive went on to say, "The problem I face in trying to move our mission toward a more contextualized approach is that I am held accountable to a board of trustees, and they don't understand *anything* about contextualization. They are interested only in extending our denomination across the face of the globe, sincerely believing that this is the best way to win the world for Christ." It was obvious that he was stuck between a theological rock and an ecclesiastical hard place. I urged him to push ahead in leading his mission to become more contextualized in its approach. With confidence, I boldly stated that if his mission chose the contextualization route, in the end they would have more churches planted and connected to their denomination than if they continued in their present noncontextual approach, even though these churches wouldn't necessarily resemble the same kinds of churches his board of trustee members attended every Sunday.

This conversation illustrates the fact that there still remains an enormous gulf between the models of contextualization that we missiologists discuss and teach in our seminary classes and the practice of contextualized mission by North American and European missionaries, both Protestant and Roman Catholic. Contextualization and denominational extension are two very different agendas, but if most of us are committed intellectually to the former, we frequently draw our paycheck from the latter, and this creates the problem. It must also be noted that this is not just a problem for Western missionaries. For example, Korean missionaries, as well as other non-Western missionaries, have the same struggle of disentangling their culture from their understanding and practice of Christianity.[14]

Another illustration of this tension between contextualization and denominational extension comes from my mission work in Melanesia. I was asked to lead a weeklong workshop on Melanesian culture and religion for Catholic missionaries working in the southern highlands of Papua New Guinea. They were wanting to pioneer a new pastoral approach called Basic Christian Communities. As we know, this concept originated in Latin America, and for this Catholic order it had spread to Tanzania and was now being brought to Papua New Guinea. As an anthropologist, I led them through the process of understanding the social structures, economic patterns, values, and worldviews of Melanesian communities. We had a wonderful week together as we got deeper into understanding things Melanesian. Then we came to the final session. I recalled how we had discussed in great detail the nature of basic Melanesian communities, and I suggested that if they would begin their new pastoral approach in this Melanesian context and let it take on a Melanesian face and be expressed in Melanesian ways, and if they would infuse this Melanesian world with Gospel values, then their pastoral plan, I predicted, would be successful. These basic Christian communities would be both Melanesian and Christian. "But," I warned them, "if you approach these communities with a prepackaged plan and lay that heavy burden on the shoulders of these Melanesian communities, I fear your approach will fail, because it will not be rooted in Melanesian soil."

A veteran missioner at the back of the room jumped up and, with anger in his voice, said, "Now you have gone too far! We are here first as—(and he named his order), and there are certain distinctive features of our Catholic order on which we must insist. We cannot forfeit those in order to adapt to the Melanesian context."

My heart sank and my blood pressure rose. After pouring myself out for a week to help them understand how these communities could be *both* Christian and Melanesian, they still did not get it. They were fearful that contextualization would lead to at best a weak church or at worst to syncretism. In fact, it is just the opposite. When we fail to contextualize, we run a much greater risk of establishing weak churches, whose members will turn to non-Christian syncretistic explanations, follow nonbiblical lifestyles, and engage in magical rituals. This is because a non-contextualized Christianity seldom engages people at the level of their deepest needs and aspirations, and so we end up with what Jesuit Jaime Bulatao in the Philippines calls a "split-level" Christianity.[15]

But the news on the contextualization front is not all bad. In fact, there is a lot of good news. We *have* made some progress.[16] Where has it been? In worship styles?

In church social organization and structures? In contextual theology? We can celebrate the incremental progress that has occurred over the past twenty-five years, but there is still a gap—and at times an enormous gap—between our scholarly books and articles on models of contextualization that we write to one another and the actual practice around the world, where in far too many corners of the globe, Christianity is still identified as a Western religion and where for various reasons people have missed the universal appeal of Jesus.

There are notable exceptions, but they tend to occur in places where Western missionaries or Western-trained national church leaders are not in control. In fact, if we look around the world to see what has happened in the past twenty-five years since the terms "contextualization" and "inculturation" came into missiological discussions, we will discover that some of the arguments about contextualization have passed us by as the Christian church's center of gravity has shifted from the North and West to the South and East.[17]

A notable exception to this lack of contextualization are some of the African Independent Churches.[18] The documentary film *Rise Up and Walk* profiles five of these churches, and it knocks the theological and ecclesiastical socks off my students every time I show it. Ecclesiastical hegemony—a carryover from colonial and political domination, and a close cousin of economic domination today—is one of the major obstacles to contextualization. Let me illustrate what I mean.

A friend of mine in a school that was about to introduce a Ph.D. program in intercultural studies complained that such a program was not needed. His reasoning was that non-Western church leaders who would be attracted to the program would be people who already understood their culture and context. He mused, "What could they possibly learn from a Ph.D. in intercultural studies that they don't already know because they were born in a non-Western context? What they really need," he argued, "is a Ph.D. in systematic theology and biblical studies so that they can return to their countries and teach and preach the truth"—which to him meant his particular denominational theological system.

Little does my systematic theologian colleague realize that until non-Western Christians learn how to exegete their own cultural context as well as they exegete the biblical text, no number of Ph.D. students trained in standard Western theological and biblical studies will automatically enable and encourage church leaders to plant and grow indigenous, contextualized, churches.

POINTS OF RESISTANCE

What are the points of resistance to contextualization? I limit my discussion to two primary sources. One source of resistance comes from the mission-sending organizations themselves. I have often observed the enthusiasm with which missionary candidates train for cross-cultural ministry. It is thrilling to see them acquire skills to begin distinguishing the universalizing Gospel from their parochial culture. They come to realize the value of their cross-cultural training and the need to express the Gospel in ways that are appropriate to the local context of their host's society. But then they arrive in their host country and are sometimes surprised, and certainly disappointed, when they discover that their mission organization is very intent on reproducing the church "over there" to look like the church back home. I have observed that this problem occurs equally with independent "faith missions," denominational mission boards, and Catholic mission orders. In other words, we are all guilty.

The first point of resistance to contextualization often comes from mission executives and denominational leaders, who frequently do not think missiologically about these issues. They nevertheless hold positions of power and influence that shape the patterns of mission work.

The second source of resistance to contextualization, and sometimes the dominant one, comes from the leaders of the very churches the missions created several generations previously. This resistance can certainly catch new missionaries by surprise. They wonder, "Why would *these* people be so hesitant and cautious about connecting the Gospel to their own context in ways that are both relevant and challenging?" I believe the primary cause is that as non-Western Christians have learned a non-contextualized Christianity from their missionary teachers and have adopted it at a formal, behavioral level, it still has not yet penetrated the deeper levels of their worldview. It has not connected with their social structure or addressed the critical questions arising from their political and economic situations. When this happens, after several generations it is not unusual for the church to be plagued with nominalism. But there is security in familiar ways of doing things, and so any newfangled talk about contextualization can be both frightening and threatening, especially to those persons who are in positions of power.

I believe the only way through this maze is to discover the tools and perspectives of contextualization and then have the courage to implement them. We must work at closing the gap between our discussions about contextualization, the training of cross-cultural witnesses and church leaders, and their actual practice of contextualization around the world.

Why, for example, does Christianity continue to be viewed as a foreign religion in much of Asia and Southeast Asia? The answer? Because frequently that is how it is practiced. For example, in China before 1949 there were about 10,000 missionaries and 1.5 million Christians. A common phrase at the time was, "One more Christian, one less Chinese," or "Gain a convert, lose a citizen." A common, if not implicit, perception by both missionaries and Chinese was that one could not follow Christ without becoming Westernized in the process. This is the old Judaizer problem in a new guise. Then Mao Tse-tung came to power, and the Western missionaries were forced to leave China. And many thought the church would now die without their presence. But it didn't. In fact it has flourished, with a rough estimate of 30-40 million Christians today. Now what is the missiological lesson to be learned here? Kick out the missionaries and the church grows? Perhaps, but I do not think so.

The lesson to be learned is that the Chinese discovered that the Gospel could be contextualized in their own contemporary Chinese experience, as oppressive as it often was. They discovered they could follow Jesus and remain Chinese. In other words, they discovered the important principle hammered out in the Jerusalem Council as recorded in Acts 15. Gentiles did not have to become Jews culturally in order to follow Christ. And Chinese do not have to become Westernized, acquiring white, middle-class values to be Christian. One of the most precious items out of China that I have held in my hands is a two-inch-thick Chinese hymnal printed on thin rice paper, containing 1,000 hymns—all created during the turbulent period following 1949. It is a beautiful symbol and vivid reminder of the importance and fruit of contextualization.

CONCLUSION

Although we can see the obvious need for contextualization, the actual practice of it is not easy. Blinded by our own ethnocentrism and ecclesiastical hegemony, we find it is very difficult to cultivate the art of listening and learning from those different from ourselves. But in a spirit of humility this is a fundamental requirement for contextualization.

The challenge that contextualization brings to us is, How do we carry out the Great Commission and live out the Great Commandment in a world of cultural diversity with a Gospel that is both truly Christian in content and culturally significant in form?

The function of contextualization in mission leaves us with three challenges:

- Contextualization changes and transforms the context—this is the *prophetic* challenge.
- Contextualization expands our understanding of the Gospel because we now see the Gospel through a different cultural lens—this is the *hermeneutic* challenge.
- Contextualization changes the missionaries because they will not be the same once they have become part of the body of Christ in a context different from their own—this is the *personal* challenge.

In our discussion and practice of contextualization, we must take our cues from the incarnation. In the same way that Jesus emptied himself and dwelt among us, we must be willing to do likewise as we enter another culture with the Gospel. The incarnation is our model for contextualization, for as J. D. Gordon once said, "Jesus is God spelled out in language human beings can understand"—I would add, "in every culture, in every context."

NOTES

1. See, for example, Charles R. Taber, "Contextualization," in *Exploring Church Growth*, ed. Wilbert R. Shenk (Grand Rapids: Eerdmans, 1983), pp. 117-31; Harvie M. Conn, "Contextualization: Where Do We Begin?" in *Evangelism and Liberation*, ed. Carl Armerding (Nutley, N.J.: Presbyterian & Reformed, 1977); Dean S. Gilliland, ed., *The Word Among Us: Contextualizing Theology for Mission Today* (Dallas: Word Publishing, 1989); Robert J. Schreiter, *Constructing Local Theologies* (Maryknoll, N.Y.: Orbis Books, 1985); Stephen B. Bevans, *Models of Contextual Theology* (Maryknoll, N.Y.: Orbis Books, 1992); Justin S. Ukpong, "What Is Contextualization?" *Neue Zeitschrift für Missionswissenschaft* 43, no. 3

(1987): 161-68, and "Contextualisation: A Historical Survey," *African Ecclesial Review* 29, no. 5 (October 1987): 278-86. For a conservative evangelical perspective, see Bruce C. E. Fleming, *Contextualization of Theology: An Evangelical Assessment* (Pasadena, Calif.: William Carey Library, 1980); David J. Hesselgrave and Edward Rommen, *Contextualization: Meanings, Methods, and Models* (Grand Rapids: Baker, 1989).

2. The term "inculturation" first appeared in Roman Catholic circles in item 12 in the Final Statement of the First Plenary Assembly of the Federation of Asian Bishops' Conference (Taipei, April 22-27,1974), where the Asian bishops noted, "The local church is a church incarnate in a people, a church indigenous and inculturated" (*His Gospel to Our Peoples*, vol. 2 [Manila: Cardinal Bea Institute, 1976], p. 332). The Society of Jesus at their Thirty-Second General Congregation in late 1974 to early 1975 focused on fostering the task of the inculturation of Christianity. For a history of the term, see Gerald A. Arbuckle, "Inculturation and Evangelisation: Realism or Romanticism?" in *Missionaries, Anthropologists, and Cultural Change*, ed. Darrell L. Whiteman, Studies in Third World Societies No. 25 (1985), pp. 171-214; Arij A. Roest-Crollius, S.J., "What Is New About Inculturation?" *Gregorianum* 59, no. 4 (1978): 721-38, and also his article on inculturation in *Dizionario di missiologia* (Bologna: Edizioni Dehoniane, 1993), pp. 281-86. See also Peter Schineller, S.J., *A Handbook on Inculturation* (New York: Paulist Press, 1990). The fullest treatment of the term to date is Aylward Shorter, *Toward a Theology of Inculturation* (Maryknoll, N.Y.: Orbis Books, 1992).

3. For a discussion of contextualization as a method in contrast to church growth strategy, see Taber, "Contextualization."

4. Schineller, *Handbook on Inculturation*, p. 3.

5. See George Hunter's discussion of the Willow Creek Community Church in *Church for the Unchurched* (Nashville: Abingdon Press, 1996).

6. See J. Wesley Bready's classic study *England: Before and After Wesley; the Evangelical Revival and Social Reform* (London: Hodder & Stoughton, 1938). Cf. Leon O. Hynson, *To Reform the Nation* (Grand Rapids: Zondervan/Francis Asbury Press, 1984).

7. Andrew Walls, "The Gospel as the Prisoner and Liberator of Culture," *Missionalia* 10, no. 3 (November 1982): 98-99, and chapter 1 of this volume.

8. Paul Hiebert, "Critical Contextualization," *International Bulletin of Missionary Research* 11, no. 3 (July 1987): 104-12.

9. Schineller, *Handbook on Inculturation*, p. 72.

10. Ibid., p. 116.

11. John V. Taylor, *The Primal Vision: Christian Presence amid African Religion* (London: SCM Press, 1963), p. 108.

12. Kosuke Koyama, *No Handle on the Cross* (Maryknoll, N.Y.: Orbis Books, 1977).

13. Lamin Sanneh, *Translating the Message: The Missionary Impact on Culture* (Maryknoll, N.Y.: Orbis Books, 1989).

14. Two recent doctoral dissertations attempt to close the gap between theory and practice. See Tereso C. Casiño, "The Text in Context: An Evangelical Approach to the Foundations of Contextualization" (Ph.D. diss., Asia Center for Theological Studies and Mission, Seoul, 1996); Hyun Mo Lee, "A Missiological Appraisal of the Korean Church in Light of Theological Contextualization" (Ph.D. diss., Southwestern Baptist Theological Seminary, Fort Worth, Tex., 1992).

15. Jaime Bulatao, S.J., *Split-Level Christianity* (Manila: Ateneo de Manila Univ., 1966).

16. Discussion of inculturation (contextualization) at the grassroots level in South Africa has been the subject of articles and letters in *Challenge: Church and People*, published by Contextual Publications, Johannesburg. See no. 26 (November 1994), no. 28 (February/March 1995), no. 30 (June/July 1995), no. 32 (October/November 1995), and

no. 34 (February/March 1996). A very practical guide to contextualization (inculturation) is Gerald A. Arbuckle, *Earthing the Gospel: An Inculturation Handbook for Pastoral Workers* (London: Geoffrey Chapman; Maryknoll, N.Y.: Orbis Books, 1990). See also Schineller, *Handbook on Inculturation*.

17. See, for example, Walbert Bühlmann, *The Coming of the Third Church* (Maryknoll, N.Y.: Orbis Books, 1978).

18. See David B. Barrett, *Schism and Renewal in Africa* (Nairobi: Oxford Univ. Press, 1968); Harold Turner, *History of an African Independent Church: Church of the Lord (Aladura)*, 2 vols. (Oxford: Clarendon Press, 1967), and *Bibliography of New Religious Movements in Primal Societies*: Vol. 1, *Black Africa* (Boston: G. K. Hall 1977); M. L. Daneel, *Old and New in Southern Shona Independent Churches*, 3 vols. (vols. 1-2, The Hague: Mouton, 1971-74; vol. 3, Gweru, Zimbabwe: Mambo Press, 1988).

4

Inculturation: Win or Lose the Future?

Aylward Shorter*

This article first describes the nature and function of culture and inculturation and the dangers of the homogenization of culture as a result of the process of globalization. It then speaks of the need for a "new evangelization" that abandons the preference for western culture as the medium of preaching the gospel. Such a "new evangelization" will demand a church that takes koinonia *and dialogue seriously, and that will allow local voices—particularly those of small Christian communities—to be heard.*

INTRODUCTION

"Today is the elder brother of tomorrow," runs a West African proverb.[1] Inculturation is the most urgent and overriding topic of the African synod, because many of those concerned are convinced that an opportunity must be grasped today, or lost forever. This paper begins by describing the nature and function of culture and inculturation. It then discusses the experience of cultural alienation in the African Church. After this, there is an examination of the threat posed to the indigenous cultures of Africa by Euro-American world culture and the need for a "new evangelisation" in which the Church abandons its preference for Western culture. This in turn demands an "evangelisation model" of Church, one that is culturally polycentric. Finally, the importance of small Christian communities in Africa is emphasised, as instruments and guarantors of inculturation.

---

* Originally published in Walter von Holzen, S.V.D. and Seán Fagan, S.M., eds., *Africa: The Kairos of a Synod—Symposium on Africa* (Rome: SEDOS, 1994). This book contains the proceedings of a symposium held at SEDOS (Service of Documentation and Studies) during the Roman Catholic Synod for Africa in 1994. Aylward Shorter is a Missionary of Africa and one of the world's most eminent authorities on inculturation. For many years he taught at various institutions of higher education in Africa and has recently completed several years as president of the Missionary Institute London.

THE NATURE AND FUNCTION OF CULTURE

Culture is part of the human phenomenon. It means that everything a human being thinks or does is an aspect of a pattern or whole. When groups of people come into contact with one another they perceive a variety of such patterns. Culture is acquired or learned by individuals as members of a human society. Culture controls their perception of reality. It offers them a system of meanings embodied in images and symbols. It shapes their understanding, feelings and behaviour. It gives them a group identity. Human beings, according to the teaching of the Second Vatican Council, "constitute large and distinct groups united by enduring ties, ancient religious traditions, and strong social relationships."[2]

A number of consequences follow. Firstly, cultures are coherent systems. They cannot be artificially broken down into "elements" or "components" without doing violence to them. Secondly, the right to culture is a human right, and the manipulation or oppression of cultures is an abuse. Although this is not to say that cultures are beyond criticism or comparative evaluation. Thirdly, evangelisation must not only respect cultures, it must address them, if it is to produce any effect on human beings.

INCULTURATION: THE EVANGELISATION OF CULTURES

The evangelisation of cultures was described by Pope Paul VI: "What matters is to evangelise man's culture and cultures (not in a purely decorative way, as it were by applying a thin veneer, but in a vital way, in depth and right to their very roots)."[3]

Pope John Paul II is even more emphatic about the need to address cultures. "The synthesis between culture and faith is not just a demand of culture, but also of faith. A faith which does not become culture is a faith which has not been fully received, not thoroughly thought through, not fully lived out."[4]

Inculturation, therefore, is an inseparable aspect of evangelisation. It means the presentation and re-expression of the gospel in forms and terms proper to a culture—processes which result in the reinterpretation of both, without being unfaithful to either. Inculturation is a creative development which, as the International Theological Commission rightly pointed out, participates in the dynamism of cultures and their intercommunication.[5] Inculturation means both that the gospel challenges cultures and that cultures re-express the gospel. Inculturation is therefore:

> The process of a deep, sympathetic adaptation to, and appropriation of, a local culture in which the Church finds itself, in a way that does not compromise its basic faith.[6] The process by which a particular people respond to the saving Word of God and express their response in their own cultural forms of worship, reflection, organization and life. This is how a local Church is born and continues to live.[7]

Syncretism is a name given to the anomalous conflict of meaning which frequently occurs when cultures interact. In the context of evangelisation it occurs when cultures "domesticate" the gospel and distort its meaning. On balance, this is more likely to happen in the case of older evangelised cultures which claim to be unfailingly "Christian," than in newly evangelised cultures. When a culture claims to be "Christian," the implication is that the process of inculturation is finished. This is impossible, because genuine inculturation constitutes an ongoing dialogue between the gospel and culture, a call to continuous conversion and renewal.

Inculturation is opposed to uniformity in the universal Church. It demands the legitimisation of diversity. The logic is inescapable: genuine evangelisation addresses cultures. Cultures are empirically diverse. Therefore evangelisation leads to culturally diverse ways of living the gospel. Inculturation produces, and is the product of, a dialogue between the gospel and diverse forms of human life in the major socio-cultural regions of the world. Genuine evangelisation therefore demands a culturally polycentric universal Church. There can be no monopoly of cultural forms in a truly Catholic communion.

Another important consequence of inculturation is that both evangelising and evangelised cultures mutually influence each other. This is a normal outcome of the intercultural process. It is to be expected that evangelised cultures acquire culture traits from the evangelisers, reinterpret them and integrate them within their own authentic systems. It is also to be expected that evangelising cultures are enriched in their turn by the new cultural expressions of Christianity they have provoked. This point was clearly made by Pope Paul VI.[8] It has also given rise to the term "inter-culturation" coined by the late Bishop Joseph Blomjous.[9] It has even been suggested that the evangelisation/inculturation process can correct cultural distortions in the message brought by the evangelisers.[10] Such interaction characterizes the communion and mutual ministry which should exist between legitimately diverse forms of Christianity.[11]

It must be emphasised from the start that the agenda for inculturation can only be set by the owners of the culture concerned, that is, the local community. Moreover, genuine inculturation demands that the interests of all sections of the community, e.g., women and youth, be represented.

THE CHURCH AND CULTURE—CULTURAL ALIENATION OF THE AFRICAN CHURCH

The discovery of culture as a plural, empirical phenomenon is one of the achievements of the twentieth century, and the Church's understanding of culture has evolved with that of humanity at large. Originally, culture was taken for granted as a single, universal, normative criterion, and Christianity in its European, Latin form was deemed to be the perfection of this culture of humanity. No allowance was made for factors of cultural diversity in doctrinal or ritual controversy. Moreover, the Church was unable to accommodate the initiatives of early missionaries, such as the Jesuits Matteo Ricci, Roberto de Nobili and Pedro Paez, when they tried to evangelise foreign cultures from within. In the twentieth century, however, first Pope Pius XII, and then, with greater confidence and clarity, Pope John XXIII, referred in official documents to a plurality of cultures.[12] Finally, the Second Vatican Council directed its attention to culture as such, explicitly considering the relationship between faith and cultures.[13] These discussions bore fruit in the 1974 and 1977 synods of Bishops with the eventual fashioning of "inculturation" as a theological concept.

In Africa these developments coincided with the first decade of political independence and with an impulse to disown the culture of the evangeliser, which also happened to be the culture of the colonial oppressor. The modern era of missionary expansion which began in the mid-nineteenth century took the form of Christianity in the shape of one or another Euro-American subculture communicating with a multiplicity of non-Western cultures in every part of the world. For the first hundred years of this expansion, there was little or no appreciation of cultural diversity. Fortunately, the emphasis of missionary founders on language learning and language recording eventually led to an understanding of language as one of the principal mechanisms of culture, and thence to an appreciation of culture as an empirical reality.

The missionary appreciation of culture undoubtedly contributed to the reflection on the relationship between faith and culture at the Second Vatican Council. However, in practice, little or no explicit dialogue between the Catholic faith and African culture had taken place by the time the call was made for the holding of an African Council by the Society of African Culture in 1977. Moreover, Euro-American culture was entrenched in the language and forms of universal communion, of the *Magisterium* and of Canon Law, as well as in the local cultural forms taken by Christianity. The result was that evangelisation entailed the kind of cultural alienation lamented by the Zairean theologian, Oscar Bimwenyi:

> [Africans] pray to God with a liturgy that is not theirs. They live according to a morality which is not the conversion of their own previous morality under the action of God's grace and the breath of the Holy Spirit. They are ruled by a Canon Law which is not a law born from the conversion to Christ of social and juridical realities inherent in the universe to which they belong . . . They reflect—when indeed they reflect—using philosophical and theological systems secreted by the meditation and reflection of the other Christian communities which evangelised them.[14]

EVANGELISATION AND THE THREAT OF EURO-AMERICAN WORLD CULTURE

Up to the present time evangelisation has been manifestly Eurocentric, accompanying a world process of Euro-American cultural domination. Historically, Euro-American culture tends to undermine and supplant local indigenous cultures. It does this especially where there is a technological culture-differential between coloniser and colonised. The culture-differential underlies the contemporary consciousness of the "global village." This refers to a totalitarian world process through which the Euro-American technocratic culture has created a global monetary system, provoked a world-wide industrial revolution and has internationalised productive capital. At the global (or macro-cultural) level cultural diversity is disappearing, and lower levels of indigenous culture and popular religiosity are seriously threatened. This is not a mere question of nostalgic romanticism, but the perception of an injustice involving genuine cultural impoverishment and the loss of human resources.

One of the major instruments of this world process is urbanisation. By the end of the twentieth century half the world's population will be urban-dwelling, and by the first quarter of the next century nearly half the population of Africa. Besides creating intractable ecological problems, urbanisation is a force for secularisation, cultural disorientation and material impoverishment. The impact of Western electronic mass media on Africa and the rest of the world is comprehensive and devastating. Although they offer many positive advantages with regard to information and education, their cultural message is also often arrogant, introspective and preoccupied with the morbid social factors of Euro-American society. Moreover, they tend to rob the viewing and listening public of the capacity to make a genuine moral response to current events. In spite of the media's own democratic self-image, the modern means of communication are essentially a vehicle of power and of cultural domination, from which religious content is usually absent, except as a story with news value.

This is not to say that the modern media can be ignored; and the *Instrumentum Laboris* of the African synod is right to point to their positive factors.[15] On the other hand, people need to be educated to use the media. The Euro-American monopoly needs to be counter-balanced by local media production, even if African countries cannot compete with it at world level.

African youth are among those most attracted by Euro-American culture, the more so since their own experience of indigenous culture is limited. This attraction can lead to cultural disorientation. It is clear that a balanced cultural education would give them greater respect for their own cultural roots and indigenous spiritual values.

Euro-American world technocracy has no substance as a genuine cultural system. In the part of the world from which it originates, it has already undermined traditional Christian culture. In Africa and the rest of the world, it also fails to meet the cultural needs of humanity.[16] It undermines human sensibility, it absolutizes the material and the technical, it renders human beings less compassionate.[17] It is, as it were, a worldwide movement of "anti-culture."[18]

It is difficult to believe that the secular Europeanisation of the world is an "innocent vehicle" for the propagation of the Church's message, and that it is not, in fact, a subversion of the gospel itself.[19] However, the claim continues to be made that Euro-American culture has a universal significance for evangelisation, through its fusion with indigenous cultures.[20] Even the Second Vatican Council took a benign view of what it called "universal culture."[21] This is not the view of African and other contemporary observers from the non-Western world. They have no faith in "universal culture." Their concern is to "uphold human and religious values as the basis and inspiration of culture in a secular and technological world," and to do this by siding with the threatened indigenous traditions, not to assist in the destructive process itself.[22]

In the 1985 report by four Vatican secretariats on *Sects or New Religious Movements*, the need for inculturation was said to be one of the lessons which the Catholic Church could learn from the sects in Africa. It is an opinion which has been reiterated in the *Instrumentum Laboris* of the African synod:

> The question of inculturation is a fundamental one. It is particularly stressed by the responses from Africa which reveal a feeling of estrangement to Western forms of worship and ministry which are often quite irrelevant to people's cultural environment and life situation. One respondent declared: "Africans want to be Christians." We have given them accommodation, but no home . . . They want a simpler Christianity, integrated into all aspects of daily life, into the sufferings, joys, work, aspirations, fears and needs of the African . . . The young recognise in the Independent Churches a genuine vein of the African tradition of doing things religious.[23]

In the eight years which have elapsed since those words were written many African independent churches have succumbed to the influence of fundamentalist, Pentecostal or faith-gospel trends from America. These trends present the Bible as a book of prophecies which purport to confirm the socio-cultural responses of evangelicals from the southern United States to current events. This is presented as "Bible Christianity" and is a tragic example of the way in which Euro-American religious trends lend support to the imposition of technocratic world culture and to the subversion of African religious values.[24]

It is doubtless true that the ultimate solution to the problems created by a secularising world culture in Africa and the South lies in confronting that culture in the Euro-America from which it emanates and in which it is now entrenched. The idea that science is the only objective truth, and that religion is merely subjective opinion has to be challenged. If secularism is to be effectively counteracted worldwide, the gospel must first become a matter of public truth amidst the pluralism and free market of opinions that characterises the Western mind.[25] Needless to say, this does not absolve the Church of its immediate responsibility to uphold, in the power of the gospel, the authentic religious values of African and other indigenous cultural traditions.

Pope John Paul II has rightly referred to the urgency of inculturation in the present situation:

> As she carries out missionary activity among the nations, the Church encounters different cultures and becomes involved in the process of inculturation. The need for such involvement has marked the Church's pilgrimage throughout her history, but today it is particularly urgent.[26]

The urgency of inculturation to which the Pope refers, is also underlined by the African particular Churches in the *Instrumentum Laboris* of the African synod. For the great majority it is "urgent, necessary and even a priority."[27]

It is clear that, in the present climate of Euro-American cultural aggression, inculturation is an urgent necessity. Many social analysts are even pessimistic about the chances of redefining the indigenous cultures of Africa, whereas the optimists, while pointing to the historical resilience of such traditions, would also admit that they are now in a critical "win or lose" situation. Historically, the Church has played an honourable role in the preservation of human cultures when these were threatened with extinction. She is no less morally obliged to assist in the preservation of African indigenous cultures today.

Furthermore, by tying evangelisation to Euro-American culture and secular domination, the future of Catholic Christianity in the non-Western world is placed in jeopardy. "Christianity, with its universal message, cannot grow as a religion today, unless it abandons its preference for Western culture . . . ."[28] As long as Western culture, Western language and the Western rational bias are privileged in the Church, its Catholicity is frustrated. The great commandment of love, which is the foundation of the Church's mission, takes account of human differences.[29] We love others in their otherness, not by denying, let alone destroying, their otherness.[30]

INCULTURATION AND "NEW EVANGELISATION" IN AFRICA

The evocative phrase "new or second evangelisation," used by Pope John Paul II in *Redemptoris Missio*, sheds further light on this argument.[31] The expression was first used by the Pope in Haiti in 1983, when he spoke of "a new evangelisation—new in its fervour, in its methods and in its expression."[32] In the Haitian context, the Pope was envisaging a scenario in which Christianity had not taken sufficient root or had not made sufficient headway. A new or second evangelisation was needed either because the original evangelisation had lost its momentum, or because it was in some sense flawed.

This is also the case with the original evangelisation of Africa, which was not sufficiently new or liberative. It sought to transplant the institutions, images, concepts and moral habits of Euro-America, and it evaded or postponed a genuine encounter between the gospel and the indigenous religious cultures of Africa. The Church in Africa remains fundamentally Euro-American in outlook and expression, and this alien character is unaffected by a patchy, piecemeal adaptation, that incorporates elements of African culture into basically foreign structures, rites and institutions.

The prospect of legitimising more thoroughgoing cultural diversity in the Church is, no doubt, daunting to leaders who have been formed by, and are at home in, a monocultural system. They fear that diversification will lead to disunity, even schism, yet the reverse is more likely. Schism is liable to occur wherever the gospel is prevented from taking deep root in local cultures, and even if it is avoided, there is a risk of internal heterodoxy under a veneer of monocultural uniformity. Such timidity on the part of Catholic leaders could lead to the loss of a positive opportunity for integrating and creatively transforming traditional African symbols and values within Christianity. A Christian anthropologist has argued that only Christianity is capable of articulating and developing African religion in ways that will ensure its survival in a modern, secularising world.[33] And a distinguished African historian has argued that Bible translation, accompanied by a valid encounter with Christianity, is a vehicle of enormous significance for the preservation of indigenous cultures and for fostering their "change-in-continuity."[34]

Until this moment, evangelisation in Africa has been vitiated by Eurocentrism. The celebration of the African synod coincides with the urgent call for a new and more effective evangelisation characterised by diversification or cultural polycentrism. Africa and the world can only be evangelised by addressing their lived cultural plurality. Effective evangelisation, therefore, demands an "evangelisation model" of Church, a Church that is better geared to the work of evangelisation, in other words a culturally polycentric Church. Such a Church may be a dream, but it is not an impossible dream.

THE DEMANDS OF A CULTURALLY POLYCENTRIC CHURCH

In such a Church, communion or *koinônia* is at a premium. It is vital to see how the "mutual enrichment" of the particular Churches, mentioned by Paul VI in *Evangelii Nuntiandi*, is to take place.[35] In the first place, diversity is not being emphasised at the expense of unity. Ecclesial maturity does not consist in self-encapsulation, but in the capacity to give, receive and mutually enrich within the *koinônia*. Moreover, this communion possesses a hierarchical structure, focussed on the Petrine ministry and its universal jurisdiction. This authority guarantees a universal bond of faith, sacrament and ministry. What is at issue is not the reality of Catholic communion, but its contingent cultural forms and functions. In an evangelisation model of Church, communion facilitates pluriform cultural expression; it does not block or impede it.

A preliminary question that must be asked is: At what level are the Church's cultural centres to be located? Although the diocese is the principal analogue of the particular Church, it can seldom be identified with a given African indigenous culture. Many dioceses, and even parishes in Africa, are multicultural. In other instances, African indigenous cultures transcend dioceses and even national episcopal conferences. Dioceses which are not even geographically contiguous may share common cultural experiences, as is the case with the nomads in the seven countries of East Africa. For these reasons, bilateral, regional and even continental relationships among episcopal conferences may be of greater cultural significance than relations between dioceses. The missionary decree of the Second Vatican Council spoke realistically of "major socio-cultural regions," as being the context for dialogue between the faith and local culture.[36] It would seem, therefore, that cultural regions or cultural clusters should provide the focal points for polycentrism in Africa, and that these can best be articulated through national, regional and continental episcopal bodies.

MINISTRY, THEOLOGY AND LAW IN THE CULTURALLY POLYCENTRIC CHURCH

Some may wonder whether it is possible for a Church that is hierarchically monocentric (that is, centred on the Successor of Peter) to become culturally polycentric. The answer lies in laying stress on the ministry of communion as a basic dimension of the Church's ministry. There are many obvious ways in which the cultural regions of the Church can develop their own spontaneous expressions of faith, worship, ministry and Christian life. Rather than reflect Euro-American technocratic domination, central authorities should scrupulously safeguard the freedom of action, initiative and responsibility of the Church in the various cultural regions. Equally, local authorities exercise a ministry of communion when they discourage cultural fragmentation and ensure that their initiatives respect the bonds of universal communion.

A culturally polycentric Church accepts as necessary a plurality of understanding, applications and expressions of Catholic teaching that are consistent with its universal tradition of faith.[37] It also accepts that this tradition makes progress in the Church through a multiplicity of initiatives and experiences and that the consequent growth of insight comes about in varied ways.[38] Without denying the unhindered right and duty of the Pope to address the whole Church as shepherd and teacher, especially when it is a question of making infallible definitions of dogma, or of offering guidance on world questions, much of ordinary papal teaching would be delegated to local bishops, or would be the direct outcome of consultation with them. Moreover, a central mechanism could be set up, through which the teaching and pastoral initiatives of the particular Churches could be shared and made available cross-culturally.[39] According to its constitution, the Pope can already confer deliberative power on the synod of Bishops, subject to his ratification.[40] This would, no doubt, take place frequently in a culturally polycentric Church.

In the realm of theology, the ministry of communion would require a mechanism through which local Churches could learn new theological interests from one another. This mechanism—perhaps a renewed international theological commission—would operate a cross-cultural hermeneutic, interpreting and disseminating such theological teaching, as well as defining the bounds of legitimate diversity.[41] It would offer guidance for the right understanding of tradition, as well as for correct cross-cultural translation.

The new Church model is inconsistent with an invasive *Canon Law* which subverts local cultures, produces cultural parallelism or which contributes to cultural domination by the West. Above all, the Church's law must not be used to hinder the progress of inculturation or to block effective evangelisation. The 1983 *Code* incorporates many pastoral insights from the Second Vatican Council and offers local Churches a variety of options in applying the law. No doubt local bishops have sometimes been slow to make use of the opportunities which the *Code* offers them. However, it remains a unified system that reflects its Western culture of origin, and which assumes that the universal Church is monocultural.

The Second Vatican Council recommended local adaptations in the field of ecclesiastical legislation.[42] Some canonists have taken up this suggestion and have called for a central legal framework, or *loi cadre*, within which local Churches could formulate their own codes.[43] This was also the recommendation of the Secretaries-General of the episcopal conferences of SECAM in 1978.[44] A culturally polycentric Church requires a fully developed local Church structure which can make the benefits of the Church's law available to all Christians and which interprets local, rather than foreign, juridical realities.

THE NEED FOR SPECIAL LITURGICAL REGIONS
OF THE ROMAN RITE

Modern liturgical inculturation takes its origin in the movement precipitated by the Second Vatican Council's constitution on the sacred Liturgy, *Sacrosanctum Concilium*, and in the establishment by Pope Paul VI of the liturgical *Consilium*, which oversaw the revision of liturgical books in the Roman rite. The crucial step was to allow the use of the vernacular in the Roman liturgy. This entailed a massive worldwide exercise of translation and also encouraged a burst of creativity in producing musical settings for the new texts. The cultural centrality of language is such that the exercise could never be merely one of verbal translation. Indeed, at the time, the work of translation was seen as foreshadowing a later, more creative, phase of liturgical adaptation.[45]

Although the liturgical constitution provided for "legitimate variations and adaptations," the substantial unity of the Roman rite was to be preserved.[46] It was unfortunate that the new constitution was drawn up before the Council had discussed the nature of the Church and human culture, and their relation to each other. It demonstrated a misunderstanding of the coherence and unity of culture in speaking, for example, of admitting "elements from the traditions and cultures" of peoples into Catholic worship.[47] This also made it easier for a reaction to set in during the 1970's and for the revision of the liturgy to become virtually a new instrument of standardisation, characterised by a preoccupation with texts and their centralised approval.

In its decree on the Oriental Churches, *Orientalium Ecclesiarum*, the Second Vatican Council offered a more mature view of liturgical diversity, and it attributed this to the Church's wish "to adapt its own way of life to the needs of different times and places."[48] Africa has been evangelised by Western missionaries of the Roman or Latin rite. Although a Catholic Coptic rite and a Catholic Ethiopic rite have been created following existing Orthodox Coptic and Ethiopic models, the suggestion by Boniface Luykx in the mid-1970's that they might become a model for sub-Saharan Africa was never taken up.[49] While they remain outstanding examples of successful inculturation, it is clear that liturgical creativity in Black Africa must build mainly on the foundations of the Roman rite.[50] This, in fact, is what has happened in the creation of African Eucharistic rites. The Cameroon (Ndzon Melen) Mass is simply a manner of celebrating the Roman Eucharistic rite.[51] The same is true of the Zaire Mass which was approved by the Congregation for Divine Worship in 1988, and which in the opinion of a commentator does not really "break the mould of the Roman rite."[52] However, both these initiatives deserve to be called inculturation, since they develop the vernacular principle and correspond to a given socio-cultural context. They transcend, by far, the limitations of a text.

When serious attention is paid to indigenous culture, it immediately becomes apparent that rites must be created for which the Roman liturgical books provide no models. A good example of this is provided by the Zimbabwe Liturgy for

Second Burial, finalised in 1982. In this case the constraints came, not from Rome but, from the local Shona culture, and the result was a *locus classicus* of African inculturation, the achievement of a sympathetic and courageous local hierarchy.[53] Yet another area of liturgical inculturation in which local freedom and creativity is presupposed is that of the liturgical homily. One example is the widespread use of the choric story format, and other literary devices of African oral tradition.[54]

If Africa—and indeed the rest of the world—is now familiar with the Roman rite, there is no sense in making an artificial break with the immediate past. On the contrary, new liturgies and sacramental rites should grow organically from the old. However, as an African liturgist has suggested, special liturgical regions of the Roman rite should be created.[55] Within such regions, local Churches would be trusted to create their own liturgical traditions and usages, without the need to submit texts for central approval. No doubt there would be room for appeals in disputed cases, and for a degree of overall supervision, but the basic initiative and responsibility would belong to the local Church. Until Africa is recognised as such a special liturgical region or regions, it must be said that the best hope for liturgical creativity in the continent lies with spontaneous, non-textual forms.

SMALL CHRISTIAN COMMUNITIES AND INCULTURATION

There are many recognised fields of inculturation, and we have already considered aspects of some of them: theology, law, liturgy, ecclesial structures and ministries.[56] The *Instrumentum Laboris* of the African synod considers a number of other fields: marriage and family living, priestly and religious life, spirituality, health care and themes from traditional religion, such as ancestor veneration.[57] In a culturally polycentric Church the emphasis is on mutual service and mutual empowerment, not on centralised approval or disapproval. Ultimately, evangelisation/inculturation comes from below. It is most effective when it operates through interpersonal relationships, and through people empowered by the Church to act through them. Such relationships are especially those of marriage, family and neighbourhood.

Several African Episcopal Conferences have adopted the formation of small Christian communities as a priority in their pastoral plan. This fact is noted in the African synod's *Instrumentum Laboris*.[58] The small (or basic) Christian community brings together several families in a given neighbourhood. It is a cell of committed Christians at the service of the Church and in dialogue with the world. It is concerned first and foremost with how to be Christian in a given life-context and with how to penetrate the local culture and bring the values of the gospel to bear upon it. It is not simply an appendage of the hierarchy or a segment of the parish structure. It enjoys a measure of structural freedom, while at the same time acting as an agent of pastoral care in the parish. In the small Christian community collaborative ministry can be realised in a manner that is not yet possible at other levels of the Church, and which is effective for evangelisation. Such witness can prepare a mentality which is more favourable towards giving women a place in Church leadership.

The small Christian community is a fundamental instrument of inculturation. This is recognised by the African synod's *Instrumentum Laboris*:

Those responsible in pastoral matters should analyse the nature of inculturation of Christianity in Africa and its capacity to constitute vibrant ecclesial communities, the role of the laity, the response to the thirst for spiritual experience and the Word of God as well as the reply to be given to the vital questions posed by suffering, sickness and death.[59]

Inculturation is essentially a community project, and it is important to realise that in the absence of a culturally polycentric Church, the spontaneous initiatives of the small Christian community will eventually bear fruit for inculturation. A statement I made five years ago is still true today: "At the present time . . . the vocation of the small Christian communities is to be the keeper of the Church's conscience for inculturation."[60] Winning or losing the future also depends on them.

CONCLUSION

Whether or not Africa becomes the Christian continent of the future depends to a great extent on the wholehearted acceptance of the need for inculturation. The synodal *Instrumentum Laboris* is right to say that this is a "new requirement" calling for a "new awareness," and that "this new requirement demands a profound change in mentality and conviction."[61] I have argued in this paper that this profound change is not for Africa only. It is one that must take place urgently at the heart of the universal Church. "Today is the elder brother of tomorrow."

NOTES

1. Ruth Finnegan, *Oral Literature in Africa* (Oxford: Clarendon Press, 1970), p. 402.
2. *Ad gentes divinitus*, n. 10.
3. *Evangelii nuntiandi*, n. 20.
4. *L'Osservatore Romano*, 28 June 1982, pp. 1-8.
5. International Theological Commission, "Faith and Culture," *Omnis Terra*, n. 198, 1989, p. 264; Pedro Arrupe, "Letter to the Whole Society on Inculturation," J. Aixala, ed. *Other Apostolates Today* (St Louis, 1981) p. 172.
6. W. Reiser, "Inculturation and Doctrinal Development," *Heythrop Journal*, vol. 22, 1981, pp. 135-148.
7. Michael Amaladoss, "Dialogue and Inculturation," *Inculturation*, n. 314, 1988, p. 22.
8. *Evangelii nuntiandi*, nn. 63-64.
9. Joseph Blomjous, "Development in Mission Thinking and Practice 1959-1980: Inculturation and Interculturation," *AFER*, vol. 22, n. 6, p. 393.
10. Anton Wessels, *Images of Jesus—How Jesus is Perceived and Portrayed in Non-European Cultures* (London: S.C.M. Press, 1990), pp. 66-80.
11. *Redemptoris missio*, n. 34.
12. *Evangelii praecones*, Raymond Hickey, *Modern Missionary Documents and Africa* (Dublin, 1982), p. 99; *Princeps pastorum*, ibid., p. 143.
13. *Ad gentes divinitus*, nn. 10, 22; *Gaudium et spes*, nn. 53-58.
14. K.O. Bimwenyi, "Inculturation en Afrique et attitudes des agents de l'évangélisation," *Bulletin of African Theology*, vol. 5, 1981, pp. 5-17 (author's tr.).
15. *Instrumentum laboris*, nn. 130-31.

16. P. Rottlander, "One World: Opportunity or Threat for the Global Church?," *Concilium*, n. 204, 1989, p. 108; J.B. Metz, "Unity and Diversity: Problems and Prospects for Inculturation," *Concilium*, n. 204, 1989, p. 80.

17. Michael Drohan, "Christianity, Culture and the Meaning of Mission," *International Review of Mission*, vol. 75, n. 299, 1986, pp. 298-99; cf. also Edmund Hill, "Christianity and Cultures," *New Blackfriars*, vol. 67, nn. 793-94, 1986, pp. 324-29, where Hill speaks of "Christianity's all too successful inculturation in a violent, arrogant and aggressive culture," p. 326.

18. Aylward Shorter, *Toward a Theology of Inculturation* (London and Maryknoll, N.Y.: Orbis Books, 1988), p. 231; Azevedo, M.de C. *Inculturation and the Challenges of Modernity* (Rome 1982) passim.

19. Metz, *op. cit.*, p. 80.

20. J. Ratzinger (with Messori, V.) *The Ratzinger Report* (Leominster, 1985), p. 103; UCAN, AS7025/705, 9 March, 1993.

21. *Gaudium et spes*, n. 61.

22. Michael Amaladoss, "Dialogue and Inculturation," *Inculturation*, n. 314, 1988, p. 24; Rottlander, *op.cit.*, p. 113.

23. *Sects or New Religious Movements—Pastoral Challenge*, (Nairobi, 1985), pp. 17-18; cf. also *Instrumentum Laboris*, n. 88.

24. Cf. Paul Gifford, *Christianity and Politics in Doe's Liberia* (Cambridge University Press, 1993).

25. Leslie Newbigin, *Truth to Tell: The Gospel and Public Truth* (London: S.P.C.K., 1991); Owen Chadwick, *The Secularisation of the European Mind* (Cambridge University Press, 1993 [1975]), pp. 21 ff.

26. *Redemptoris missio*, n. 52.

27. *Instrumentum laboris*, n. 50.

28. S.M. Michael, "The Role of the Church in the Transformation of Culture," *Indian Missiological Review*, vol. 11, n. 1, 1989, pp. 75-95.

29. *Redemptoris missio*, n. 23.

30. Efoé-Julien Pénoukou, *Eglises d'Afrique: Propositions pour l'Avenir* (Paris, 1984).

31. *Redemptoris missio*, n. 33.

32. Aloisio Lorscheider, "Nova evangelizaçâo e vida religiosa," *Irmâo Sol*, December 1988, pp. 2-3.

33. Marja-Liisa Swantz, *Ritual and Symbol in Transitional Zaramo Society*, (Uppsala: Gleerup, 1970), p. 341.

34. Lamin Sanneh, *Encountering the West—Christianity and the Global Process: The African Dimension* (London: Marshall Pickering and Maryknoll, N.Y.: Orbis Books, 1993), p. 246.

35. *Evangelii nuntiandi*, n. 63.

36. *Ad gentes divinitus*, n. 22.

37. Bernard Lonergan, *Method in Theology* (London: Darton, Longman and Todd, 1975), p. 276.

38. *Dei verbum*, n. 8.

39. Cf. the current attempt to do this for the social teaching of local bishops. Peter Hebblethwaite, "The Bishops' Part," *The Tablet*, 15 May, 1993, pp. 609-610.

40. *The Code of Canon Law* (London: Collins, 1983) can. 343.

41. Metz, *op. cit.*, p. 85.

42. *Ad gentes divinitus*, n. 19; *Ecclesiae Sanctae, III*, 19, §2.

43. Michel Legrain, "Young Churches and the New Code of Canon Law," *Theology Digest*, vol. 31, 1984, pp. 217-218.

44. *Acts of the Fifth Plenary Assembly of the Symposium of Episcopal Conferences of Africa and Madagascar* (Nairobi, 1978), p. 225.

45. Cf. *Notitiae*, n. 44, 1969, p. 12.

46. *Sacrosanctum concilium*, n. 38.

47. *Sacrosanctum concilium*, nn. 40, §1, 65.

48. *Orientalium ecclesiarum*, n. 2.

49. Boniface Luykx, *Culte Chrétien en Afrique après Vatican II* (Immensee, Switzerland) *Neue Zeitschrift für Missionswissenschaft*, 22, 1974.

50. African Synod, *Instrumentum laboris*, n. 63.

51. The author assisted at the Ndzon Melen Mass in Yaoundé on Sunday, 3 December, 1972.

52. Raymond Moloney, "The Zairean Mass and Inculturation," *Worship*, vol. 62, n. 5, 1988, pp. 440-41.

53. Zimbabwe Catholic Bishops' Conference, "Liturgy for the Second Burial," (mimeographed translation from the Shona), 1982.

54. Cf. Aylward Shorter, "Form and Content in the African Sermon: An Experiment," *African Ecclesial Review*, vol. 11, n. 3, 1969, pp. 265-79; Aylward Shorter, *Priest in the Village* (London: Geoffrey Chapman, 1979), pp. 173-79; Donald Sybertz and Joseph Healey, *Kueneza Injili kwa Methali* ("Spreading the Gospel through Proverbs"), (Ndanda-Peramiho, 1984).

55. Eugene Uzukwu, "Food and Drink in Africa: The Christian Eucharist," *African Ecclesial Review*, vol. 22, n. 6, 1980, p. 383.

56. Cf. *Evangelii nuntiandi*, n. 63.

57. *Instrumentum laboris*, nn. 68-73.

58. *Instrumentum laboris*, n. 45.

59. *Instrumentum laboris*, n. 89.

60. Aylward Shorter, *Toward a Theology of Inculturation* (London: Geoffrey Chapman, 1988), p. 270.

61. *Instrumentum laboris*, n. 74.

5

Inculturation of Faith or Identification with Culture?

*Robert J. Schreiter**

An enduring problem in the process of inculturation, points out Robert J. Schreiter in this essay, is whether Christians should take faith *or* culture *as starting point of and ultimate norm for a contextual theological expression. Schreiter then goes on to elaborate several possible understandings of both "faith" and "culture," and argues that the solution to the problem of faith* or *culture depends on particular situations in which cultures find themselves. Situations that seem to commend starting and validating inculturation from the perspective of culture are those of cultural reconstruction, cultural resistance and cultural solidarity. Situations commending "faith" as starting point and validation are those in which a particular culture sanctions injustice, or in which culture seems to be unable to meet contemporary challenges. Schreiter concludes by enunciating three principles over against which to judge the validity of a particular expression of inculturation: the principle of* metanoia *or change, the principle of gospel integrity and transcendence, and the principle of necessary risk.*

THE BASIC ISSUE

As one follows discussions of the process of inculturation in the past number of years, one is struck by a basic issue that surfaces time and time again: in developing a genuinely inculturated faith or in constructing a local theology, how much emphasis should be placed on the dynamic of faith entering into the process, and how much emphasis should be given to the dynamics of culture already in place?

---

*From *Concilium* 1994/2: "Christianity and Cultures." Robert J. Schreiter is Professor of Doctrinal Theology at Catholic Theological Union (CTU) at Chicago and Director of the Cardinal Bernardin Center of Theology and Ministry at CTU. He is the author of *Constructing Local Theologies* (1985) and *The New Catholicity: Theology between the Local and the Global* (1997), both published by Orbis Books.

Church documents—beginning with the discussion of culture in Vatican II's *Gaudium et Spes* and continuing with the writings of Paul VI and John Paul II—have stressed the role of faith encountering the culture. In this scenario, the gospel enters the culture and examines it thoroughly: affirming what is good and true and in turn elevating that goodness and truth to an even more exalted level, but also challenging and correcting what is evil and sinful so as to purify the culture. There is also always a reminder that, while the gospel can indeed become inculturated in every human situation, it also transcends every culture. It is not beholden to or circumscribed by any single human culture. Even cultures where the gospel has been known and faith practised for a very long time (as in the case of European cultures) cannot make a proprietary claim on the gospel. This approach affirms the potential of culture and (especially in the addresses of John Paul II) asserts the right to culture, but consistently and insistently emphasizes the sovereign power of the gospel to move freely and autonomously in its transformation of culture in the process of inculturation of faith. It should be noted that such an emphasis is more than church authority exercising its responsibility to preserve the faith; it is grounded in a consistent theology of revelation that understands God's word as intimately bound up with creation yet always transcending it.

Another approach prefers to emphasize the dynamics of culture as the starting point. It does not deny the transcending character of the gospel or the power of faith to criticize and transform culture. It shares the same theological commitments as the first position. But it questions whether a scenario of the gospel operating over against culture can really bring about the inculturation of faith that is sought. It stresses that the gospel never enters a culture in pure form; it is always already inculturated—embedded in the culture of the evangelizer. This already inculturated faith will emphasize some features of the message and necessarily de-emphasize others. Moreover, imagining the gospel working in such an autonomous manner over against the culture seems to misunderstand the dynamics of how intercultural communication takes place. It assumes that a message communicated by someone from one culture will be received and understood by someone in another culture precisely in the way that its sender intended. There simply is no guarantee of that—in fact, one can almost count on some measure of miscommunication, mainly because the cultural worlds of the sender and receiver of the message are always in some measure different. Even the most carefully crafted modes of evangelization will always fall somewhat short of the mark. There simply is no plain and pure presentation of the gospel.

Moreover, to the extent that the evangelizer is unaware of how the gospel message is embedded in his or her culture, effective communication—and therefore inculturation—will be in some measure defective or incomplete. Consequently, for genuine inculturation to take place, one must begin with the culture to be evangelized, and imagine a more dialectical approach to the relation between gospel and culture in which the presentation of the gospel is gradually disengaged from its previous cultural embeddedness and is allowed to take on new forms consonant with the new cultural setting.

But, counters the first position, does not such an approach lead to too close an identification of the gospel with culture, and thereby run the risk of diluting or even changing the gospel message? By what criteria can we judge whether this new inculturation is a genuine expression of the gospel and not some false rendering of the gospel message? Might not such an approach render the gospel powerless to judge the sin of a setting because of the demands for a close identification of the gospel with culture? Doesn't this approach foster a dangerous syncretism? Examples of close identification ending in a false presentation of the gospel message are easily conjured up: perhaps the 'German Christians' of the Nazi period in 1930s Germany is the most notorious example.

How would one go about mediating between these two positions? Each affirms an important point: the transcendence of the gospel and the complexity of human cultures. And each position acknowledges the validity of the other's concerns. But neither position has been able to answer the objection of the other: just how does the first position assure that its approach to inculturation is not a form of cultural domination? How does it answer the objection that much so-called Christianization has really been a Westernization? And when will the second position articulate criteria that will assure that close identification with culture does not end in a false inculturation of the gospel?

Satisfying answers to these questions cannot be given in the short compass of an article; nor, probably, would several books suffice to accomplish the task. The reasons for this are several. First of all, we still do not understand the inculturation process all that well. Secondly, we are increasingly aware that differing models of the inculturation process can answer the question differently.[1] And thirdly, there are no agreed-upon definitions of either 'faith' or 'culture' in these discussions.

Some reflections will be presented here on how one might go about working through the complexities surrounding these issues. They begin by focussing on operative definitions of both faith and culture, and then move on to examine what kinds of situations may make one position or the other more desirable as an effective means of inculturation. Finally, there will be a brief look at the question of criteria for judging whether an inculturation is a true one.

IMAGES OF FAITH, IMAGES OF CULTURE

The key to mediating the issue of inculturation of faith or identification with culture is how we understand 'faith'—that which is to be inculturated—and 'culture'— the context or situation in which inculturation takes place. How faith is understood affects what we see as needing to be inculturated, what cannot be substantively changed, and what are the limits of change that can be permitted.

The boundaries of what needs to be inculturated are not as easily drawn as might first seem to be the case. One does not want to be too minimalist in this, and the very fact that we hold to a hierarchy of truths rules out an uncritical maximalist position as well. The debates surrounding the *Universal Catechism* point to how difficult it is to circumscribe Christian belief.

Perhaps the greatest danger is to begin with a reified understanding of faith— that faith is a series of propositions that need to be transmitted. Propositional thinking itself is a culture-bound exercise. And while it can help clarify issues within the context of a single culture, it frequently does not travel well across cultures, even within the same historical period. The great christological controversies in the early history of the church give ample evidence of this. Nor does such thinking respect the fact that our language never captures adequately the mystery of God nor what God has done for us in Christ. The rich theological traditions of the church give testimony to the polysemic density of Christian faith.

This does not, of course, mean that nothing can be defined. But taking again the experience of the early church in the christological controversies—which were often controversies about the meaning of words embedded in different cultures— one can imagine a hermeneutic that would be useful for understanding faith as it moves across cultural boundaries.[2] Just as the bishops at the early councils were reluctant to develop formulae for encompassing the faith, so too perhaps we should follow their lead and read our efforts to define the faith by seeing those pronouncements as negative statements, i.e., boundary language about what *cannot* be said. Such an approach can be seen as an effort at once to preserve the *regula fidei* while at the same time not foreclosing the density of meaning that the faith brings to us. Church teaching would thus be seen not so much as exhaustive statements on a particular issue as at once preserving the integrity of the faith and demarcating it from what cannot be said.

For faith not to be seen in a reified manner will require a more complex understanding, embracing symbol, ritual and ethos. Faith has to be seen as being as much a way as a view of life. This more complex understanding is called for not only because of the rich reality of faith itself, but also because communication in multiple ways and by multiple media enhances the possibility of understanding across cultural boundaries.[3]

How we construe faith affects what we expect to see reproduced in the newly inculturated situation. Is it a matter of getting the words right? Or a matter of symbolic enactment? The replication of certain values? A representation of the Christian story? Our sense of what constitutes an acceptable or effective inculturation will have much to say about what we consider to be 'faith'.

Similarly, how culture is construed has a profound effect on the inculturation process. There is no agreed-upon definition of culture, so again how culture is seen makes a difference. If culture is seen as a worldwide system of rules governing behaviour, then faith has to engage itself with that system. If it is seen as a set of values that offer guidelines for making decisions, then faith enters the culture as values to be upheld or virtues to be achieved. Both of these general approaches see culture largely as a cognitive system, and would evoke a similar cognitive structure from faith. These are among the more traditional understandings of culture. More recent theories emphasize action and performance as models for understanding culture. For example, culture is best understood as a conversation, constantly being constructed by those who participate in it. Or culture is a tool kit that we reach into when we have a problem, but we think little about it when things are going smoothly. Or culture is primarily a performance, understood only when it is enacted.[4]

If one takes a more action-oriented or performance-oriented approach to culture, elements of faith as ethos, ritual and praxis play a larger role. Here perhaps the inculturated faith would best be served by narrative theologies which interlace the local community's story with the larger Christian story.

Which theory of culture we choose will best be determined by the kind of situation the culture finds itself to be in at a given time. This will be explored in the following section. Here it is important to see that there are a variety of understandings of what both faith and culture can be, so when trying to mediate the question of the inculturation of faith or the identification with culture, we must be aware not only of how we define faith and culture, but also of how those definitions carry with them implications that shape the direction of the inculturation process.

THE SITUATION OF A CULTURE AND THE CHOICE OF EMPHASIS

It was noted above that the situation a culture finds itself in may have an effect on one's choice of definitions of faith and culture. This observation is prompted by any examination of Christian experience both in the present and in the past: at times, Christians have felt called to challenge radically a culture, whereas at other times they have defended a culture out of Christian principle. What shapes the choices in these circumstances?

One way of sorting through these choices is to see an inculturated theology addressing alternately the need to affirm the identity of the culture and the need to address social change in a culture.[5] Roughly speaking, decisions to identify with a culture cluster around theologies affirming identity, and decisions to challenge culture with faith around the need for social change. This is not, of course, an absolute distinction, but one that can be helpful in seeing not only how or when such decisions are made, but also something of the principles that motivate those decisions.

There are at least three kinds of situations that seem to prompt a decision to identify strongly with the culture. The first is a situation of *cultural reconstruction*. In this situation, a culture has been so damaged by outside cultural forces that a people has to engage in a conscious reconstruction of their culture. This happens when a culture finds itself in the minority against a larger and more powerful culture and is threatened with extinction. An example would be the situation of indigenous cultures in the Americas. In parts of Canada, for example, peoples in the western part of that country have been borrowing rituals from their neighbours to the south in the United States because their own cultural memory has been so depleted by a century of exploitation and genocide. Another kind of example is the reconstruction of African cultures after the experience of colonialism. That African calls for inculturation seek strong identification with the culture grows out of the need to reinstate the dignity of those cultures as worthy vessels of Christian faith. The reconstruction is different from the first example in that the colonial history must also be confronted and negotiated in a way different from historical patterns of extermination.

A second kind of situation is one of *cultural resistance*. This is the case where a culture is threatened by an alien force and needs to take a posture of resistance in order to survive. One of the clearest examples of this type is the church's intense identification with Polish culture over several centuries of occupation by alien forces. Such patterns of resistance create deep bonds of solidarity, because Christian faith is so intricately bound up with preserving a culture's sense of its own identity and humanity. Similar patterns can be seen in the close identification that grows up in resistance to dictatorships, as was the case in the Philippines and in Chile in the 1970s and 1980s.

A third type of situation is one of *cultural solidarity*. This is a situation where the church is a tiny minority in the population and is suspected of being alien to the majority. In these situations Christians are at pains to show their loyalty and do so by a strong affirmation of the culture. Such would be the case for Christians in China who have had to struggle to show how they are truly Chinese yet part of a universal church.

In all of these situations the identity of a culture needs to be attended to. The church, with its understandings of culture since Vatican II, has affirmed again and again a people's right to culture. If one would want to search for a principle behind these identifications with culture, one could suggest that, without a culture having its own integrity and dignity, as well as the participation of its people, there can be no inculturation of the faith. That is because without these conditions of integrity and participation, the culture that the faith is inculturated into is fundamentally alienating to the people involved and so cannot speak to their hearts and minds. Thus an identification that bespeaks a care for the culture would seem to be an important component for the inculturation process to take place at all.

On the other hand, there are situations when faith seems called to stand over against the culture. The most obvious kind of situation is when injustice is perpetrated and sanctioned by the culture. Here Christian faith must speak out against the injustice. It must resist explanations that injustice and violence are necessary for the integrity of the culture. To be sure, cultures have particular and even peculiar configurations, but long-term violence does not make it a cultural necessity. Moreover, even if these patterns of injustice could be internally justified, cultural boundaries are now porous because of modern communications; therefore such explanations and justifications of injustice will no longer be believed. An example of this kind of injustice is the treatment of women in many parts of the world. More and more it has become apparent that justifications of their subjugation not only now no longer hold, but were probably only believed by men in those cultures in the first place. Racism is another injustice that simply cannot be tolerated.

A second set of situations where Christian faith seems called upon to engage in a more autonomous critique of culture is when a culture faces strong challenges and does not seem to have the inner resources to meet those challenges, either because of the challenge from without or because of disintegration from within. An example of this might be some of the Eastern European countries whose social values were so corroded by forty years of Communism that they find it difficult to marshall the resources for living in a very different kind of world.

Is there an underlying principle in these sets of situations that guide a decision in the direction of a more autonomous role for faith *vis-à-vis* culture? It might be formulated thus: when a culture experiences a profound lack (no resources for a formidable challenge) or refuses to acknowledge a lack (legitimated injustice), then Christian faith must assume a more autonomous role in the inculturation process.

CRITERIA FOR EVALUATING INCULTURATION

The five sets of situations just discussed—three calling for identification with culture and two for a more autonomous critique of culture—are in some measure limit cases; i.e., they represent the extremes of possibility. What about all the cases in between? How should one mediate identification and critique in those situations? And how should one judge the results of efforts at inculturation?

Although the situations just described are limit cases, they do provide insight into the cases that fall in between. A useful set of cases might be found in the different strategies of the new evangelization in Latin America, Europe and North America. If a culture does not feel itself to be under acute challenge, yet is faced with an evangelization that is largely a jeremiad against it, or hears a call to faith that seems patently unable to understand the complexities of its situation, that kind of evangelization is likely to fail. There can be no critique of culture without a prior identification with that culture. Otherwise the gospel voice is simply experienced as an alien sound unrelated to reality. One could surmise that the failure of Christianity to reach many Asian peoples has come from this inability to identify.

But on the other hand, an identification with culture that does not offer criticism is an empty one. The gospel, after all, is about *metanoia*, about change. Not to be willing to see a culture grow is not to care about that culture. The deepest commitments of Christianity seem to call both for profound identification, modelled on the incarnation, and transformation, modelled on the passion, death and resurrection of Christ.

Can all of this be translated into criteria for evaluation? Attempts have been made to do this, and while there is some convergence, differences in tradition will cause differences in emphasis.[6] One thing seems certain: no single criterion can be adduced that will give a quick and tidy answer to whether or not the results of inculturation are true to the gospel. We need a number of criteria, working in concert, to answer that question. This is based on what was seen above, namely, that construals of faith and of culture evoke different models and different emphases.

Beyond those criteria that have already been articulated elsewhere (such as consistency with Scripture and the subsequent tradition, the resulting practice, the liturgical life, the quality of discipleship, and so on), I shall conclude with a mixture of principles—two theological and one cultural—that may offer some general orientation to answering the question of the truth of inculturation when used in conjunction with other principles.

First of all, the gospel is about *metanoia*—conversion, change. Consequently, if the gospel enters a culture and nothing changes, then there is no effective inculturation. 'Nothing changes' describes a state in which either the gospel never connects with the culture, or it is allowed to be absorbed into the culture.

Secondly, the culture cannot homogenize the gospel. By this is meant that the culture cannot be permitted to choose which parts of the gospel it chooses to hear and which it chooses to ignore. Cultures must deal with the whole gospel, not simply one with which they feel to be comfortable. This is based on the principle that the gospel transcends every culture and cannot be domesticated by any one of them.

Third, inculturation remains subject to the perils and the possibilities of intercultural communication. An important principle here is that any message communicated across culture boundaries risks both the loss and gain of information and intelligibility. Thus, emphases shift, nuances change, things are forgotten, and new insights are gained. The history of the development of theology and doctrine is testimony to this process. Thus inculturation remains a risk, but it is also a necessary one. Without it, faith cannot take root. With it, the possibility of new and deeper insights into the meaning of the mystery of Christ is always present.

CONCLUSION

From what has been said here, it should be clearer why the inculturation of faith and the identification with culture cannot be seen as an either-or proposition. They represent two moments in the inculturation process which, depending on circumstances, require greater or lesser emphasis. Either acting alone will not suffice. Within the process, how faith and how culture are understood is pivotal to ascertaining the nature and level of inculturation that is taking place. And that ascertainment will continue to require multiple criteria to be adjudicated effectively.

NOTES

1. For a review of these models, see Stephen B. Bevans, *Models of Contextual Theology*, Maryknoll, N.Y. 1992.

2. Alois Grillmeier, *Jesus der Christus im Glauben der Kirche*, Freiburg 1986, II/I, 19, speaks explicitly of the christological controversies as a process of inculturation.

3. Useful here is Clifford Geertz, 'Ethos, World View and the Analysis of Symbols,' in *The Interpretation of Cultures*, New York 1973, 126-41.

4. For culture as conversation, see David Tracy, *The Analogical Imagination*, New York and London 1981; for culture as tool kit, see Ann Swidler, 'Culture in Action: Symbols and Strategies,' *American Sociological Review* 51, 1986, 273-86; for culture as performance, see Sam Gill, *Native American Religious Action: A Performance Approach to Religion*, Columbia 1987.

5. This is described in greater detail in Robert Schreiter, *Constructing Local Theologies*, Maryknoll, N.Y. and London 1985.

6. For a set of criteria from a Catholic perspective, see ibid., 117-21; for a Reformed perspective, see Anton Wessels, *Images of Jesus: How Jesus is Perceived and Portrayed in Non-European Cultures*, Grand Rapids and London 1990, 158-92.

6

Hearing and Talking

Oral Hermeneutics of Asian Women

*Kwok Pui-lan**

In this exploratory essay, Chinese (Hong Kong) biblical scholar Kwok Pui-lan makes use of the emerging insights of scholarship on the importance of orality to propose several "strategies" of biblical interpretation that might be employed by Asian women to appropriate the Bible and Christian faith in the context of their own culture and identity. "Hearing" and "Talking" the Bible, rather than reading a text, might well be the key to authentic articulation of faith by people—especially women—who live in cultures (like those of Asia) that prize living oral tradition over fixed literary texts.

In women's groups, at church meetings, and in the Y.W.C.A., Christian women in Asia study the Bible and discuss enthusiastically its implications for their lives. They dramatize biblical stories, retell gospel messages, and pose critical questions to the Bible from their own experiences. Bible study among Asian women is a communal event; they gather to talk about their own stories and the stories of the Bible, constructing new meanings and searching for wisdom for survival and empowerment. They treat the Bible as a living resource rather than as an ancient text closed in itself.

The importance of the aural/oral dimension in cultural and religious life has been emphasized by theologians and scholars in other cultural contexts. Teresa Okure of Nigeria has observed that the Africans were traditionally "a people of the word, not of the book."[1] Renita J. Weems points out that during slavery, black people in America were forbidden by law to learn to read and write. An aural hermeneutics emerged as the slaves evaluated the contents of the Bible through the critical lens of their harsh reality.[2] Likewise, Cornel West emphasizes the "kinetic

---

* From *Discovering the Bible in the Non-Biblical World* (Maryknoll, NY: Orbis, 1995). Kwok Pui-lan, formerly of the Chinese University in Hong Kong, is currently a member of the faculty of the Episcopal Divinity School, Cambridge, Massachusets, USA.

orality" in black sermons, songs, prayers, and hymns. Its fluidity, rhetoric, and flexible oral stylizations of language, West maintains, "gave black church life a distinctively African-American stamp."[3] In Latin America, grassroots Bible study plays a crucial role in the life of the basic Christian communities, providing food for thought and sustenance for their ongoing struggle against injustice.[4]

In the past several decades interdisciplinary studies of oral and written traditions have yielded fruitful results, but such research has not been appropriated by the majority of biblical scholars. In *The Oral and the Written Gospel*, Werner H. Kelber suggests the main reason for this neglect lies in "the tendency among biblical scholars to think predominantly, or even exclusively, in literary, linear, and visual terms."[5] In order to study the strategies of oral hermeneutics by Asian women, we have to shift our attention from the written text to the women who are talking about the text. We need to emphasize that ordinary Christian women are interpreters of the Bible, and the insights they offer are no less important than biblical scholarship contributed by scholars in the academy. Furthermore, the study of oral hermeneutics requires us to learn from disciplines including linguistics, translation, anthropology, history of religions, and cross-cultural studies.

In this chapter I explore the strategies of oral hermeneutics by Asian women based on my own participation in women's Bible studies and relevant written resources. The first part presents a gender analysis of the transmission of scriptures in Asia, with special focus on the Bible, to provide a cultural and religious context to understand the oral hermeneutics of Asian women. The implication of orality and textuality for biblical interpretation will be examined in the second part. Finally, I shall analyze some examples of oral hermeneutics from Christian women in Asia.

TRANSMISSION OF SCRIPTURES IN ASIA—A GENDER ANALYSIS

On the diverse continent of Asia some of the religious traditions do not have scriptures; I shall limit the discussion here to those historical religions with a scriptural tradition. In the West *scripture* often means a written text—the Latin *scriptura* means "writing." The same is not true in Asia, where scripture can assume diverse forms. For example, the Vedas of the Hindu tradition have been transmitted orally from generation to generation, although writing was invented two and a half millennia ago in India. Scripture was considered more often to be spoken words rather than written texts.[6] Indian theologian Stanley J. Samartha has noted: "One has to go behind the written texts to the *sound* of the Word, recited and heard over long periods of time by the community, in order to see how words have functioned religiously in matters of faith."[7]

Comparable to the Bible, many Asian scriptures went through a period of oral transmission, some for a long period of time, before they assumed written form. The Confucian *Analects*, a compilation of the sayings of Confucius and his disciples, were recorded long after the death of the master.[8] The Daoist classic *Dao de jing* consists of sayings that embodied the spirit of a living tradition.[9] Shortly after the Buddha's death, his disciples met to recite his teachings in order to establish an authoritative body of doctrine for the future.[10] But the actual writing down of the Dharma was not achieved until hundreds of years later. The notable exception to this pattern of early oral transmission seems to be the Qur'an, which consisted from the outset as a written collection of Allah's revelations through his prophet Muhammad.

The question as to whether women participated in or played a role in the creation of Asian scriptures requires more study in the future. Tradition does not recount that women numbered among the seventy-two disciples of Confucius. In the case of Daoism, some of the basic motifs or concepts in *Dao de jing* date back to ancient times, when shamans—both male and female—played essential religious roles.[11] But the exact circumstances leading to the compilation of *Dao de jing* are still debated. In early Indian Buddhism women and men listened to the teaching of the Buddha and many women asked to be admitted to the monastic order.[12] It is not clear, however, whether they participated later in the writing and compilation of the sayings of the Buddha. In the Muslim tradition women did not participate in any meaningful way in recording and compiling the Qur'an, as far as we know.

Although the written text was revered in some Asian traditions, the dominant mode of scriptural transmission among the populace has been oral in most cases. Multiple relationships exist between scripture and its diverse receiving and interpretative communities, dependent on caste, class, and gender. The Hindus have developed elaborate techniques for verbatim memorization of the Vedas,[13] while the written texts are often regarded as the "defilements of the sacred sound."[14] The recitation of the Vedas was for centuries the responsibility of male priests of the brahmin caste to the exclusion of women and other castes.[15]

Islam is often referred to as a religion of the book, but in the everyday lives of the Muslim community, recitation of the Qur'an is far more wide-reaching and permeating than the study of the written text. In fact, the root meaning of Qur'an is "to recite" or "read aloud."[16] While Muslim scholars devote their energy to produce commentaries and studies of the book, common people recite and memorize oral texts. Until recently, Muslim women in general have not had equal opportunities to study the Qur'an. Attempts by women to challenge the teachings of the Qur'an have been suppressed, as in the recent death threat against the outspoken feminist writer Tasleema Nasreen of Bangladesh.

As for Confucianism, learning the classics has shaped the entire civilization of East Asia. Much of the learning has been done not simply through silent and private reading but through recitation, rote memorization, and conversation with teachers. While the masses learn portions of the classics, detailed exposition and exegesis of the words of the sages have been the responsibility of members of the literati. In China, girls who belonged to the upper class, or the families of literati, had opportunities to learn to read and study classical texts through private tutoring.[17] But until female education was made available in the nineteenth century, the number of women who could read and interpret classical texts was limited.

In the multifaceted tradition of Buddhism there are marked differences in the ways believers treat the sacred texts. On the one hand, the Buddhist scriptures are respected as authoritative, and for centuries scholars have been preoccupied with copying, translating, and interpreting the texts. In popular Buddhism scriptures sometimes assume a magical character, not unlike relics in the West. On the other hand, there is a deep-seated suspicion of texts, and words are seen by some as obstacles to direct religious experience, especially in the Zen tradition. Zen Buddhism emphasizes: "A special transmission outside the Scriptures; no dependence upon words and letters."[18] The recognition of the limits of human language and the embodiment of truth in ordinary things in everyday life is found also in Tibetan Buddhism. In some folk Buddhist traditions in China women have been religious leaders, custodians of secret scriptures from one generation to the next, and teachers of religious doctrines.[19] Buddhist nuns have opportunities to learn and study the *sutras* and helped to explicate them for the laypeople.[20]

The accent on oral traditions and transmission of sacred texts implies that the study of literary texts is not so important. Today, three-quarters of the world's illiterate population live in Asia, the majority of them women. Until female education becomes wide-spread and affordable, many Asian women, especially those in rural areas and poverty-stricken districts, will have access to sacred texts only through the aural/oral media: listening to religious texts recited at home, in the temples, and during religious ceremonies and festivals. Parts of the sacred texts are also told as myths, legends, epics, and performed as plays and festive dramas.

When the Bible was introduced into Asia, it encountered a cultural world with different understandings of sacred texts and diverse modes of transmission. During the century of mission the Protestant missionaries who arrived to preach the Gospel in many parts of Asia were influenced by the print mentality of the western world and invariably understood *scripture* to be a written text. Protestant missionaries, much more than their Roman Catholic predecessors, were engaged in translating the Bible into the languages of the people. Mission presses were set up and portions of the Bible, catechism, and religious tracts were widely distributed.

While Muslims regard Arabic as the revealed language, insisting that non-Arab believers learn to recite the Qur'an in its original language, Christianity assumes no single revealed language, and the Bible has been translated into different languages during the history of Christian expansion. As Lamin Sanneh has pointed out, the "success of Islam as a missionary religion is founded upon the perpetuation of the sacred Arabic."[21] In sharp contrast, the vitality of Christianity depends on the degree that its tradition is translatable into the local setting, and the radical pluralism and diversity of the biblical tradition.[22]

Because Asian languages usually include many different spoken dialects, missionaries decided to translate the Bible into the written languages and also the vernacular. The decision of the missionaries to render the Bible into the vernacular had significant repercussions. First, it elevated the status of the vernacular language. The printing press set up by William Carey in India produced religious materials in forty-four languages and dialects, and his linguistic research contributed to the renaissance of Bengali prose literature.[23] In China the Bible was translated into the literary style, Mandarin, regional dialects, and minority national languages.[24] Second, the use of the vernacular necessarily entailed borrowing the terminologies and concepts of the common people. In translating concepts such as heaven, hell, devil, soul, and repentance into Asian languages, missionaries had to borrow many of the terms from folk traditions. Third, the option for the vernacular also meant that the biblical text had to be recast in the spoken language and in the style that the common people would have told it orally.

Since most denominations required some knowledge of the Bible as a prerequisite for baptism, Christian missions were heavily involved in a literacy campaign. Sunday school for children, mission station courses, and catechism classes were offered to help prepare the candidates. For people who had not learned to read and write, the Bible looked mysterious and intimidating. For Asian women, who were excluded from any formal schooling, the process of learning to read the Bible could be both frustrating and liberating.

Much of the early missionary activity among women depended on the spoken word: for example, house-to-house visits, telling the gospel stories, singing hymns, and reciting the Lord's Prayer. Women were taught to read the Bible and a written catechism in Bible study classes, Sunday school, mission station classes, or catechism classes. Missionary work among women was initially led by women missionaries, but as mission work began to grow "Bible women" were employed to help teach women, especially in the rural areas. The involvement of Bible women and other lay women in the transmission of the Bible created women's fellowships, helping to nurture personal bonding among women within the patriarchal church and society.[25]

Christian missions were often the first to organize girls' schools in Asia to provide education for girls of the lower classes. Early girls' schools were meant to train future Bible women and the wives of pastors and evangelists. Both the Bible and religious instruction featured prominently in the curriculum. As time went by, the curriculum was expanded to include other subjects in the liberal arts, but the teaching of the Bible still occupied an important place. Among Christians the rate of female literacy was generally much higher than in the general populace. In some places Christian mission schools for girls served as catalysts moving local people to provide education for girls. The education of women remains one of the important legacies of the Christian mission in Asia.

The emphasis on female literacy and education reveals not only the gender dimension of the church's "civilizing" function, but a class dimension as well.[26] The Christian church and mission schools helped to nurture an emerging class of school teachers, female evangelists, Y.W.C.A. workers, medical doctors, and nurses. These women leaders, usually from urban areas, were instrumental in spreading new ideas of womanhood, which they learned from the Christian church and from their missionary teachers. But they have also been criticized for being westernized and identifying too much with the culture of the foreigners. Espousing middle-class values, these female leaders had a worldview very different from rural women and less educated women.

The tension between different classes of Christian women continues to exist today and manifests clearly in the ways they approach the Bible. Women who are more educated and who have received theological training tend to focus more on the written text. Some use western exegetical methods learned in seminaries to analyze the Bible. The majority of Asian Christian women, however, use free association and creative retelling of biblical stories to appropriate the Bible in their life situations. While academic study of the Bible can help clarify the androcentric language and worldview of the texts, oral hermeneutics of Asian women should not be ignored in our examination of feminist interpretation in Asia.

ORALITY AND TEXTUALITY IN BIBLICAL INTERPRETATION

The analysis of the Asian situation calls for closer attention to the implications of orality and textuality in the interpretation of the Bible. These implications are numerous: 1) the influence of the oral tradition on the written text, 2) the power dynamics behind the inclusion of some voices and suppression of others in the written account, 3) the relation between the oral and the written in the transmission process, 4) the influence of the medium of transmission on the various modes of biblical interpretation, and 5) the importance of understanding oral hermeneutics in feminist biblical interpretation. Trying to understand the implications of orality and textuality for biblical interpretation in Asia, I benefit from the insights of scholars who have studied the interaction between the oral and the written text of the Bible as well as from anthropologists, linguists, and cultural historians who have investigated the cognitive significance of orality.

In *The Oral and the Written Gospel*, Werner H. Kelber examines the complex process by means of which the oral kerygma was rendered into the written form. Contrary to Bultmann's presupposition that the written text was an automatic evolutionary progression from the spoken word, Kelber shows that the earliest canonical gospel, Mark, was actually a textual *interpretation* of the oral kerygma. Based on the growing research in the field of orality-literacy of many other disciplines, Kelber investigates the implications of the change of medium, the shift from a nonliterate to a literate and educated audience, and Mark's contribution to this process in producing the first unified narrative. Kelber reminds us that Jesus was an oral performer "moving from one place to another, surrounded by listeners and engaged in debate.... His message and his person are inextricably tied to the spoken word, not to texts."[27] But when these stories were written down, the concrete *event* that found expression in the oral exchange was lost, and the stories assumed a new medium, "in words that floated context-free, visually fixed on a surface, retrievable now by anyone anywhere, as the utterances of the oral kerygma had never been."[28]

But it is a mistake to think that once the gospels were written down, the oral stage was superseded, leaving few traces on the written accounts. In her study of the Gospel of Mark, Joanna Dewey notes that it lacks a tight plot structure, unlike the modern novel; instead, it has a more loose and additive plot development. This is because the gospel was composed with a listening audience in mind. Likening Mark to a piece of "interwoven tapestry," Dewey emphasizes that "we need to pay more attention to oral hermeneutics in studying the Gospel."[29] Similarly, Charles H. Lohr has shown how oral techniques influenced the actual composition of the Gospel of Matthew. Such techniques include the use of formulaic language and repetitive devices for elaborating unifying themes, the grouping of similar materials into individual sections, the development of a leading idea through repetition of key words, and symmetry in structural arrangements.[30]

From a feminist point of view, the study of the relationship between oral kerygma and written gospel expands our historical imagination of the roles played by women in shaping the biblical tradition before it was fixed as texts. We can easily imagine the women telling the stories of Jesus and how their voices were largely suppressed in the written account. Dewey has argued that although the gospels include stories about women, the actual voices of the women who followed, listened to, and were healed by Jesus did not survive in the writing process, because the gospels were written from an androcentric perspective. Even when the stories do include women, Dewey observes, they often present women in a skewed manner. For example, in the stories of the anointing woman (Mark 14:3-9) and the widow's mite (Mark 12:41-44), the women act but do not speak. Their actions became the subject of male discourse between Jesus and others.[31] In her study of the social make-up of the Matthean community, Antoinette Wire maintains that the gender roles presented in the Gospel of Matthew reflect the assumptions of the community of scribes who put the gospel in written form. At the same time, the inclusion of stories about marginal individuals, especially those about women, seems to her to suggest an underlying oral tradition in which "peoples' voices still directly challenge others to faith."[32]

As the Bible assumed written form, the written text became primary. Oral instruction was transformed into exegesis of this canonical body of literature. Having traced the development of a primary oral culture, through a manuscript culture, to a print culture in the West, Walter J. Ong elucidates the impact of this process on biblical interpretation.[33] It is noteworthy that before Johannes Gutenberg introduced printing with movable metal type in Europe in 1447, the circulation of costly Bibles in handwritten form was limited to the clergy, theologians, monks, and the aristocracy. The social and historical location of such persons influenced the interpretative process. The Bible was often used as a proof-text for their own doctrinal positions, as a refuge for their ecclesiastical interests, and as divine sanction for their privileged positions within the church and society. Ordinary people, who could neither read nor write, were systematically excluded from participating in the creation of meaning and knowledge that grew out of the study of the biblical text.

Since popular literacy in the West became a reality only during the last two hundred years, for some eighteen centuries Christian common folk had access to the Bible primarily through the oral, aural, and visual media. Women's knowledge of the Bible, whether in the East or in the West, came largely through worship and preaching. In the liturgical setting of the church, the Bible was never read in its entirety; instead, parts of the Bible were used to illustrate theological statement and principle.[34] Women were not encouraged to develop a comprehensive and critical understanding of the biblical message. Furthermore, their oral and aural hermeneutics of the Bible were dismissed as unimportant and were not subjected to careful study. To understand the divergent ways women have interpreted the Bible, feminist scholars cannot simply rely on the historical-critical method, literary criticism, and reader-response criticism, because these methods give primacy to the written text of the Bible.[35] Such methods fail to provide tools to analyze the negotiation of meaning in discursive contexts, the retelling of stories to meet the particular needs of an audience, or the thought processes that lie behind oral transmission. Moreover, many contributions of Third World Christians, especially women, who do not understand scripture rigidly as a "book," will be overlooked.

I have found the discussion of oral and literate cultures and the relationship between spoken and written languages that takes place today in the fields of anthropology, linguistics, and social and cultural history helpful for raising new questions about biblical interpretation. Instead of assuming the text to be fixed and given, these disciplines challenge us to problematize the nature and boundaries of a given text. Recent biblical scholarship distinguishes three different worlds to a specific text: the world *behind* the text, which may be uncovered through historical, archaeological and sociological methods; the world *of* the text, created by its use of language, narrative, and discourse; and the world *before* the text, constituted by the presuppositions and interpretative processes of its readers.[36] Such differentiation, though helpful, still assumes the primacy of the written text and reading as a largely silent act of the individual. It fails to take into consideration the performative function of sacred texts and the reconstruction of stories in a communal setting. As Ong has pointed out, in some oral cultures the stories are not memorized and repeated word for word each time. Instead, they are reconstructed and adapted to a particular context.[37] The text is considered to be dynamic and open-ended, not rigidly fixed by the written word.

The issue of orality and textuality has implications for the creation of meaning and the process of interpretation. Scholars who have studied oral and literate traditions point out that in an oral tradition, meaning is negotiated in the discourse, whereas in the literate tradition, meaning is often seen to exist in the written text. The former sees meaning as growing out of shared experience of the interaction between the communicator and the audience, while the latter focuses exclusively on the content of information or message. Understanding, in oral tradition, is more involved and subjective, achieved through a sense of identification with the speaker. In literate culture, it is more detached, logical, and analytical.[38]

Finally, there is the question of the thought process and assumptions about knowledge. Ong has observed that in oral tradition the thought process is more formulaic, elaborated, and "rhapsodic," whereas in literate tradition the thought process is analytical, linear, and sequential.[39] According to David R. Olson, truth in oral tradition lies more in common-sense reference to experience, while in literate tradition it resides in logical and coherent argument.[40] Jack Goody, an anthropologist who has studied oral and written cultures in West Africa, distinguishes between two different paths to knowledge. In oral culture the bulk of knowledge is passed on orally, in face-to-face contact among members of the family, clan, and village. In written culture knowledge comes from an outside, impersonal source (book) or is acquired in an extra-familial institution, such as a school.[41] He further observes that religious organization in oral cultures tends to be less rigid and more open, whereas religions that claim a written revelation tend to be more stratified and closed.

While there are differences between oral and literate traditions, these scholars are quick to point out that in many settings an interplay between the spoken and the written exists. The invention of writing did not end oral tradition, and the oral and literate coexist as a continuum. Furthermore, strategies learned from one medium can be used and applied to another. In the past, biblical interpretation has been largely an intertextual matter. I am arguing that an awareness of the different strategies in both oral and literate traditions will open new avenues for "listening" to the voices of Christians from the Third World, especially where the oral dimension is still paramount in people's lives.

EXAMPLES OF ORAL HERMENEUTICS BY ASIAN WOMEN

In this section, I will discuss strategies drawn from oral hermeneutics based primarily on my own experiences of Bible study with women in Asia and from other examples of biblical interpretation. My sources include Bible studies presented orally, conversations about biblical passages, and biblical reflections that show the use of oral style. These conversations and reflections are by literate women with a feminist consciousness. I recognize the need for future explorations of how women in oral cultures interpret the Bible. In citing these examples, I acknowledge the limits of written records in fully capturing the rhythm, tone, and emotional intensity of spoken language. On the other hand, these examples clearly show that an understanding of the oral tradition helps us to appreciate Asian women's interpretation of the Bible.

The first strategy is to give voice to women in the Bible. When Asian women gather to discuss and dramatize the stories of women in the Bible, they frequently imagine what the women would have said and acted in the situation. The reimagining of women as speaking subjects is important; as we have seen, the voices of women were often left out in the androcentric written account. There are several ways this silencing of women occurred, including 1) women's speech is left out, as in Mark's Gospel,[42] 2) women are admonished not to speak, as in the story of the Syrophoenician woman (Matt. 15:21-28), 3) women talk only to themselves; they are allowed private speech but not public speech. For example, the woman with a flow of blood speaks to herself: "If I touch even his garments, I shall be made well" (Mark 5:28), and 4) in extreme situations, women "voice" accusations of injustice done to them most powerfully through their abused or dead bodies, as in the cases of Hagar, Tamar, and Jephthah's daughter in the "texts of terror" studied by Phyllis Trible.[43]

Asian women theologians are well aware of the silencing of women in the Christian tradition. Lee Oo Chung, Sylvia Jenkin, and Mizuho Matsuda write in the introduction to *Reading the Bible as Asian Women*:

> During all these centuries, in the Biblical stories and texts, and in Christian documents, women's voices were silenced. With few exceptions, they are excluded from any opportunity to speak to the church. . . . Even the women in the Bible themselves gained no hearing, were misinterpreted or disregarded. But now, at the touch of Christ, by movement of his Holy Spirit in our time, the voices of women are crying out from the pages of Scripture.[44]

They encourage Asian Christian women to use creative ways to express their biblical reflections: through poems, pictures, dance, music, mime, storytelling, and testimonies. An example of recovering women's voice is a dramatization of the stories around Moses' birth in the book of Exodus by a group of Asian women. In Exodus 2, Moses' mother has no name and has no speech. In the dramatization by the Asian women she talks about the suffering of the Jewish people with other mothers, one of them Susannah:

Susannah: How our children suffer!
Jochebed: (Deep sigh) Yes. Their suffering breaks my heart more than anything. Our husbands work in the building site; we work in their homes as servants and yet our income is not enough for our livelihood.[45]

When Jochebed hears the decree to kill newborn baby boys, she laments:

Jochebed: It is a death sentence to my baby. The death sentence is on me and my family, on all Hebrew babies and families. God have mercy. Have mercy.[46]

Instead of giving up her son helplessly, as in the biblical account, the new version describes how Jochebed plans to save her baby with the cooperation of the midwives.

Another strategy drawn from oral hermeneutics is reframing the discourse and reconstructing the dialogue. An example is the revision of the conversation between the angel Gabriel and Mary (Luke 1:26-38) by Pearl Drego from India.[47] The story of the annunciation and Mary's response, in particular, has been subjected to various interpretations. Traditionally, Mary's reply has been taken to mean her submission and obedience to God. Feminist theologians have tried to reclaim Mary as a model of the new human being, a true disciple and an active participant in the drama of God's incarnation, who accepts her role through active consent.[48] But the discourse between Gabriel and Mary in the Lukan narrative is not framed on an equal basis. Gabriel does most of the talking and is clearly the more active partner in the conversation. Mary's words are few, and she is the one responding.

In her new version, Drego presents Mary as a full partner in the conversation, making her a full talking subject. Mary is portrayed as one who can read, draw, and play a musical instrument, and she is reading a book when Gabriel visits her. Drego reconstructs Mary's inner speech after Gabriel informs her that she will give birth to the Divine Child:

Mary: Somewhere deep within I knew I was being cared for in a special way and I cared for myself in a special way too. I am ready. It would have been nice to be just ordinary, to marry Joseph and have six or seven children. Yet, this choice has been stirring in my heart for some years. I've known it. I have seen you in dreams. I know that it will be much harder than I can tell. And yet if I don't say yes, the women of this earth will never be free, nor the men either. I can hear the women of the centuries, millions upon millions, their spirits call to me, "Maria, say yes, say yes, on behalf of all of us, you are doing it for all of us. God has chosen us and has chosen you from among us."[49]

Drego portrays Mary's response and transforms her act of submission to God into a positive response to the outcry of the women. When Gabriel warns that people will make up stories about how she was chosen for her compliance and obedience, Mary's reply is unequivocal:

Mary: Me, obedient? When I have defied so many of the laws and sayings of our Jewish patriarchs?[50]

In the course of the conversation Mary is invited to decide whether to give birth to a boy or a girl. After weighing the pros and cons, Mary gives her free consent to the birth of a boy. She rejoices that her virgin privacy will be protected and that God has bypassed rabbis and scribes to extend this invitation to her as a woman.

The retelling of stories and epics from the women's point of view is common in folk traditions in India. For example, women's songs may tell their own version of the Indian epic of Ramayana with characters and incidents not found in the written Sanskrit texts. While the text celebrates the birth of the hero, women's oral traditions in Telugu talk about the birth pangs of his mother and the suffering of his wife.[51] Using such oral technique in her culture, Drego reconstructs the episode of the annunciation. The reclamation of the voice of women in biblical narrative, the imaginative reconstruction of these women's encounters with God, and the presentation of these women as strong and defiant in respect to the patriarchal system play a significant role in the creative hermeneutics of Asian women,[52] and other oppressed women as well.[53]

The third strategy of oral hermeneutics is the blending of different narratives as if making a quilt or weaving a tapestry. I would like to use the Bible study I presented at the Asian Mission Conference organized by the Christian Conference of Asia in Indonesia in 1989 as an example. The Bible study, originally presented in dramatized form with movement, dance, and costumes, is reprinted as the Prologue of this book. I explain my background and women's way of doing Bible study, trying to establish rapport with the audience. The Bible study is not meant so much to convey information as to evoke a response. The oral performance tells simultaneously the story of the women in the ministry and passion of Jesus and the story of the courageous students who were massacred on the fatal night of June 4, 1989, at Tiananmen Square in China.

The Bible study tries to capture and express my double consciousness of my Chinese background and of the biblical tradition. It shows the "internal dialogization"[54] that weaves the two stories together. The contemporary story of Chinese students is not subordinated to the biblical story, nor is the Bible the text and the Chinese situation the context, as commonly understood in the process of contextualization in theology. On the other hand, the Chinese experience is not treated as the text, with the Bible and church tradition as the context for understanding, for there are many possible contexts. In oral performance the text is neither stable nor fixed. In retelling the story I have tried to *voice*, or speak, the Chinese *into existence* in an otherwise alien narrative.[55] Here, the meaning of both stories is negotiated and constructed precisely at the margin or boundary where one context pushes against another, alien context.

By framing the story in a new way, by playing with the borders, and by creating stylizing variants, this example shows that meaning is not fixed, but negotiated in the discourse. Oral representation retells the story in *one's own words*, transforming an external authoritative discourse into an internally persuasive discourse, as Bakhtin describes it.[56] For him, the latter's semantic structure is not fixed; its context is shifting, and its meaning is inexhaustible, inviting further dialogic interaction.

The last example is a Bible study I participated in at the Shanghai Y.W.C.A. A group of women theologians from Asia, Europe, and the United States visited churches and seminaries in China in the summer of 1990.[57] We had a Bible study on Genesis 2 with a group of Chinese Y.W.C.A. workers and local women leaders of the churches. Before the Bible study took place, we had spent a few days in China and learned about the changes in women's status after the revolution of 1949. The Chinese women leaders repeatedly told us that equality of women and men was guaranteed by the Constitution and the law, though women were still discriminated against in terms of jobs and educational opportunities.

In our discussion of the creation story in Genesis 2, the other Asian women theologians and I were conscious of the fact that the story was sometimes used against women because Eve was created second and she was to be Adam's helper (Gen. 2:18). But the Chinese Christian women in my group did not read the story in terms of male domination over female. One Chinese woman said that the term *helper* implied that Eve was a capable woman, that she could offer help to others. Living in a socialist country where equality between the sexes is emphasized in public discourse, these Chinese women focused on the complementarity of the two sexes in their interpretation. The experience has reminded me of the different social locations of women and the implications for our interpretation strategy. Coming from different cultures and societies, the women discussing the Genesis story have multiple subject positions and produce multiple interpretations. There is no single women's point of view and the meaning of the text is negotiated in the discursive practice.

These examples of strategies drawn from oral hermeneutics raise new questions about the text, context, and the process of interpretation. The Bible is understood to be a talking book, constantly eliciting further conversation and dialogue, instead of an external, privileged text handed down from a distant past. Building on the oral traditions indigenous in their culture, the oral hermeneutics of Asian women offer insights to women's creative appropriation of the Bible. Yet we have learned very little from such insights, because women's voices have not been taken seriously. I hope that biblical scholars and theologians can pay more attention to oral hermeneutics in the future, so that voices from the margins, including those of women, will not continue to be ignored.

NOTES

1. Teresa Okure, "Feminist Interpretations in Africa," in *A Feminist Introduction*, vol. 1 of *Searching the Scriptures*, 83.

2. Renita J. Weems, "Reading *Her Way* through the Struggle," in *Stony the Road We Trod: African-American Biblical Interpretation*, ed. Cain Hope Felder (Minneapolis: Fortress, 1991), 66; see also Vincent L. Wimbush, "Historical/Cultural Criticism as Liberation: A Proposal for an African American Biblical Hermeneutic," *Semeia* 47 (1989): 45.

3. Cornel West, *Prophetic Fragments* (Grand Rapids, Mich.: William B. Eerdmans, 1988), 5.

4. Carlos Mesters, "The Use of the Bible in Christian Communities of the Common People," in *The Challenge of Basic Christian Communities*, ed. Sergio Torres and John Eagleson (Maryknoll, N.Y.: Orbis Books, 1981), 197-210.

5. Werner H. Kelber, *The Oral and the Written Gospel: The Hermeneutics of Speaking and Writing in the Synoptic Tradition, Mark, Paul, and Q* (Philadelphia: Fortress, 1983), 2.

6. William A. Graham, *Beyond the Written Word: Oral Aspects of Scripture in the History of Religion* (Cambridge: Cambridge University Press, 1987), 67-77; and Thomas B. Coburn, "'Scripture' in India: Towards a Typology of the Word in Hindu Life," in *Rethinking Scripture*, 102-28.

7. Stanley J. Samartha, "The Cross and the Rainbow: Christ in a Multireligious Culture," in *The Myth of Christian Uniqueness: Toward a Pluralistic Theology of Religions*, ed. John Hick and Paul F. Knitter (Maryknoll, N.Y.: Orbis Books, 1987), 78.

8. Arthur Waley, *The Analects of Confucius* (London: George Allen and Unwin, 1938), 21-26.

9. D. C. Lau, *Lao Tzu: Tao Te Ching* (New York: Penguin Books, 1963), 12; Ellen M. Chen, *The Tao Te Ching: A New Translation with Commentary* (New York: Paragon House, 1989), 19.

10. Miriam Levering, "Scripture and Its Reception: A Buddhist Case," in *Rethinking Scripture* (Albany, N.Y.: State University of New York Press, 1989), 61.

11. Joseph Needham, *Science and Civilization in China* (Cambridge: Cambridge University Press, 1956), 2:134.

12. Rita M. Gross, *Buddhism after Patriarchy: A Feminist History, Analysis, and Reconstruction of Buddhism* (Albany, N.Y.: State University of New York Press, 1993), 32.

13. Jack Goody, *The Interface between the Written and the Oral* (Cambridge: Cambridge University Press, 1987), 121-22.

14. Harold Coward, *Sacred Word and Sacred Text: Scripture in World Religions* (Maryknoll, N.Y.: Orbis Books, 1988), 120.

15. Ibid., 118; Goody, *The Interface between the Written and the Oral*, 119.

16. Graham, *Beyond the Written Word*, 88-90; Frederick M. Denny, "Islam: Qur'an and Hadith," in *The Holy Book in Comparative Perspective* (Columbia, S.C.: University of South Carolina Press, 1985), 96-97.

17. Female literacy rates in China after the sixteenth century have been rising. See Susan Mann, "Learned Women in the Eighteenth Century," in *Engendering China: Women, Culture, and the State*, ed. Christina K. Gilmartin, Gail Hershatter, Lisa Rofel, and Tyrene White (Cambridge: Harvard University Press, 1994), 27-46.

18. William Barrett, ed., *Zen Buddhism: Selected Writings of D. T. Suzuki* (Garden City, N.Y.: Doubleday Anchor Books, 1956), 9.

19. Susan Naquin, *Millenarian Rebellion in China: The Eight Trigrams Uprising of 1813* (New Haven: Yale University Press, 1976), 41.

20. Levering, "Scripture and Its Reception," 68.

21. Lamin Sanneh, *Translating the Message: The Missionary Impact on Culture* (Maryknoll, N.Y.: Orbis Books, 1990), 213.

22. Ibid., 233-34.

23. Ibid., 101-2.

24. Wang Weifan, "The Bible in Chinese," *China Theological Review* 8 (1993): 100-23.

25. For a detailed study of the Chinese case, see Kwok Pui-lan, *Chinese Women and Christianity, 1860-1927* (Atlanta: Scholars Press, 1992), 65-100.

26. I benefit from the analysis of Evelyn Brooks Higginbotham of the black Baptist church (see *Righteous Discontent: The Women's Movement in the Black Baptist Church, 1880-1920* (Cambridge: Harvard University Press, 1993), 14-15).

27. Kelber, *The Oral and the Written Gospel*, 18.

28. Walter J. Ong, "Text as Interpretation: Mark and After," *Semeia* 39 (1987): 11.

29. Joanna Dewey, "Mark as Interwoven Tapestry: Forecasts and Echoes for a Listening Audience," *Catholic Biblical Quarterly* 53 (1991): 235.

30. Charles H. Lohr, "Oral Techniques in the Gospel of Matthew," *Catholic Biblical Quarterly* 23 (1961): 403-35.

31. Joanna Dewey, "From Storytelling to the Written Text: The Loss of Early Christian Women's Voices," Unpublished paper.

32. Antoinette Clark Wire, "Gender Roles in a Scribal Community," in *Social History of the Matthean Community*, ed. David L. Balch (Minneapolis: Fortress, 1991), 121.

33. Walter J. Ong, *The Presence of the Word: Some Prolegomena for Cultural and Religious History* (New Haven: Yale University Press, 1967).

34. Elisabeth Schüssler Fiorenza, *Bread Not Stone: The Challenge of Feminist Biblical Interpretation* (Boston: Beacon, 1984), 27.

35. Mary McClintock Fulkerson observes that many of the proponents of reader-response criticism rely upon the objective text to control meaning; see *Changing the Subject: Women's Discourses and Feminist Theology* (Minneapolis: Fortress, 1994), 135.

36. See Sandra M. Schneiders, *The Revelatory Text: Interpreting the New Testament as Sacred Scripture* (San Francisco: Harper SanFrancisco, 1991), 97-179.

37. Ong, *The Presence of the Word*, 24-26.

38. See the discussion in Deborah Tannen, "The Oral/Literate Continuum in Discourse," in *Spoken and Written Language: Exploring Orality and Literacy*, ed. Deborah Tannen (Norwood, N.J.: Ablex, 1982), 1-3.

39. Ong, *The Presence of the Word*, 25-29.

40. David R. Olson, "From Utterance to Text: The Bias of Language in Speech and Writing," *Harvard Educational Review* 47:3 (1977):277.

41. Goody, *The Interface between the Written and the Oral*, 164.

42. See Susan Lochrie Graham, "Silent Voices: Women in the Gospel of Mark," *Semeia* 54 (1991): 145-58. Graham suggests we listen to the language of the body, figured by touch, instead of the language of the mind (speech and hearing).

43. Phyllis Trible, *Texts of Terror: Literary-Feminist Readings of Biblical Narratives* (Philadelphia: Fortress, 1984).

44. Lee Oo Chung, Sylvia Jenkin, and Mizuho Matsuda, "Introduction," in *Reading the Bible as Asian Women* ed. Christian Conference of Asia (Singapore: Christian Conference of Asia, 1986), 1.

45. Crescy John, Susan, Sun Ai Lee Park, Pearl Drego, Pauline, Mary Lobo, and Margaret Shanti, "The Exodus Story," *In God's Image* (September 1988): 43.

46. Ibid., 45.

47. Pearl Drego, "Annunciation," *In God's Image* (December 1989): 11-14.

48. Marianne Katoppo, *Compassionate and Free: An Asian Woman's Theology* (Geneva: World Council of Churches, 1979), 22-24; Chung Hyun Kyung, *Struggle to Be the Sun Again* (Maryknoll, N.Y.: Orbis Books, 1990), 74-84; Rosemary Radford Ruether, *Mary—The Feminine Face of the Church* (London: SCM, 1979), 27.

49. Drego, "Annunciation," 12.

50. Ibid.

51. A. K. Ramanujan, "Tell It to the Walls: On Folktales in Indian Culture," in *India Briefing, 1992*, ed. L.A. Gordon and P. Oldenburg (Boulder: Westview Press, 1992), 167-68.

52. For example, "The Samaritan Woman," *In God's Image* (September 1988): 40-42; "The Exodus Story," ibid., 43-48; and "Waiting to Be Recognized," ibid., 49-50.

53. Elsa Tamez, "The Woman Who Complicated the History of Salvation," in *New Eyes for Reading: Biblical and Theological Reflections by Women from the Third World*, ed. John S. Pobee and Bärbel von Wartenberg-Potter (Oak Park, Ill.: Meyer Stone Books, 1987), 5-17; and Delores Williams, *Sisters in the Wilderness* (Maryknoll, N.Y.: Orbis Books, 1993), 15-33.

54. I find Bakhtin's expression "internal dialogization" very illuminating, though he refers more specifically to his philosophical understanding of language. See Bakhtin, *The Dialogic Imagination*, 280-84.

55. The idea of "voice into existence" is from Henry Louis Gates, Jr., "Talkin' that Talk," in *"Race," Writing, and Difference*, ed. Henry Louis Gates, Jr. (Chicago: University of Chicago Press, 1985), 403.

56. See M. M. Bakhtin, *The Dialogic Imagination: Four Essays*, ed. Michael Holquist (Austin: University of Texas Press, 1973), 342-47. The fact that I use Bakhtin's work on the novel in the context of biblical hermeneutics illustrates the possibility of further dialogic interaction with Bakhtin's work.

57. A report of the visit is found in *In God's Image* 10:3 (Autumn 1991).

7

Theses on Inculturation

*Theological Advisory Commission
of the Federation of Asian Bishops' Conferences**

Presented here are five theses on the relationship of gospel and culture in the inculturation process. Inculturation involves gospel and culture in a mutually critical interaction, one in which "culture" is understood not only as a set of enduring values and a particular world view, but is seen also as a historical process of change and—especially in Asia—as intimately formed by the world's religious traditions. The entire Christian community is the primary "subject" of inculturation, with the basic Christian communities being "especially significant places" of inculturation and the building up of the local church.

THESIS 5

A local Church comes into existence and is built up through a deep and mutually enriching encounter between the Gospel and a people with its particular culture and tradition. In current theological and magisterial language, this is known as inculturation. Inculturation consists not only in the expression of the Gospel and the Christian faith through the cultural medium, but includes, as well, experiencing, understanding and appropriating them through the cultural resources of a people. As a result, the concrete shape of the local Church will be, on the one hand, conditioned by the culture, and, on the other hand, the culture will be evangelized by the life and witness of the local Church.

5.1 Inculturation is a must for the self-realization and growth of the Churches. In every part of the world, therefore, attempts are being made to contextualize the

---

* Taken from "Theses on the Local Church: A Theological Reflection in the Asian Context," prepared by the Theological Advisory Commission (TAC) of the Federation of Asian Bishops' Conferences (FABC). The TAC is composed of theologians from every bishops' conference that has membership in the FABC. Originally from J. Gnanapiragasam and F. Wilfred, eds., *Being the Church in Asia: Theological Advisory Commission Documents (1986-92)*, Vol. I (Quezon City, Philippines: Claretian Publications, 1994).

life and mission of the Church by bringing faith and culture into closer relationship. This is particularly evident in the developing countries. In fact, in their First FABC Plenary Assembly the Asian bishops described the local Church as "a Church incarnate in a people, a Church indigenous and inculturated. And this means concretely a Church in continuous, humble and loving dialogue with the living traditions, cultures, the religions—in brief, with all the life-realities of the people in whose midst it has sunk its roots deeply and whose history and life it gladly makes its own" (12). For the Churches of Asia the task of inculturation is as challenging as it is urgent against the background of long centuries of cultural estrangement that marked their histories of mission during the colonial period, and in the context of contemporary cultural awakening among various Asian peoples.

5.2 In this task of inculturation we can derive much inspiration from the examples of Matteo Ricci in China and Roberto de Nobili in India, in spite of their limitations in the understanding of the relationship between the Gospel and culture. These great missionaries of Asia followed basically the method of adaptation which is an effort to transmit the Gospel and the truths of revelation by employing the language and concepts drawn from the culture of a people. Inculturation is something much deeper than adaptation. It implies *encounter* with the Gospel, and is much more *comprehensive*, for it defines the genesis and growth of the Church among a people.

5.3 Our efforts at building up authentic local Churches through inculturation are guided today by the vision, spirit and techniques of Vatican II, especially as found in *Lumen Gentium, Gaudium et Spes* and *Ad Gentes. Lumen Gentium* sees the relationship of the Church to cultures and traditions in the horizon of the unity of the whole of the human race (of which the Church is a sacrament), and of the universality of the Church in which each individual part with its different culture, heritage and riches is in communion with each other (LG 13). *Gaudium et Spes*, on its part, far from confining itself to a narrow understanding of culture as cultivation of mind through education, study of humanities, etc., in contrast to uncivilized persons and "primitive peoples" (*Naturvoelker*), has included in its description of culture its historical, social and ethnological dimensions. These dimensions are of paramount importance in understanding the relationship between local Churches and cultures. Finally, the Decree on the Church's Missionary Activity (*Ad Gentes*) has envisaged the local Churches as emerging from the encounter of God's Word with the culture and traditions of peoples and has underlined the necessity of pursuing inculturation in various areas of Christian life and mission (AG 19-22). Much attention has been given to the theme of inculturation by the various Roman synods of bishops, especially the one on evangelization, and by the Apostolic Exhortation *Evangelii Nuntiandi* that followed it. Through his various pastoral journeys particularly to Asia and Africa, and through his discourses on these occasions, Pope John Paul II has highlighted the necessity of inculturation of local Churches as well as the evangelization of cultures.

5.4 Local Churches are born and are built up only when there is an encounter with the culture of a people. *Encounter means mutuality and reciprocity.* The various traditions, symbols, institutions, customs, manners, etc., of a people spring forth from the soul, the spirit of a people. The encounter of the Gospel with the culture takes place not simply by adopting the external forms and symbols but by reaching deeply into the spirit and soul of a people of which these are expressions and manifestations. Dialogue and encounter of the Gospel at the level of the spirit and in the "cave of the heart" of a people will enable the emergence of authentic local Churches. Such an encounter is also a meeting with the *worldview* of a people, which is the matrix for the various cultural forms. It is also through the worldview that the various parts of the culture are organically interlinked and exist as a whole. The worldview expresses itself in the local organization of the cultural group, its institutions, structures, etc.

5.5 To understand the relationship between the Gospel and culture in terms of *encounter* means that we acknowledge that culture has its legitimate autonomy and proper identity. For culture, as the product of the human spirit acting on nature and creating various instruments, institutions, social relationships, ways of living, etc., forms part of God's design of creation. Besides, the culture of every people has a vocation: to contribute, each one in a unique way, to the life and well-being of the one human family. Every culture manifests in a singular way the richness of the *humanum*. As such it should be respected and fostered.

5.6 In the light of what has been said, it should be clear that culture, which has its basis in God's creation of man and nature, should be respected in its inner purpose and goal and should not be viewed simply as a means for something else. Nor should individual elements of culture be isolated from the organic whole. Hence, inculturation cannot be a process in which particular elements of a culture are selected to serve as a garb for the Gospel. This will be a very external and superficial kind of inculturation since it does not respect the inner soul of the culture and its organic character.

5.7 Each culture not only provides us with a new approach to the human but also opens up new avenues for the understanding of the Gospel and its riches. When the Gospel encounters the tradition, experience and culture of a people, its hitherto undiscovered virtualities will surface; riches and meanings as yet hidden will emerge into the light. That is why it is so important to reinterpret the Gospel through the cultural resources of every people; this reinterpretation truly enriches the Christian Tradition. Seen in this light, the local Church itself may be viewed as a fresh and creative reactualization and reintrepretation of the Gospel and faith. Such a reinterpretation will not be a break with the Tradition, but will be in organic continuity with it, inasmuch as the past will be repossessed and reactivated in the present experience of a local Church. In turn, the Tradition and the heritage of the past, instead of being a hindrance, will support the present life of the local Church, where the Risen Lord and his Spirit are living and active.

5.8 A deeper encounter will take place only when the Gospel and faith themselves are experienced and understood through the cultural resources of a people. This is not only something desirable but also a necessity. For, given the historicity of human existence in a determined context and tradition, it is inescapable that our perception of truth, understanding and experiencing of reality—including the Gospel and faith—be bound up with a particular culture. In other words, true understanding of God's Word and the response of faith can take place among a people through the cultural resources they possess, which are the embodiment of their experiences and traditions. It is with reference to these that new experiences and events are interpreted, assimilated and absorbed. There takes place, in other words, an organization or rather reorganization, a restructuring of the new materials, events and experiences in terms of the cultural genius and specific ways of thinking of a group or people. All this is applicable also to the encounter of the Gospel with the culture of a group, nation or people.

5.9 If such is the encounter between the Gospel and culture, then, it follows that the concrete form of a local Church is conditioned by the culture of a people among whom it is rooted. The enfleshment of the local Church in the cultural body of a particular people distinguishes it and marks it off from other Churches. Each local Church, then, will bear the stamp of the culture where it is incarnated. Thus, according to the varieties of cultures there will be also diversity in the local Churches, in spite of the fact that they share the same Gospel, faith, eucharist and so on. Thus the universal communion of Churches is also a communion in the diversity of cultures and traditions. Pope John Paul II in an address on December 21, 1984 stated: "It is difficult to express oneself with greater clarity and depth. The universal Church is presented as a communion of (particular) Churches, and indirectly as a community of nations, languages, cultures . . ." (*Doc. Cath.* 1889 (1985), pp. 167-72).

5.10 In the self-realization of the local Church through a process of inculturation, the following two aspects should be held in mind. First, the Gospel is always found in inculturated form. Gospel is not an abstraction. It exists in the concrete as the faith of a people appropriated and expressed in their cultural context. Hence, the encounter of a people with the Gospel, in practice, happens to be also a meeting with another culture animated by faith. Because of this fact, some authors prefer to speak of "interculturation" than inculturation. But we adopt in our commentary consistently the term inculturation, including in its scope also implied meeting of cultures.

5.11 A second point to be noted is that the encounter of the Gospel need not always be with one homogeneous culture. It could be with a diversity of ethnic, linguistic or cultural groups living in the same locality. In fact, in some countries in Asia we have in the same local Church the presence of various ethnic and cultural groups. This mosaic of various languages, cultures and peoples is a great enrichment for the local Church. The process of inculturation must take into account this concrete situation as well as the evolution and growth which these diverse human groups undergo as part of a region or nation. In situations of conflict of ethnic or cultural identities, the local Church can serve as an agent of unity and reconciliation. It will foster the communion of various cultures and traditions and thereby shape its own specific identity as a local Church. In multiracial, multilinguistic and pluricultural situations the task of inculturation would involve also the promotion of harmony and communion.

5.12 If the local Church is the fruit of the interaction between the Gospel and culture, it is not enough to say that culture conditions the shape of the local Church. In the same breath we should also add that the Gospel too acts on the culture. As God's Word it enhances and elevates the culture as well as challenges some of its values, institutions, customs, ways of life, etc. Cultures bear also the mark of human sinfulness. They can contain dehumanizing and enslaving elements. The evangelizing mission of the local Church should move today more in the direction of transforming the culture from within as a leaven. Pope Paul VI underlined the importance of evangelization of cultures when he stated in *Evangelii Nuntiandi*: "What matters is to evangelize man's culture and cultures, not in a purely decorative way, as it were by applying a thin veneer, but in a vital way, in depth and right to the very roots. The split between the Gospel and culture is without doubt the drama of our times, just as in other times. Therefore, every effort must be made to ensure a full evangelization of culture, or more concretely, of cultures. They have to be regenerated by an encounter with the Gospel" (EN 20).

5.13 The concrete manner in which this evangelization of cultures takes place is very important. Gospel can truly evangelize cultures to the extent it is lived and borne witness to by men and women who believe in it and who are guided by it. Further, such an evangelizing action should be free of all kinds of triumphalism. It should be done as a humble service to culture, all the time being aware that the Gospel itself can receive, for its understanding and appropriation, much from culture. The Second Vatican Council has clearly recognized this.

THESIS 6

A local Church lives in an ongoing historical process of inculturation, since the Church is a community of faith in growth and the culture itself continues to evolve and change. Today a local Church realizes itself by effectively responding to the challenges of new historical forces, which give birth to the process of modernization and which affect all areas and aspects of the life of a people.

6.1 After speaking of the emergence of the local Church through encounter with culture, the present thesis views this encounter from a dynamic perspective, looking at culture as a constantly evolving reality in relation to the developments in society. In our considerations the process of modernization will be given particular attention, since it affects deeply both culture and society. All this has consequences for the self-understanding, life and mission of the local Churches of Asia.

6.2 Culture is not a static but a living reality. It continues to grow, evolve and change due to factors from within and without. Change takes place in every culture. The difference consists in the extent and speed of change. One significant force for change in a culture is its encounter with other cultures. When this process of transformation through encounter ceases to take place a culture is isolated and dies out, as has happened with many cultures and civilizations of the past. What is remarkable about the enduring cultures of Asia is not only their antiquity but also the fact that through the millennia and centuries they have evolved and absorbed new elements, responding to the manifold challenges and vicissitudes of history. Inculturation in Asia, as elsewhere, demands that the local Church grow by listening, perceiving and responding to the evolution of culture. If the Church considers inculturation as something to be achieved once and for all and fails to interact with the culture in its evolution, it is bound to be alienated and estranged from the hopes, aspirations and expectations of the people. This is what the experience of the Churches in various parts of the world teaches us.

6.3 What is striking about culture today is that the extent of its transformation is something unprecedented. This is very much accelerated by the process of modernization which has its own consequences. By modernization we mean the process of rapid transformation in society caused by modern science, technology, industrialization, modern means of communication, urbanization, new educational, economic and political systems, which all have profoundly affected the traditional culture, institutions, way of life, etc. And even more deeply, the process of modernization has brought about transformations in attitudes, values, and in the consciousness of individuals and groups. These changes and transformations are immediately visible in our Asian cities, which are growing at an alarmingly fast pace through mass-mobilization and urbanization.

6.4 The meeting of traditional cultures and modernization in Asia has produced wide varieties of situations and responses. In some Asian societies and in some areas of life, we find modernization juxtaposed to traditional cultures and ways of life. In such societies, Asians, accustomed as they are to living with contradictions, live with one foot in modernity and the other in the traditional ways. Another response has been to try to discard the traditional culture—lock, stock, and barrel—and to replace it with modernity. In yet other cases, we have staunch opposition to modernity and its values, coupled with defense of traditional culture, institutions, ways of life, etc. In some other situations, we have a transference of traditional attitudes and values onto modern systems, tools, etc. Or, reversely, superimposition of the modern onto the traditional. It is undeniable, however, that the mainline response in Asia has been a profound desire to reap the benefits of modern culture without losing the identity of one's traditional heritage and its long-cherished values and ideals.

6.5 The encounter between tradition and modernity presents an immense challenge to the Church (cf. GS 56). In an address to the Pontifical Council for Culture, Pope John Paul II characterized the present situation of change and transformation in this way:

> It is obvious that the emergence of new culture calls for courage and intelligence on the part of all believers and of everyone of goodwill. Social and cultural changes, political upheavals, ideological ferment, religious questioning, ethical probing, all show a world in gestation, in search of form and direction, organic wholeness, prophetic renewal (*L'Osservatore Romano*, English edition, 16 December 1985).

All this is very true of the Asian situation. It is by responding to the complex situations in our Asian countries with their challenges that the Churches in this continent will become authentic local Churches.

6.6 In seeking to respond the Church should in the first place acknowledge and accept both the validity of tradition and of culture, as well as the important role being played by the process of modernization. A defensive attitude towards them, evidently, will not contribute to the emergence of the local Church and the fulfilling of the mission to which God calls it today. The riches of Asian cultures and traditions are to be positively promoted because God and his Spirit have been active in the history of Asian peoples. Their variegated cultural expressions reflect his light, truth, and beauty. Similarly, modernization is a process which manifests the continued presence of God in our contemporary history. The local Church should then manifest the great openness which Vatican II has shown both to the cultures of peoples and to the modern world and its developments.

6.7 One of the crucial problems faced in Asia and elsewhere has been articulated well by the *Pastoral Constitution on the Church in the Modern World*: "How can the vitality and growth of a new culture be fostered without the loss of living fidelity to the heritage of tradition?" (GS, 56). To this concern and aspiration widespread in Asia, the Asian local Churches should respond. The response should take into account the fact that a deep and lasting change in a culture does not take place by simple superimposition of new elements from without or through a heterogenetic process. Change in a culture or society takes place when it proceeds from within, that is, when it is orthogenetic. The meeting of tradition and modernity must be such that the change in culture activated from within is able to respond creatively to modernity and make it its own through a new synthesis.

6.8 In order to contribute towards an harmonious blending of tradition and modernity, the Church in Asia needs to exercise critical discernment. For Asian cultures are ambiguous, in the sense that, along with many lofty ideals, visions, and values, they contain also oppressive and anti-human elements, such as caste, which goes against the equality of all human beings, discrimination towards women, etc.

On the other hand, modernity, in spite of its great and marvelous contributions to humanization, contains profound contradictions. It is eroding some of the long-cherished values of Asian societies, causing commercialization of immorality, creating new, ruthless and large-scale exploitation of the poor and the weak. Modernization with its advanced industrialization is causing serious damage to the natural environment in Asian countries. It has victimized the poorest sections in our societies, like the tribals and fishermen who live on the natural resources of forest and sea. Modern industrialization weighs most heavily on the Asian women who are displaced, exploited and sexually commercialized.

6.9 It is in this context of the meeting of tradition and modernity that the local Church has to exercise a critical discernment by being aware of the limitations and strengths both of tradition and of modernity. It should contribute to the evolution of a humanism that will be truly Asian; a humanism that will result from the encounter of the best elements of traditional culture and modernity. Thus, the active participation of the Church in the past and contemporary history of the peoples of Asia, critical identification with their tradition, culture, their present aspirations and hopes will make it truly Asian. The shape of the local Churches of Asia of tomorrow will depend upon the process of inculturation that takes place today in the context of the meeting of tradition and modernity in Asia.

THESIS 7

In Asia a local Church realizes itself by entering into new relationships with neighbors of other faiths and by involving itself in concerns of justice, human

dignity and human rights, and in the concrete fulfillment of the preferential love for the poor.

7.1 Two areas which are particularly important to Asian local Churches for their self-realization in their own milieux are *dialogue* and *inculturation*; these two concerns (as the FABC I declaration so strongly affirmed) must form part and parcel of their life and mission. If the Church is a sacrament of communion with God and solidarity among men (LG 1), then all local Churches in our part of the world must relate to our neighbors as they concretely experience that communion and that solidarity in their own religious traditions. *Dialogue with other religions* is intimately linked with the process of inculturation of our Asian Churches because among many Asian peoples culture is animated by religious experience and religious belief and practice. Religion and culture are so closely linked together that to talk about one is necessarily to talk about the other. (We have addressed this and related issues in our *Theses on Interreligious Dialogue*.)

7.2 Most of our Asian countries are characterized by massive poverty and misery, with millions of people deprived of the basic necessities of life: food, water, shelter. After the pattern of the Incarnation, our local Churches must, in a spirit of solidarity, truly share the lot of the poor, the marginalized and the exploited in the society wherein they live. Announcing the Good News to the poor (cf. Lk. 4:18) demands that our local Churches become Churches of the poor. We note with joy the recent efforts undertaken to move toward an increasing solidarity with the poor and even, among some, to become identified with them. And yet we are so painfully aware that many of our institutions project an image of wealth and power, that often our schools, hospitals, etc., benefit mainly those who are affluent. The life-styles of some Church leaders, of some priests and religious, do not manifest an evangelical simplicity and detachment.

7.3 FABC I in 1974 called upon our local Churches in Asia to engage in dialogue with the poor:

> A local Church in dialogue with the people, in so many countries in Asia, means dialogue with the poor. This dialogue has to take shape in what has been called a "dialogue of life." This involves a genuine experience and understanding of this poverty ... of so many of our people. It is our belief that it is from the material deprivation of our peoples, as well as from their tremendous human potential and from their aspiration for a more fully human and brotherly world, that Christ is calling the Churches in Asia (FABC I, 19, 20, 22).

7.4 This kind of inculturation into the context of the life of the people opens up the local Church to the horizon of the Kingdom—the Kingdom which is larger than the Church and of which the Church itself is an instrument. It sets the local Church in an evangelizing dynamism and leads to its self-realization by bringing into the life of the poor and the oppressed true human dignity, justice and freedom. We recall the words of the Synod of Bishops in 1971, which stated: "Action in behalf of justice and participation in the transformation of the world fully appear to us as a constitutive dimension in the preaching of the Gospel."

7.5 Culture is very much bound up with the social and political areas. We assist today at the central role culture is increasingly playing in the socio-political order. It is important, therefore, that the local Churches pay attention to the following two aspects in the process of their self-realization through inculturation. In many of our societies or nations there are generally two types of culture: that of the politically and economically powerful and that of the weak and powerless. (Cultural domination accompanies political and economic domination, and helps to sustain it. The culture of the poor and the marginalized is neglected, if not suppressed, by political and economic domination.) This "little tradition" of the poor and the powerless must become the object of special concern for the local Church that wants to be in "dialogue of life" with the poor of Asia. Inculturation should not be identified with the culture of the dominant and powerful groups but must become a process through which the local Church lives in solidarity with the poor, their traditions, customs, ways of life, patterns of thought, etc.

7.6 There is also a second point to be noted. The process of modernization should not become an exclusive concern of the powerful in society and pursued to their advantage. Modernization has to be filtered through the concern for the poor and the marginalized in the Asian societies, so that it can be detoxicated of its dehumanizing effects and made to serve the goals of justice and freedom. Integral to the process of inculturation for us, then, must be this effort to address the challenges of modernization in dialogue with the multitudes of the poor and the powerless among us.

THESIS 8

The Christian community is the active subject of inculturation which takes place in all aspects of Christian life, witness, and mission.

8.1 Inculturation is a task in which the whole Christian community must involve itself. This is so because, in the first place, Church is a people. Hence, in all its activities all sectors of the people must participate in one way or another. Secondly, inculturation is something integral; it affects every aspect of the people's Christian life and mission. Thus, genuine inculturation cannot be effected merely through the work of an elite group or of experts.

8.2 By living within their particular context according to the "sense of faith aroused and sustained by the Spirit of truth" (LG 12), the faithful will learn to express their faith not only in fidelity to the apostolic tradition, but also in response to their cultural situations. This response is the responsibility of the whole community which discerns God's Word and Spirit in its culture and history. This responsibility is unique; it cannot be delegated or substituted. Since the context of one local Church differs from another, every local Church enjoys a legitimate autonomy, while maintaining the universal communion, to shape creatively its own life and structures, and fulfill its God-given mission in its cultural environment: "In the face of such widely varying situations it is difficult for us," said Paul VI in *Octogesima Adveniens*, "to put forward a solution which has universal validity. Such is not our ambition, nor is it our mission. It is up to the Christian communities to analyze with objectivity the situation which is proper to their own country, to shed on it the light of the Gospel's unalterable words" (OA 4). These words of Pope Paul VI acknowledging the responsibility of the local Church in relation to social quetions can be applied to the task of inculturation as well.

8.3 A very important area of inculturation is the liturgy of the Christian community. Liturgy expresses the faith of the Church (*lex orandi lex credendi*). Liturgy must be the outcome of the faith-experience in a particular cultural environment. In turn, such liturgical experience should flower in a Christian life that is fully inculturated. Therefore, true liturgical inculturation of the Christian community cannot be done from without and introduced through an external and artificial process; it should spontaneously spring forth from the life of the faith lived fully in the context of the culture and the life-realities of the people. Nevertheless, given the long estrangement of the liturgical life of Asian local Churches from their cultural traditions, at this stage of transition to a fully inculturated ecclesial life, certain liturgical experiments and models are very legitimate and necessary in order to facilitate the process of inculturation by the whole community. These experiments, however, should not reflect only the concerns of a few experts, but rather should be in dialogue with the whole Christian community.

8.4 Another area of inculturation is the faith-formation or catechesis which initiates the faithful into the life of faith and helps them to achieve maturity in it. In its content, method, and terminology, catechesis must be attuned to the experience, pedagogical traditions, psychological make-up, and linguistic genius of the people. As an integral part of the life of the local Church, faith-formation should reflect all the dimensions of its life and mission. While holding firmly to the truth of affirmations of faith, it should not be reduced to a set of doctrinal and catechetical formulations made out to be immutably valid for the appropriation and expression of belief, for all times and all cultures. The Holy Father, Pope John Paul II, himself insisted on this necessary process of inculturation in catechesis when, in his Apostolic Exhortation, *Catechesi tradendae*, he said:

> The term "acculturation" or "inculturation" may be a neologism, but it expresses very well one factor of the great mystery of the Incarnation: We can say of catechesis, as well as evangelization in general, that it is called to bring the power of the Gospel into the very heart of cultures and its essential components; it will learn their most significant expressions; it will respect their particular values and riches (53).

8.5 The life in the Spirit, which is spirituality, must be attuned to and reflect the experience of the Spirit by a people in their culture and tradition. For we know that the Spirit is present and active among peoples of Asia, in their histories, traditions, cultures and religions. Inculturation will be thus a meeting of the Spirit with the Spirit, fostering the bonds of spiritual communion and solidarity with the people among whom the local Church lives and grows. The spiritual riches and religious values by which the people of our continent have been nourished through millennia and centuries must flow into the life of the local Church to enrich it. Deep awareness of God, meditation, contemplation, interiority, asceticism, self-denial, simplicity of life, deep faith, silence, the spirit of surrender, sense of mystery, deep communion—these are some of the spiritual values highly prized and fostered in our traditions. The Second Plenary Assembly of FABC, which dealt with the theme "Prayer: the Life of the Church of Asia," underlined the need to integrate into the life of the Asian local Churches the ways of prayer and worship of our peoples. The bishops stated:

> We are daily more convinced that the Spirit is leading us in our time, not to some dubious syncretism, (which we all rightly reject), but to an integration—profound and organic in character—of all that is best in our traditional ways of prayer and worship, into the treasury of our Christian heritage . . . These many indigenous riches will at last find a natural place in the prayer of our Churches in Asia and will greatly enrich the prayer-life of the Church throughout the world (31,33).

8.6 There is no need to say that the Christian life and mission involvement of our local Churches in Asia must be accompanied by theological reflection which will be attentive and respond to the questions and problems arising from experience and praxis. Vatican II's Decree on Missionary Activity, *Ad Gentes*, acknowledged the importance and necessity of such contextualized theological reflection.

> Theological investigation must be necessarily stirred up in each major sociocultural area, as it is called. In this way, under the tradition of the universal Church, a fresh scrutiny will be brought to bear on the deeds and words which God has made known, which have been consigned to Sacred Scripture and which have been unfolded by the Church Fathers and the teaching authority of the Church (22).

8.7 For a profound inculturation of theology it is important that new theological methods and ways of interpretation be devised which will reflect the culture and traditions, the mindsets and ways of thought of Asian peoples. In this regard we must single out the place of experience. All Asian philosophical traditions accord particular importance to experience and/or immediate relationship with reality. Thus, experience should provide the starting point for any genuine Asian theology. Conceptual elaboration should be firmly rooted in experience. Theological reflection, thus enrooted in experience and life, will help our local Churches to understand and interpret their faith and express it in authentically creative ways.

8.8 Another area which calls for a fuller "enrooting in the native soil of our Asian cultures and traditions" is religious life in our Churches. Religious life is meant to make more visible the significance of a way of living which is totally dedicated to the values of our Christian faith. Religious men and women should manifest in their worship and witness, in their common life and service, how the followers of Jesus incarnate his life and mission in the heart of a people and a culture in the most authentic way.

In ways worthy of praise, many religious communities and individuals have been in the forefront of the efforts toward significant inculturation and solidarity with the poor. Unfortunately, however, there remain areas and situations where religious communities retain much that is foreign and alien in relation to the milieux surrounding them. This is seen in language and lifestyles, in formation programs (often dominated by foreign members), in ongoing importation of frequently alienating culture-bound elements. For instance, sometimes psychological processes used in other cultures are uncritically imposed on Asian members. Sometimes adapting to these becomes a norm of acceptance. Not infrequently local members must put on Western ways if they wish "to belong." Decision-making centers are often located abroad, where decision-makers are incapable of discerning essentials of religious life from merely culturally-conditioned attitudes and practices. Thus, inculturation is hindered, or even blocked, in the name of a false universality, by superiors and others who cannot or do not resonate with the aspirations and needs of Asian members, or who even now (perhaps only half-consciously) bear within them attitudes of cultural superiority.

8.9 Formation programs, above all, must be immersed in the language and life-style of the poorer sectors in our countries. The preferential option for the poor, worked out in daily life, is often the best way of bringing about an authentic inculturation of religious life. An estrangement from the Christian piety of the poor and the humble is often the result of styles of formation which mistake what is current in Western societies (often highly secularized) as mandatory for all. This must be studiously prevented.

8.10 In the ongoing revision of religious life in our Asian local Churches—a revision still quite necessary in most countries—some aspects of the spiritual traditions found within local cultures, such as the ideals of *sannyasa* (life of renunciation) in Hinduism, or the monastic life in Buddhism, can offer much by way of inspiration, enrichment, and example. A more earnest, more discerning inculturation in Asian religious life can lead the way to a more authentically evangelical witness and service among peoples.

THESIS 9

Basic ecclesial communities are especially significant "places" of inculturation and the building up of the local Church.

9.1 In many parts of Asia today Basic Ecclesial Communities (or small faith communities) have been proliferating in response to the needs of Christian life and mission. In these communities, through prayer centered on the Word of God and the eucharist, through meetings, mutual service and sharing, the Christian faithful experience what it is to be the Church. Here, too, where Christians know each other by name, they strengthen each other's faith; communion and participation become lived realities. And since they grapple with life-issues in the light of the Word of God, they are able to appropriate personally for themselves the meaning of the Word of God and recognize its concrete challenges and demands. While many BECs concentrate on the cultivation of community prayer and mutual help, others have sought to address and correct basic causes of underdevelopment and injustice, and bring about societal transformation.

Thus BECs become especially potent places and agents of the inculturation of the Gospel. In them the Gospel of Jesus Christ becomes the Gospel of the people.

9.2 So that BECs may not become isolated and instrumentalized by ideologies, and so that they may preserve their ecclesial character, they must maintain their communion with the pastors of the Church. One very important means to this communion is the ongoing formation of the community leaders (cf. *Evangelii Nuntiandi* 58).

9.3 In many parts of our countries, where Christians are few and far between, they are often confronted, together with adherents of other faiths, by common problems. As they live and struggle together to face these problems Christians and those adherents of other faiths can be seen as basic human communities. In these human communities, the faith-life of the Christian members can grow as they engage in a dialogue of life with adherents of other faiths, and together with them confront life-issues, like the struggle against poverty, the struggle for justice and human rights, and the efforts to build a world of peace in diversity. Basic human communities can be special places for experiencing and witnessing to the presence of the Spirit in the midst of persons of goodwill. They also provide opportunities for authentic Christian witness to peoples of other faiths. Further, in their interaction with these peoples of other faiths with whom they constitute these basic human communities, Christians can act as leaven for human and societal transformation.

8

Cultural Barriers to the Understanding of the Church and Its Public Role

Robert N. Bellah*

This article by sociologist Robert N. Bellah is a stunning example of what Andrew F. Walls calls the "pilgrim" principle in Christianity, the principle that points to the transforming, counter-cultural dynamic within Christianity. Written within the context of the culture of the United States, Bellah cites the notions of freedom of the solitary individual and the establishment of government (civil, social, or ecclesial) by social contract—both traceable to the philosophy of John Locke—as the root causes of inauthentic Christianity in the United States today. The church's calling within this context is to demonstrate convincingly that authentic human—and therefore Christian—existence is radically different from the surrounding culture. Christian faith and contemporary United States culture need to be in opposition, so that both culture and Christian practice in the United States can be called back to authenticity.

THE LEGACY OF JOHN LOCKE

There are difficulties inherent in some of the central presuppositions of American culture for the understanding of the church, of priesthood, and so necessarily of the episcopacy. These difficulties present problems for the bishop as leader in the church and in society. In the successor book to *Habits of the Heart* (1985) entitled *The Good Society* (1991), we develop the commonly accepted idea that if there is one philosopher behind the American experiment, it is John Locke. Locke, as we know, begins with a state of nature in which adult individuals who have worked

---

* Taken from *Missiology: An International Review*, XIX, 4 (October, 1991). An earlier version of the essay was presented to the 1990 Annual Meeting of the House of Bishops of the Episcopal Church in the United States, with a similar presentation given to the National Conference of Catholic Bishops several months previously. Robert N. Bellah is Elliot Professor of Sociology at the University of California at Berkeley.

and gained a little property by the sweat of their brow, decide voluntarily to enter a social contract through which they will set up a limited government, one of the chief responsibilities of which is the protection of their property. There are many peculiarities about this myth, which is one of the fundamental myths of origin of American society (fortunately, not the only one). Where did these adults come from? Did they have no parents? Who took care of them when they were little? How did they learn to speak so that they could make their social contract? Locke leaves us in the dark about all these matters.

Our founders were certainly devoted to the idea of the freedom of the individual, but they linked that freedom to an understanding of economic life that would have consequences they did not expect. It is remarkable how much of our current understanding of social reality flows from the original institutionalization at the end of the eighteenth century (the "founding") and how much of that was dependent on the thought of John Locke. Locke's teaching is one of the most powerful, if not *the* most powerful, ideologies ever invented. Indeed, it is proving to be more enduring and influential, which is not to say truer, than Marxism. It promises an unheard of degree of individual freedom, an unlimited opportunity to compete for material well-being, and an unprecedented limitation on the arbitrary powers of government to interfere with individual initiative.

Locke exemplifies the right to life, liberty, and the pursuit of happiness in the act of appropriation by the solitary individual of property from the state of nature. Government is then instituted for the protection of that property. Once men agree to accept money as the medium of exchange, the accumulation of property is in principle without any moral limit. Locke rejects all limits on the freedom and autonomy of individuals other than those they freely consent to in entering the (quite limited) social contract. He specifically attacks the patriarchal family, arguing implicitly for the rights of women and explicitly for the lack of obligation of children to parents. Limited government exists to provide a minimum of order for individuals to accumulate property. All traditional restraints are rejected and nothing is taken for granted that is not voluntarily agreed to on the basis of reason. That is an overly condensed but not unfair statement of Locke's position, or at least how Americans have come to understand Locke's position. In many respects this vision has turned out to be as utopian as Marx's realm of freedom.

The Lockean myth conflicts with biblical religion in essential ways. It conflicts fundamentally with the Hebrew notion of covenant. The covenant is a relation between God and a people, but the parties to the covenant, unlike the parties in the Lockean contract, have a prior relation: the relation between creator and created. And the covenant is not a limited relation based on self-interest, but an unlimited commitment based on loyalty and trust. It involves obligations to God and neighbor that transcend self-interest, though it promises a deep sense of self-fulfillment through participation in a divinely instituted order that leads to life instead of death.

Again the Lockean myth conflicts profoundly with the Pauline understanding of the church as the body of Christ. If through participation in the crucifixion and the resurrection of Jesus Christ we become one with his body, members one of another, we are freed from the bondage of sin and enabled to live in harmony with God and our neighbor. Christian freedom is very different from the negative

Lockean freedom to do whatever we want as long as we do not violate the limited contract entered into on the basis of self-interest.

The problem is that the Lockean notion of contract does not exist only in the economic and political spheres. It influences our understanding of all human relations, including both family and church. With respect to the family, a legal scholar has recently written, "Instead of the individual 'belonging' to the family, it is the family which is coming to be at the service of the individual." With respect to the church, the Lockean contract model, itself historically descended from, though I think a profound perversion of, the Protestant idea of voluntarism in the church, has become widely accepted. Consumer Christians shop for the best package deal they can get, and when they find a better deal, they have little hesitation about switching.

In a Lockean culture it is very hard to get people to see that the church is objectively there, rooted in the very structure of reality, and that our membership in it is formative of our very identity. Even American Catholics have been known to say, "As long as I'm all right with Jesus, I don't need the church," and such a sentiment is widespread in Protestant churches. One wants to know how they know they are "all right with Jesus," but I am afraid the answer is clear enough: they know if they "feel" they are all right with Jesus. In a Lockean culture religion becomes radically subjective and privatized. But how can such subjective Christians understand the role of the priest or the role of the bishop? How can they understand leadership in the church, or, dare we use the word, authority? Clearly the answer is, not very well.

Under these cultural conditions, the teaching role of the church is placed under a considerable strain, and tact and prudence are certainly necessary. It seems to me the first problem is at the same time theological and sociological—how to communicate the deep social realism of biblical religion to an individualistic culture. To understand, in our bones, so to speak, Paul's great organic metaphor of the body of Christ is to understand that there are many gifts, that we all have our gifts and the body cannot function without all of us, but that the gifts are nonetheless different.

The role of the priest, and of the bishop who represents priesthood in its fullness, is a special calling. We are all called and yet we are not all called in the same way. The priest is called by God and ordained by the church to represent, in the administration of the sacraments and in the preaching of the Word, the objective reality of God's presence in the world. The priesthood, and therefore the episcopacy, carries an objective authority that cannot be shirked, even when, as individuals, those who carry this authority may feel uncertain and unworthy. We know enough about the prophets in the Old Testament and the disciples in the New Testament not to confuse the calling with the individual merit of the called.

Yet it is this whole complex of ideas that Americans have great difficulty in understanding. If religion is a purely private matter, and essentially a matter of subjective feeling, then one person's feelings are as valid as another; there is nothing objective against which to test them. Thus there can be no such thing as authority in religion. Indeed, to individualistic Americans there is little sense of valid authority in any sphere, certainly not in politics, or even in law. Perhaps the only exception is science, where something indubitably objective is generally admitted. Even within the family any notion of legitimate authority is remarkably weak.

It is indeed an exacting discipline to try to be the church in a culture such as ours. All the assumptions upon which we could rely, which we could take for granted in other times and places, are missing. It is therefore necessary to demonstrate, in the face of cultural skepticism, what a community of loyal and committed believers is really like. In the midst of a culture of divorce, it is also very important that we have families who can demonstrate what lasting commitment and mutual devotion in family life are really like. In fact, the church, in manifesting its own essence, strengthens all those communities that are based on loyalty and commitment, on covenant rather than contract.

But in demonstrating what the church as the body of Christ is really like to an individualistic culture, we have the delicate task of showing that the stereotypes of the culture are mistaken. In its mistaken stereotype of authority, an individualistic culture confuses it with power, with the exercise of arbitrary coercion. Authority is based on consent, and consent is gained through persuasion, not coercion. Even God, Creator of all that is, has dealt with us through persuasion, through his prophets, and through his crucified Son. He does not arrange for everything on this earth to turn out right, as some immature believers wish he would, but leaves us free to make our mistakes and to accept his freely offered grace. So leadership within the church, though it carries a legitimate authority, also recognizes the legitimate gifts and concerns of everyone within the body of Christ.

As I understand it, authority belongs to the whole church, just as Karl Rahner says that it is the church itself that is the essential sacrament. But bishops and priests have a special responsibility to represent that authority, which comes from God and belongs to the whole church. Thus in including the laity in the decision-making process, the bishops do not dilute their authority, they enhance it. Yet, unlike a democratic official, the bishops do not just represent the opinions of the people, whatever they happen to be. What is particularly difficult for an individualistic culture to understand, within the church or without it, is that the authority with which the bishop speaks is not his own, that it is his obligation to represent as best he can an authority that transcends us all, that is the authority of reality itself. It may be precisely the responsibility of the bishop or the priest to say things that most people do not want to hear, not because of arbitrary opinions of his own, but because that is what he understands God to be saying to us now. But just because of the caricature of authority in our culture, where it is generally confused with the arbitrary exercise of power, it is especially important that the bishops make clear that they speak out of their understanding of Scripture and tradition as part of the obligation of their role, not out of any desire to exercise personal power. And it is important that they remain in dialogue with those whose opinions differ, both because new light can come from any quarter, and because without conversation there can be no persuasion.

Words are very important. I believe the task of interpreting Scripture and tradition to our society and applying them to our present need (and I agree with Hans-Georg Gadamer that if we cannot apply the words to our present situation we have not understood them) is particularly urgent today. Biblical literacy is in decline in our society, and it is part of the responsibility of the church to restore it. But I know as a teacher in a secular institution what others probably have also discovered as teachers in a sacred institution, that we teach most powerfully by what we are, whatever we say. If there are many of us who do not understand very well what it is to be a Christian today, then it is probable that there are some priests who are not entirely certain about what it is to be a priest, and there may even be some perplexity about what it is to be a bishop here and now in this society. Nevertheless, I hope bishops will have the courage to be what they are as authentically as they understand what that is, and will not be too intimidated by the confusions of our culture, or will not fall back too readily on our central cultural stereotypes of leadership— the manager or the therapist. For if we are to demonstrate what the church is as a community based on unlimited loyalty in a covenant, and membership in the same body, we must all, with the grace of God, fulfill the particular gifts with which we have been entrusted, to the best of our ability. Bishops have indeed been pastors, prophets, and leaders in this society in a way that demonstrates what the people of God is. The remaining part of this essay will attempt to encourage them to continue what they have been doing, not only in the church but in public life as well.

THE TOTALITARIAN AUTHORITY OF THE STATE

One of the ironies of a Lockean culture is that it has unleashed such extraordinary energy that, like the sorcerer's apprentice, it seems to have gotten beyond human control. This is true in the economy, as I will discuss in a moment, but it is also true in the state. The uncontrolled forces of economic and technological dynamism have led in the twentieth century to the rise of a defensive nationalism to try to control the chaos, but this in turn has led to the rise of totalitarian statism, one form of which was destroyed in the Second World War and another form of which only recently (1989) we saw crumble before our eyes in the Soviet Union and Eastern Europe. But we have not in the United States so far faced the degree to which we have participated in demonic nationalism and statism.

In 1990-1991 the United States was involved in one of the most serious international crises since World War II. In August 1990, Saddam Hussein took our attention away from bringing the cold war to an end, and we found ourselves mobilizing again instead of demobilizing. It would certainly have been preferable if we could have avoided a major military crisis for a few years after the collapse of communism, but history does not often act as we might wish. In the face of the military aggression of Iraq against Kuwait, Americans were torn between the impulse to adhere to and strengthen the international rules of the game as we hoped they might work when the United Nations was first established, and the impulse to go it alone at whatever cost to ourselves or others. Each day we anxiously watched for signs of which way things were going. But regardless of how things developed in the Middle East, there are features of the national security state that came into existence at the beginning of the cold war that must be challenged, that must not be sheltered from criticism by this Gulf crisis. Because we are faced with a ruthless and repellent aggressor, we cannot let ourselves off the hook and suppress what the theologian Johann-Baptist Metz calls the "dangerous memories" of our own past.

In our democratic certainty that we always represent the good and the right, the United States has traditionally fought its wars with particular ferocity. In the Second World War, in the light of the correct perception of the evils of our enemies, we engaged in actions that rivaled the worst horrors of this most horrible of centuries. I am thinking of the carpet bombing of Dresden and Hamburg, and of the use of napalm in Japan, where in one night in Tokyo we incinerated 185,000 civilians far more efficiently than the Germans were able to do in Auschwitz. And we were, of course, the only nation to use atomic bombs against defenseless civilian populations; indeed, the only nation to use them at all. While the Russians are apologizing for so many horrors in their own past, it might be well for us to make some apologies of our own.

But what concerns me even more at the present is that national mobilization on a totalitarian scale did not end in the United States at the end of the Second World War. Rather, we saw the emergence of the cold war as the dominant preoccupation of the executive branch of government in the years of the Truman administration leading to a new and unprecedented level of centralized state power, one the Lockean founders of our republic would have been horrified to see. The report written in 1950 by Paul Nitze for the National Security Council (NSC-68) became a kind of blueprint justifying the emergence of a national defense state within a state for the next 40 years. Nitze's logic was that America had to use Soviet means to counteract the Soviet threat. The ironic consequence was to create a powerful apparatus of centralized authority outside the normal constitutional structures of democratic accountability that curiously mirrored the Stalinist state itself.

I am personally involved in contesting one part of this structure at the moment because my own institution is deeply implicated with it. The University of California manages the Lawrence Livermore and Los Alamos National Laboratories where atomic bombs and other advanced weapons systems, including Star Wars, are designed and produced. But university management is a facade for secret and arbitrary decisions, not subject even to scientific review and criticism, and certainly not subject to any ethical debate. The faculty at all nine campuses has voted to end this unholy connection and to urge democratic review and oversight of the laboratories, but it is doubtful if the regents will listen to us.

Up until the present all congressional and public efforts to control the national defense state structure have been successfully resisted in the name of a constitutionally dubious claim of the president's "sole power" over foreign affairs. America had known something close to national mobilization in both World War I and World War II, and indeed Lincoln assumed extraordinary powers during the Civil War. But only since the late 1940s has such a centrally mobilized power as the national security state been able to continue decade after decade to exert powerful and arbitrary influence over every aspect of American society.

In Eastern Europe the churches played a key role in the collapse of totalitarian statism. In Poland, for a long time it was only in Catholic parishes that there was space to question the arbitrary control of Communist state power. Catholics and Protestants both have played key roles in the changes in East Germany, Czechoslovakia, Hungary, and Romania.

The American churches have for a long time raised questions about United States military policy from the position of the ethical understanding of the Christian church. To this day those questions have not been answered. We have made significant advances toward arms control, yet atomic bombs continue to be manufactured on a large scale. What is worse, the quasi-Stalinist structures of the cold war national security state remain in place. They are compatible neither with a democratic nor a Christian understanding of social life. Yet we have not seen a dramatic challenge to the continuation of these structures at a time when their objective necessity, in spite of events in the Middle East, has become doubtful, and when other needs for the resources they consume are so pressing.

The invasion of Kuwait is only one of a long series of disturbing military conflicts in the Third World, though one that concerned us more directly than most because of our dependence on oil. But it is not part of a gigantic worldwide "Communist conspiracy" which was used to justify the creation of the national security state in the first place, and it should not be used as an excuse for its perpetuation. That the United States will need an effective defense establishment for a long time, I do not question. That we need a secret state within a state, I doubt very much. These are questions that it is very hard for politicians to raise, especially in the midst of a military crisis. It is therefore all the more the responsibility of the churches to point out the deeper problems and realities and not be stampeded by momentary feelings.

THE TOTALITARIAN POWER OF THE MARKET

But the United States today is not only threatened by a quasi-totalitarian national security state. I would argue it is threatened by another kind of totalitarianism, one that, with our Lockean presuppositions, we find it hard to recognize, namely, market totalitarianism. For over a decade now the errors of Lockean economic individualism and thin contractualism have been pushed to unheard of extremes. The result is an unprecedented polarization of wealth and poverty in our society and public evidence of widespread misery which amazes visitors from other advanced industrial nations and reminds them of Third World countries.

In a situation where economic advance has slowed and fewer people are willing to bear the burden of helping the weaker neighbor, the market metaphor has taken on a singular power in the American consciousness. The weakening of the languages of biblical religion and civic republicanism which traditionally moderated Lockean individualism (*Habits of the Heart* provides a full-scale description of this situation) has led to a situation in which the market maximizer has become the paradigm of the human person.

One powerful version of the market paradigm derives from the teachings of Milton Friedman and the school of economics he founded. In the view of Friedman and his successors, human beings are exclusively self-interest maximizers, and the primary measure of self-interest is money. Economics becomes a total science that explains everything. Alan Wolfe (1989) in his book, *Whose Keeper?*, describes the Chicago school of economics, suggesting how in its teachings economics is attempting to become our new moral philosophy or even our new religion:

> When neither religion, tradition, nor literature is capable of serving as a common moral language, it may be that the one moral code all modern people can understand is self-interest. If social scientists are secular priests, Chicago school economists have become missionaries. They have an idea about how

the world works. This idea seems to apply in some areas of life. It therefore follows, they believe, that it ought to apply in all. . . .

Chicago school theorists insist that the tools of economic analysis can be used not just to decide whether production should be increased or wages decreased, but in every kind of decision-making situation. Thus we have been told . . . that marriage is not so much about love as about supply and demand as regulated through markets for spouses; . . . and a man commits suicide "when the total discounted lifetime utility remaining to him reaches zero." From the perspective of the Chicago school, there is no behavior that is *not* interpretable as economic, however altruistic, emotional, disinterested, and compassionate it may seem to others. (1989:36, 32)

Wolfe cites an extreme example of two economists of this school who argue that a free market in babies would allow the solution of many current social problems in this area. They hold that women should be allowed to sell their babies on the open market and suggest that our situation would be better if "baby prices were quoted as soybean future prices were quoted" (1989:37-38). We may not be surprised that the French speak of American capitalism as "*le capitalisme sauvage*," savage capitalism.

These bizarre ideas are not, unfortunately, just theoretical. They influence many aspects of our lives. They have a powerful influence, for example, on government. Ann Swidler, one of my co-authors in *Habits of the Heart*, when doing interviews for our new book, *The Good Society*, talked to an expert at the Environmental Protection Agency about how they figured the trade-offs in the costs of human lives saved versus the costs of the safety devices that would save them. Ann suggested, "Some people believe human life is priceless." The government expert replied, "We have no data on that."

In spite of a long history of governmental measures taken to alleviate the harshest consequences of rapid industrialization, compared to most other advanced industrial nations, the United States has emphasized economic opportunity for individuals (and corporate "individuals") at the expense of public amenities. Indeed, David Popenoe (1985), in a book comparing the United States with Sweden and England, says that, relatively speaking, "Americans live in an environment of private affluence and public squalor," where a "very high standard of private consumption represents a trade-off with public services" (1985:82). Since we have much lower levels of taxation than West Europeans, we can use our "saved taxes" to purchase more consumer goods than English or Swedes of comparable income, but we do so at considerable cost:

> The environmental squalor of American metropolitan communities stems in part from their dispersed character and the associated dominance of the automobile. But the relative lack of public funding dooms public services of all kinds—parks and playgrounds, public housing, public transportation—to a level of quality that is meager at best by European standards. The poor quality of older communities, for example the inner-city slums in most older American cities of even modest size, also results from the lack of publicly

financed planning efforts to direct urban growth and renew town centers. (1985:82)

Popenoe recognizes that most Americans seem to be not unhappy about "this trade-off of public services for private consumption." We like our spacious homes and our automobiles, and we don't like taxes. Yet for all but the strongest, our way of doing things makes us extremely vulnerable:

At least as compared with life in European societies (and Japan) American life is also marked by a high degree of economic insecurity. American society has the character of a gambler's society: You may hit the jackpot and become really rich (something that is extremely difficult today, for example, in Sweden), but you can also with relative ease find yourself "out on the street." American employment policies are much less geared to job stability than are European policies. Many health care costs require private payments to the extent that a serious medical problem can be financially disastrous to the individual. And the pressures for ever-expanding personal consumption can quickly lead to indebtedness and even bankruptcy, to cite but a few examples. (1985:84)

Differences between income brackets are much greater in the United States than in Britain or Sweden. Whereas Americans in the top five percent income bracket earn 13 times as much as those in the bottom five percent, the difference in Britain is a factor of six and in Sweden merely three. Yet, as Popenoe points out, even this disparity is not the whole story, for the poor in America can count on much less community support than in Europe.

Thus to be reasonably well-off in the United States with job stability and economic security in old age, is to have a life of great personal freedom and affluence. But to be poor, or even economically marginal, is to be a second class citizen in a way that is not found to be acceptable by the English or Swedish societies. (1985:84)

No sphere is immune to market pressures. A student of mine who is a Lutheran minister brought me a story from a suburban newspaper in the Bay Area:

The members of St. John's Lutheran Church have a money-back guarantee. They can donate to the church for 90 days, then if they think they made a mistake, or did not receive a blessing, they can have their money back. The program is called "God's Guarantee" and the pastor is confident it will work. "We trust God to keep his promises so much that we are offering this money back policy," the pastor said. . . . The program is modeled on a similar program at Skyline Wesleyan Church in San Diego.

When my student called this pastor to remonstrate that there was nothing in the Bible compatible with a 90-day, money-back guarantee, the pastor gave a theological defense but also indicated that the program seemed to be popular with the congregation. Unfortunately there are many churches today that see themselves as competing for market shares of believers and will try whatever seems to work to make sure that they compete successfully.

For those of us in the university, these pressures are also very evident. The research university has grown in tandem with the business corporation, yet for all the interpenetration, there has always been a difference in structure and a difference in aims. Now that difference itself is under attack. The prospectus of Stanford University's new Stanford Institute for Higher Education Research states:

> Advances in economic theory and empirical analysis methods, developments in organizational behavior, and refinements of managerial technique have reached the point where we can hope to understand the complexities of nonprofit institutions—including colleges and universities—to a degree approaching that for business firms.

William Massy, Stanford's vice-president for finance and a member of the School of Business, is the chief instigator of this new institute and now holds a professorship in the School of Education as well. Massy, in a recent interview, said: "Ever since I joined the central administration in the early '70s, I have become really fascinated with higher education as an industry where institutions with many interconnections interact in a kind of marketplace."

Massy's new institute has placed high on its list of research questions "an examination of the productivity and cost effectiveness at universities. Are universities delivering the product that the public expects?" Central to this concern is the question of, in Massy's words, "the effectiveness of teaching and learning. What is a good set of measures for each of those?" Much of the public, Massy recognizes, sees university education as primarily "job preparation," and he feels the university is obliged to meet that concern. For him the university is just one more element in the market system:

> It's hard to deny that when students come for a particular service, someone will supply it. Tastes have changed: people used to be interested in the classics; now they are interested in making money. In the end, we have fundamental and deep social changes—and they are what they are. I do believe in the market. If there is a demand, we have an obligation to meet it.
>
> We need to provide an interesting menu at the university—a menu of where we think the world is going—but we can't dictate what people are going to want. If they don't like the menu, we have an obligation to change it. . . . (All these Massy quotes are from *Stanford School of Education*, a supplement to the *Stanford Observer*, January, 1989, p. 2.)

In Professor Massy's view, the education industry should be responsive to market demand. If people used to be interested in the classics but now are interested in making money, so be it. He rejects any notion of the university as a community of discourse which might prepare citizens for participation in our common world. In this market model, students are seen as consumers with fixed preferences to which we, as teachers, are passively to respond. In this conception of the university, there is no room for the idea that we might have anything to say that would surprise the students, perhaps challenge them to think more deeply about themselves and the world. Instead, education is merely a market for the skills and methods to get ahead in the world.

What is clear is that this economic ideology which turns human beings into relentless market maximizers is destructive to everything we can call community, to family, to church, to neighborhood, to school, and ultimately to the world. In *Habits of the Heart* we documented what this kind of thinking does to our capacity to sustain relationships in every sphere, private as well as public. But the final irony is that this apparently economic conception of human life turns out to be profoundly destructive to our economy! If a sense of community would make us poorer, I would still advocate it. But the embarrassing fact is that community turns out to be a much stronger basis for an effective economy than the individualistic pursuit of self-interest. We have only to look at the Japanese case to see that.

Let me give an illustration of what I mean, one that applies particularly to our high-tech industries. The old neoclassical categories of capital and labor no longer apply. The productivity of a high-tech company resides in the quality of its work force, in the competence and responsibility of individuals, but also, critically, in the trust and confidence they have in each other so that they can nurture and support creativity and innovation. What is required today is not "hands," labor in the old sense of routine manual performance. What is required is brains, but not just brains but also persons, persons who trust each other and genuinely enjoy working together. A company that has that will outperform many times over another with the same amount of financing and the same kind of physical equipment, but where the workers are not responsible and where no one trusts anyone or is willing to take any risks.

But what is happening to our companies under the logic of interest-maximization? We have over the last ten years seen an advance of what is called the commodification of the corporation. Any effective company will be looked at hungrily by those who would make an immediate profit by buying it, stripping it of its assets, firing managers and employees, and reorganizing for immediate gain. What the commodification of the corporation does is to destroy the corporation as a community, to make everyone suspicious, ready to bail out, looking out for number one, looking to make the next quarterly statement look good at whatever cost so that one can get another job. By strip-mining our most valuable economic asset, namely the creative interaction of people who have grown to understand and trust each other, we sink our long-term economic viability. And then we set up another commission to study American "competitiveness"!

But the principle that cripples our economy weakens every aspect of our lives together. People in our large urban areas are worried about the high cost of housing and the problem of clogged transportation arteries. But if every affluent person is simply intent on buying the best possible house for his or her family with no concern for the provision of low- and middle-income housing in the community, then the cost of housing will soon go out of sight and even the affluent will become indentured servants of their mortgages, while the disappearance of low-cost housing means many will go homeless. If we all think only of our own convenience in driving our individual cars to work, then we all spend ever more time on the freeway breathing the polluted air our cars are creating, rather than working on better public transportation that would serve the good of all.

In short, our individualistic heritage has taught us that there is no such thing as the common good except as the sum of individual goods. But in the complex interdependent world in which we live, the sum of our individual goods produces a common bad, that eventually erodes our individual satisfactions as well.

There is, thus, much to be done if Americans are to see that our market idolatry is not good for our own society and not good for the world. The collapse of command economies in the Communist world in no way justifies the evils of market capitalism operating with no moral constraints. So here, too, where others are slow to speak, it is important for the churches to point out how far our society needs to go to realize the dignity of the individual through shared economic participation in a good community. This again is to demonstrate what the church really is by showing how different its understanding of human existence is from that of the surrounding culture.

CONCLUSION

Let me close, if I may, by quoting some words of Frederick Borsch, Bishop of Los Angeles, based on a study of Episcopalian parishioners. Borsch argues that there is a new receptiveness to serious theological education. "We can no longer rely on our attractive liturgy nor the warmth of our congregational life to draw people in," he said. "People are hungry for fellowship to find meaning in life, and they are seeking answers" (*Episcopal Life* 1990:19).

He suggests that parishes today must certainly be alive with the presence of the Holy Spirit, but they must also "be involved with the real problems in our society and seeking to make a difference in their neighborhood and the lives of the people who are there. Our studies show that baby boomers want to know whether the churches are concerned with real societal problems." Ecology, peace, and social justice are all on people's minds, and, says Borsch, "I don't think people expect the church to have answers to all questions, but I do think that people expect the church to be seriously concerned with these questions" (*Episcopal Life* 1990:19).

Borsch emphasized the educational role of the clergy: "It is terribly important that the clergy of the future see themselves as educators," he said. "All sorts of wonderful people can do the administrating, can do the pastoring—but clergy may be the only people in the parish trained to do the education at a high level—to be the teacher of the teachers, to supply the energy for the whole program" (*Episcopal Life* 1990:19). What Borsch says of the clergy is even more true of the bishops, who are indeed the teachers of teachers. Finally, Borsch emphasized that education is not just for the formation of the individual student, but must move to a new understanding of the formation of the community of faith.

So to sum up my argument, I would say that the bishop as leader must help the whole church demonstrate what it is, to show forth to itself and the world what a covenant community based on faith and love is like. For people caught up in the ideology of self-interest and minimal commitment to anyone else, the very presence of a community based on radically different premises can be salvific. But if the church is to be the church, it must not only practice its beliefs within the community, it must show forth what they imply for the larger society, not to coerce acceptance and not to be swept up into activism at the expense of spirituality, but to hold up an alternative vision of reality, to give witness to what, as best we can discern it, God is saying to the world today. It is our responsibility as clergy, and laity, not only to help the church show forth in its life what we profess by our faith but to engage in public discussion with all others in our society about pressing matters of the common good.

REFERENCES CITED

Bellah, Robert N., Richard Madsen, William M. Sullivan, Ann Swidler, and Steven M. Tipton
    1985   *Habits of the Heart: Individualism and Commitment in American Life.* Berkeley, CA: University of California Press.
    1991   *The Good Society.* New York: Alfred A. Knopf.

Episcopal Life
    1990   "Borsch says seminaries are key to growth." *Episcopal Life* (April):19.

Popenoe, David
    1985   *Private Pleasure, Public Plight: American Metropolitan Community Life in Comparative Perspective.* New Brunswick, NJ: Transaction Books.

Wolfe, Alan
    1989   *Whose Keeper?: Social Science and Moral Obligations.* Berkeley, CA: University of California Press.

9

Doing Theology as Inculturation in the Asian Context

*José M. de Mesa**

In this essay, José M. de Mesa answers the question "How to do theology in Asia?" by proposing that an Asian theology emerges from (1) mutually (2) respectful and (3) critical interaction between the two poles of (1) the Judaeo-Christian tradition and (2) Asian culture. While the starting point for an Asian theology could theoretically be located at either of these poles, de Mesa believes that in the present situation of Asia the interaction should start "with the contemporary human experiences within the culture which call for a Christian interpretation." More specifically, the starting point should emphasize the positive resources and potential within Asian culture, even though some cultural critique will eventually and inevitably be in order.

This exposition will be a Philippine perspective of inculturation in Asia. It will neither deal with the task of inculturation in its entirety nor encompass the whole of Asia. Inculturation is more than theologizing, and the Asian reality which is the Philippines is not fully representative of Asia. Asia is a diversity of peoples and cultures, experiences and traditions, situations and histories. These cannot be lumped together as one and reduced to a single category to be referred to as the "Asian reality." But insofar as there are similarities shared by a number of countries in terms of experiences and issues, the Federation of Asian Bishops' Conferences has considered a number of situational challenges to be truly common enough to warrant the qualifier "Asian." One of these is inculturation.

Inculturation, the concern and the process for making the Gospel meaningful and challenging within a specific cultural context, has always been part of the Church's life and mission. Throughout the centuries of her existence, the Church

---

* Taken from *In Solidarity with the Culture: Studies in Theological Re-rooting* (Quezon City, Philippines: Maryhill School of Theology, 1991). José M. de Mesa is a Filipino lay theologian who is associate director of the East Asian Pastoral Institute in Manila, Philippines.

has been challenged time and again to put into practice the principle of cultural catholicity after its recognition at the Council of Jerusalem; to transcend her present historical form and her culture-bound self by going beyond the national, cultural, and ethnic boundaries. Repeatedly, it has responded courageously to such challenges. Church history is replete with such examples. Saints Boniface, Cyril, Methodius, and Augustine are outstanding figures in mission history in this matter. The advice of Gregory the Great to Abbot Mellitus, a fellow missionary of St. Augustine of Canterbury, concerning pagan temples and sacrifices remains a classic document of the Church's continuing struggle for cultural rootedness.

Nearer to our times, during the sixteenth and seventeenth centuries, we can point to Matteo Ricci's attitude toward the Chinese ancestor cult and Confucianism, and Roberto de Nobili's involvement in Hindu thought, as other instances. Right from its very beginning, the Congregation for the Propagation of the Faith stood for inculturation, strongly admonishing missionaries not to interfere with traditional ways and customs, unless they clearly conflict with Christian faith and morals. In 1659 this was emphasized by the Congregation in its instructions to missionaries in China and Indo-China: "Can anyone think of anything more absurd," it stated, "than to transport France, Italy or Spain or some other European country to China? Bring them your faith, not your country."[1]

During the Second Vatican Council (1962–65) the Church once more spoke vigorously for a catholicity that is more qualitative than quantitative: she preferred the verification of religious expression within every people and within every culture to a mere juxtaposition of cultures and sensibilities seen as variations of one and the same model. In other words, the Church, in Vatican II, once again reiterated her commitment to re-root the Good News within specific socio-cultural contexts just as Jesus enfleshed himself within the Jewish culture. It expressedly stated that "theological investigation must necessarily be stirred up in each major socio-cultural area" (A.G. 22) if cultural rootedness of the Gospel and of the Church is to be achieved.

Almost ten years after the Council, when the bishops gathered together for a synod in Rome in 1974 on "Evangelization of the Modern World," the process of incarnating the Gospel in the context of the local Churches was again emphasized. As though the point had not been made strongly enough by Vatican II, the element that was stressed the most in the synod was the socio-cultural integration of the local Church.[2]

For Asia today, according to the Federation of Asian Bishops' Conferences, evangelization has for its primary task the building up of the local Church.[3] This connotes that the Churches in Asia are aware of their being already local Churches to a certain extent, and that they intend to become more so. The task, of course, implies many things ranging from institutional renewal to creative theological reflection, all of which contribute to the deeper inculturation of the Church into the socio-cultural milieu. As the Asian Colloquium on Ministries in 1977 put it:

> Asian Churches then must become truly Asian in all things. The principle of indigenization and inculturation is at the very root of their coming into their own. The ministry of Asian Churches, if it is to be authentic, must be rele-

vant to Asian societies. This calls on the part of the Churches for originality, creativity and inventiveness, for boldness and courage.

And, as though anticipating an objection about the interdependence of Churches, it stated immediately: "Our Churches are called upon to take into their hands their own destiny not in attitude of self-sufficiency and independence but with a deep sense of responsibility for the here and now."[4]

DOING THEOLOGY IN THE CONTEXT OF THE LOCAL CHURCH

It is within this framework that indigenous theological reflection, which is the shared responsibility of the whole community, becomes significant. Not only is it a fruit of this indigenous presence and mission of the local Church, it is also an invaluable aid towards it. It is a contribution towards the Asian goal of inculturation of the Church and, as such, should be considered as part and parcel of the efforts of evangelization in Asia today. It can help the Church become more Asian and Asian Churches can help facilitate the enrichment and integration of the national cultures in Asia.

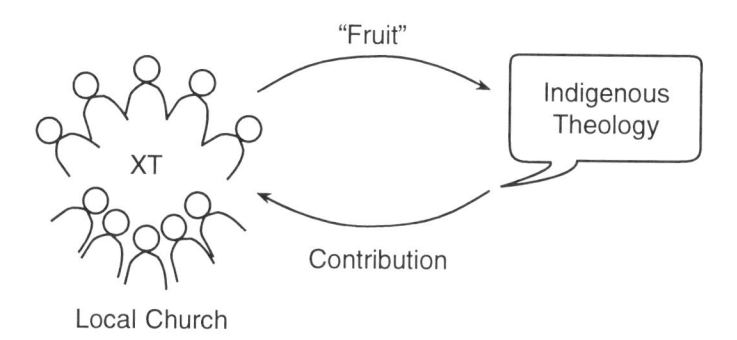

With these in mind it is important for us to answer the question, "How then should theology be done in Asia?" Surely, doing theology cannot mean the simple transfer of theological ideas and systems from elsewhere into Asia. And yet this very thing was done in the past with the imposition of neo-scholastic theology on various countries. It was not any different among the Protestants. The Chinese theologian Choan-Seng Song has complained that "christian theology has suffered from a state of 'teutonic captivity'—seldom getting the chance to break out of the Western historical and cultural framework to which the Word of God in the Bible has been made captive."[5] We should bear in mind, moreover, that doing theology in Asia is not merely a matter of expressing the Christian faith in culturally intelligible categories—though this should not be underestimated. Theology must also respond to the actual challenges of the situation where the Church finds herself. A ghetto mentality ought to be avoided by not being unduly preoccupied with internal Church affairs. A Catholic writer has observed that the Christian community in Asia has been more like glue than leaven. The Churches have been preoccupied with their own existence and organization, and correspondingly they have lagged behind in prophetic concern for the social relevance and outreach of the Gospel into the mainstream task of nation building.[6]

So what does it mean to do theology as an expression of and a contribution to becoming a local Church in Asia? I would like to suggest that doing theology in this context means the *mutually respectful and critical interaction between the Judaeo-Christian Tradition and Culture*.[7] Theology is precisely born from this interaction between two traditions of experiences. It is important to bear in mind that the two poles, that of the Judaeo-Christian Tradition and that of the culture, affect and influence one another. This is not a question of the Judaeo-Christian Tradition being simply translated or even transplanted into the culture or of the culture creating its own faith tradition without any connection or reference at all to our Jewish-Christian faith heritage. Neither is this to be seen as the kind of dialectical procedure whereby the questions raised from the pole of the human situation (culture) are given answers by the Judaeo-Christian Tradition.

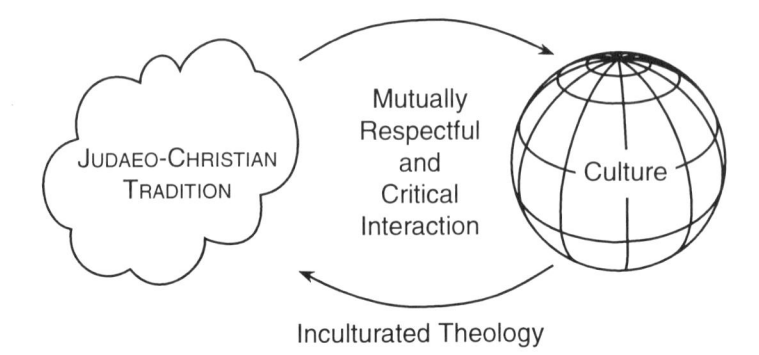

JUDAEO-CHRISTIAN TRADITION ⇄ Mutually Respectful and Critical Interaction ⇄ Culture

Inculturated Theology

The interaction is *mutually respectful* because each pole, each tradition of experiences, has something positive to contribute towards the well-being of people (i.e. salvation) and each ultimately derives its roots from the same source, God. I believe that insisting on a *respectful* stance helps us not only to discover the positive, life-giving aspects but also to appreciate them. An appreciative awareness of the wisdom and genius found in the cultural tradition of a given people as well as in the Judaeo-Christian Tradition is indispensable to the task and process of inculturation. Culture that integrates a system of beliefs, values, customs and institutions binds a society together and gives it a sense of identity, dignity, security and continuity. Not surprisingly, *Gaudium et Spes* acknowledges that "it is a fact bearing on the very person of man that he can come to an authentic and full humanity only through culture . . ." (G.S. 53). The Judaeo-Christian Tradition of faith, for its part, embodies and sacramentalizes the experiences of people with a God who is "mindful of humanity" in Jesus Christ. A respectful attitude enables each of the poles to offer its life-giving and life-enhancing potential.

It would be naive, however, to think that a respectful stance is adequate. The perspective has to include a critical component also because the culture and the Faith Tradition both contain ambiguous and at times ideological aspects or elements. The Judaeo-Christian Tradition, which includes "everything which contributes to the holiness of life and the increase in faith of the People of God" (D.V. 8), notably Scripture, is only accessible to us through a specific cultural and historical embodiment. This means that its concrete manifestation is not exempt from ambiguity. One has only to consider the ideologically structured perspective regarding the role of women in the life and the mission of the Church to see this. With regard to culture, it is widely recognized that not everything in culture enhances the humanity of a given people. A number of elements too have to be critically assessed and challenged.

Thus, in this mutually respectful and critical interaction the Judaeo-Christian Tradition and culture serve as a "source" and "target," as it were, one to the other. Each pole serves as interpretative and critical guide to the other. The pole of culture makes it possible for us to interpret meaningfully the Judaeo-Christian Tradition as well as critically assess the present cultural expressions of this Tradition. The pole of the Judaeo-Christian Tradition, on the other hand, enables us to understand the culture in the light of our faith and reassess its value vis-à-vis our Christian vocation. Both poles are essential for they serve reciprocally hermeneutic and critical functions which provoke further understanding. Allow me to spell these out in more detail.

THE STARTING POINT FOR DOING THEOLOGY AS INCULTURATION

Since the interaction which is envisioned between the two poles is mutually respectful and critical, it is possible to begin doing theology from any pole. The reason for this is that one cannot do theology with just one pole without considering the other. I do believe, however, that for the present situation of Asia and for methodological reasons, the correlation should start with the contemporary human experiences within the culture which call for a Christian interpretation. We should be aware that when we speak of such experiences we are considering, in fact, culturally defined experiences. Culture, that organized system of knowledge, of belief, is the means whereby a people structure their experiences and perceptions.[8] So we can either refer to our starting point as issues, questions or concerns within a given socio-cultural context or as contemporary human experiences. This methodological option is justified for a number of reasons.

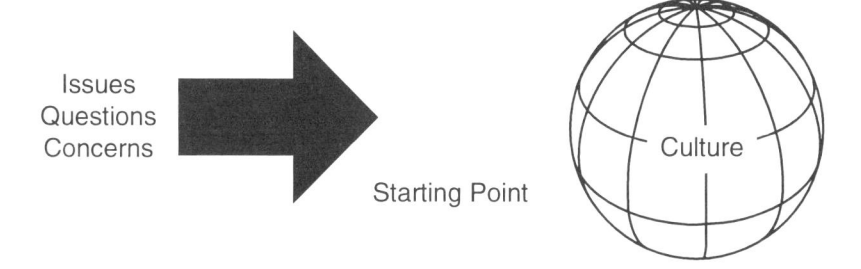

Issues
Questions
Concerns

Starting Point

Culture

Firstly, it cannot be denied that the pole of our Christian Tradition tends to be absolutized, and becomes the sole source of all theologizing. We have here a sociological phenomenon of almost every group identity. Christians in the recent past, for example, started to talk about "the end of revelation" with the consequence that theology degenerated into a compilaton of truths, which were considered as *the* answers to all possible questions people can and will ask. Only the challenges from our new experiences (if we are open to them) can help us to escape from this cut-and-dried solution that imprisons the vitality of the Good News.

Secondly, the very situation of the present-day world demands a *renewed* interpretation of the Christian message. We are not living in a world in which Christianity is a quiet possession, but in a world of crisis in which any message of salvation is questioned by the suffering of people without work and food, dignity and rights.

In connection to this the Christian message of salvation has still to free itself of its Western embodiment in Asia, which could hardly be questioned during the Western colonial invasion of the Third World. This does not imply by any means that an inculturated theology is simply the organized collection of criticisms of Asians against theology from the West. While it may begin as a reaction, surely it cannot be expected that the reaction will sustain a continuous serious effort at inculturation. So freeing the Gospel of its Western form in Asia means, rather, the rootedness of the local Churches in their own situations. Attention to our specific concerns in Asia, to be sure, lessens the danger that we will be trying to answer the wrong questions (because they are not ours), as has happened in the past. For then, not only did we import the theological answers of the West, we were even convinced that we had the same issues and questions to reflect upon.

There is still another reason why attention should initially focus on the human situation. Theology, as faith seeking understanding, does not arise in the abstract. It is born and developed in a concrete setting, culture and history. It is, therefore, culturally and historically relative. This, of course, does not merely spell limitation. It means that, too. But being relative means it is *related to* the particular culture and history of a given people. This relevance and meaningfulness to a specific context is, to be sure, the first imperative which theology ought to fulfill.

Lack of rootedness in the human experience of people has—if we examine the preponderance of neo-scholasticism in many places prior to Vatican II—precipitated a crisis in theology. Theology has come to the point where it hardly makes any sense vis-à-vis the contemporary situation. Not only did it fail to seriously consider and address the issues, it also utilized a theological language foreign to the experiences and cultures of people in Asia.

Theological language in Asia, in order to be meaningful, has to have a *recognizable reference* to the lived-experience of Asians, to their search for well-being, for what is worthy of humankind. Let me stress the need for its being a *recognizable* reference and not just a reference to the lived-experience of people. Since culture is the way of life of a given people, it is only to be expected that local theological language ought to be cultural theological language to ensure as much as possible its recognizability.

The basic condition for every interpretation of faith which is faithful to the gospel is the *meaningfulness* of that interpretation. This meaningfulness is present when an interpretation reflects real experience within the culture. In other words, the experiences of our everyday existence in the world must give meaning and sub-

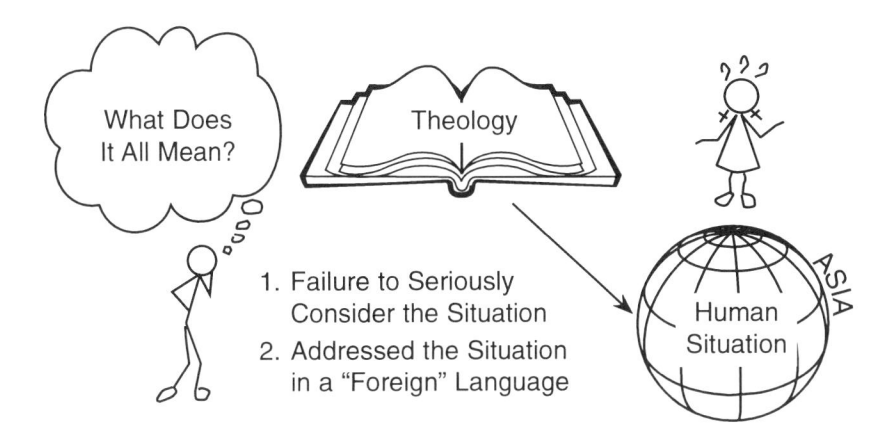

[Figure: Diagram showing a stick figure thinking "What Does It All Mean?" next to an open book labeled "Theology", with an arrow pointing to a globe labeled "Human Situation / ASIA" and a puzzled stick figure. Listed: 1. Failure to Seriously Consider the Situation; 2. Addressed the Situation in a "Foreign" Language]

stance to our theological talk. If this basic condition is not expressed in theological language, then such theological talk is meaningless, and the question whether the new interpretation is either orthodox or heretical is *a priori* superfluous. Human experience in a given situation—the issues, questions and concerns of people in a specific socio-cultural context—is the only place where a faith-understanding has a chance of becoming meaningful. This is probably the reason why the Japanese theologian Kosuke Koyama insists that "Third World Theology begins by raising issues, not by digesting Augustine, Barth and Rahner."[9] We have only to recall the opening paragraph of *Gaudium et Spes* to realize that it is the human situation of people that sets, as it were, the agenda for theology: "The joys and the hopes, the griefs and the anxieties of the people of this age, especially those who are poor or in any way afflicted, these too are the joys and hopes, the griefs and anxieties of the followers of Christ. Indeed, nothing genuinely human fails to raise an echo in their hearts" (G.S. 1).

WHAT IS THEOLOGY'S AGENDA IN ASIA?

What is theology's particular agenda in Asia? We have already mentioned that the Federation of Asian Bishops' Conferences considers the building up of the local Church as a priority. In this spirit they urged on all in the early 1970s "a deep respect for the cultures and traditions of (their) peoples" and expressed "the hope that the catholicity of the Church, the root of our diversity in the oneness of faith, may serve to help Asians remain truly Asian, and yet become part of the modern world and the one family of mankind."[10] Underlying this is the realization that to preach the Gospel in Asia today it is imperative to make the message and life of Christ incarnate in the minds and lives of people.

It is obvious, of course, that local theologizing cannot tackle the total situation all at once or provide a comprehensive analysis of it. Rather it will have to focus on certain thematic issues which arise from the reading of the situation.[11] In this way, the specific concerns that need to be attended to will be attended to. This really means that doing theology as inculturation in Asia, precisely because it wants to respond to the vital questions in the situation, is to be considered an occasional enterprise, one dictated by circumstances and immediate needs rather than the need for system building.[12] But was not theology like this among the early Christians? The wide range of theological formulations and literary forms contained in the New Testament, for instance, is neither accidental nor haphazard. The different forms are functional; i.e., the form and theologies came into being in response to different needs of communities in the early Church and were attuned to the wide variety of socio-cultural background. The realization that Tradition is in fact a series of local or inculturated theologies is an important step towards local theologizing.[13]

To expect that a complete systematic theology is afoot today in Asia would be unrealistic. Besides, who would profit from such a system, even were it feasible, if it did not address the actual needs of the local Churches? Creating theological systems like that right now would be like saying that theology exists for its own sake. It is, of course, possible that from these occasional reflections may emerge an inculturated theological system. But everything has its proper time.

Speaking about particular thematic issues raised by the situation(s) in Asia, one could zero in on the search and struggle for national identity in the context of an industrial and technological society. This has been considered as one of the situational challenges to the Christian Church in Asia, one that is directly related to cultural matters.[14] This particular issue stems, to a very large extent, from the colonial experience of a number of Asian countries.

Colonization had led to, among other things, the depreciation of the native culture and consequently of its dignity. To be more specific, allow me to illustrate from the Philippine experience the colonial attitude that negatively influenced the natives' own perception of their culture. A couple of relevant examples of the unfortunate presumption of superiority would, perhaps, be sufficient: In 1720 a letter concerning the intellectual poverty, cultural backwardness and moral depravity of the natives authored by Fray Gaspar de San Agustin of the Augustinian Order was widely circulated and *believed*, to the detriment of the natives' dignity. In that letter Fray Gaspar spoke about the natives thus: "Those wretched beings are of such a nature that they live a purely animal life, intent solely on its preservation and convenience, without the corrective of reason or respect or esteem for reputation." Such a conclusion is not surprising if one considers the various allegations Fray Gaspar hurled onto the natives: ungrateful, lazy, stupid, rude, curious, and impertinent, insolent towards Spaniards, "they do not know their place," proud and arrogant, tyrannical, excessively fond of feasts, vain, lustful, vengeful, ignorant, cowardly, and ate a lot.[15]

The tenacity of this bigotry was also reflected during the Bishops' Conference of the Philippines more than a century and a half later in 1900, when the Philippines was already under the American regime. In that meeting the Archbishop of Manila argued the case for an absolute need of the European clergy by asserting that the Filipino clergy were incapable of faithfully fulfilling their sacred ministry because the Filipino priest (emphasis, I suppose, on Filipino) was laboring under these defects: extreme shallow-mindedness, uncontrolled propensity to vices of the flesh, lack of talent which incapacitated him from obtaining a thorough and proper training. Furthermore, the very narrowness of soul of the Filipino priest, for which reason he was reduced to almost nothing in the estimation of any European, would only give his enemies, the American Protestants, cause for mockery. The Bishop of Cebu was convinced that the Filipino clergy would simply disappear by itself because Filipino priests did not have the desire for self-denial and work, and the decreased pious offerings to the Church would discourage very many from embracing the clerical life.[16]

Whatever one might say about the effects that the two processes of cultural contact in the context of colonization and change brought about, and however one would evaluate the two colonial regimes, one thing is sure. These colonization and acculturation experiences have produced an overall effect of disequilibrium; this has upset the traditional balance of the indigenous society. The Western influence on the natives is not entirely negative. But while Filipinos may succeed in giving the impression that at times they are quite proud and happy to wear the political and cultural finery of their former colonial masters, they are really not quite at home in the West. Despite their appreciation for the benefits of western thought, science and technology, they are driven by nostalgia to revisit the ancestral home of the spirit and to rediscover their real identity. Filipinos need to find themselves, re-establish continuity with their own past history and culture, gain status in their own eyes as a distinct people, and re-evaluate their achievements and potentialities in view of the future. The recent manifestations of nationalistic fervor indicate that the growing awareness of "identity" is driving them to clarify who they really are.

This issue of search and struggle for national cultural identity requires the process of conscientization (raising of awareness). The effort at conscientization is necessary in view of the colonial experience; the riches and potential of our culture have been obscured by this experience and remain to be rediscovered even by our native people. I am convinced that our Faith Tradition can help us discover and enhance both our identity and dignity as a Filipino people, and critically deepen that identity as well as ennoble that dignity. When theology tackles this concern in relation to the Judaeo-Christian Tradition it is showing how "by the very fulfillment of her own mission the Church stimulates and advances human and civic culture" (G.S. 58). Inculturation must mean not only the rootedness of the Christian faith within the culture but also the promotion of cultural identity of peoples, for culture as a way of life cannot be excluded from that offer of wholeness from God which is salvation.

It would be incorrect, moreover, to consider the reference to human experience and culture in doing theology as an attempt merely to give our understanding of the faith a semblance of modernity. The role that human experience (which is culturally conditioned) plays in theological reflection is not just incidental, but essential. The actual situation in which we live today is an intrinsic and constitutive element for understanding God's revelation in the history of Israel and of Jesus. No one is really in a position to rediscover precisely what the message of the Gospel now means to us except in relation to our present situation. It is clear that doing theology as inculturation is not a matter of applying to our present situation what we think we have discovered from the biblical tradition.[17]

EMPHASIS ON THE POSITIVE RESOURCES AND POTENTIAL OF THE CULTURE: A METHODOLOGICAL OPTION

It is in this context that we have to situate a specific emphasis or approach to promote inculturation in the Asian scene. Within the general principle of a mutually respectful and critical interaction between the Judaeo-Christian Tradition and the human situation, there is room and possibility to give it a particular form and focus depending on the actual needs of the community. So just as the issues, questions and concerns of a local Church are culturally and historically conditioned, so is the methodology utilized for actual doing of theology. Both the questions being tackled and the method opted for are geared towards the actual situation which calls for a Christian interpretation.

For this reason, I believe that a methodological approach to inculturation in Asia, and specifically in the Philippines, should *emphasize the positive resources and potential of the culture* to interpret and respond to the questions of contemporary society. It calls strongly for the retrieval (rediscovery and recovery) of the strengths and riches of the cultural wisdom and genius of a people, which may have been obscured not only by the colonial experience but also by modernization of society. So that approach intends to make us keenly and persistently conscious of these cultural resources. An "appreciative awareness" of this sort acts as a regulative principle in thought which, as an orientation of mind, can make for a maximum degree of receptivity to what these resources have to offer.[18] Moreover, it leads us to consistently utilize these in the task of interpreting not only the Judaeo-Christian Tradition but also the concrete situation in Asia. But, perhaps, this is only making very explicit what we already do implicitly and unconsciously—to interpret reality in the way the culture taught us to do. After all, any given situation is necessarily a culturally defined situation. This is, of course, not new. The New Testament is a tribute to the immense effort exerted by the early Church to make its preaching intelligible to the various cultural groups it encountered. In the unity of its proclamation and the diversity of forms in which this proclamation was expressed, the early Church as seen through the New Testament stands as a model of inculturation.

This is why Vatican II can state: "Living in various circumstances during the course of time, the Church, too, has used in her preaching the discoveries of different cultures to spread and explain the message of Christ to all nations, to probe it and more deeply understand it, and to give it better expression in liturgical celebrations and in the life of the diversified community of the faithful" (G.S. 58). The way of inculturation is the only way of making Christianity really our own within the culture. Rightly has the late Filipino historian, Horacio de la Costa, S.J., written: "Christianity must not only be *expressed* but *thought* and *lived* in terms of the cultural tradition of the people to whom it is preached, for only thus can it be their own Christianity."[19]

At this juncture I would like to make clear that a theological concern and method oriented towards the promotion of a people's cultural identity by way of emphasis in no way implies that other current issues are, therefore, to be set aside or ignored. One is quickly reminded here of the widespread preoccupation of many Asian countries

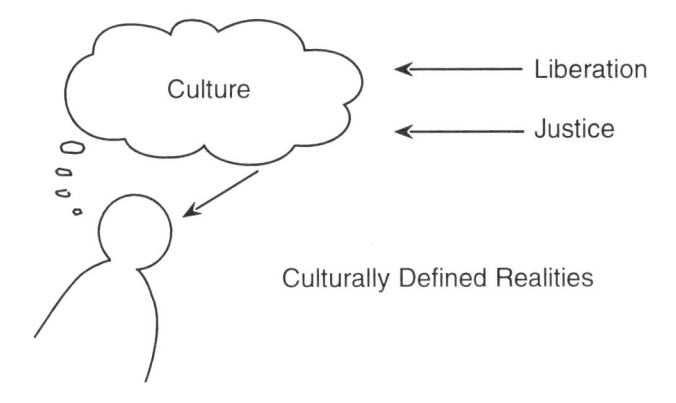

[Diagram: A thought bubble labeled "Culture" above a figure of a person. Arrows from "Liberation" and "Justice" point toward the Culture bubble. An arrow points from the bubble down to the person, labeled "Culturally Defined Realities".]

regarding the matter of justice and liberation. A Christianity solely occupied with its cultural identity in a given locality would be wanting, no doubt. We must always bear in mind that the cultural identity of a given people must seriously take into account the actual context in which this identity is to be lived out. Identity does not exist in a vacuum, but is forged precisely in the concrete social life of a people. Likewise, the specific society in existence would put itself in jeopardy if it ignored the psychological and social need of people for a cultural identity. The imperative for cultural identity and attention to burning issues like liberation and justice are, I am inclined to think, both important soteriological concerns, for both are concerned with wholeness. Not only are they complementary one to the other, they also interpenetrate each other. The concern for liberation or justice, to give an example, must be included indeed within the culture, but it must not also be lost to us that there is no notion of liberation or of justice which is not culturally defined or is acultural. Hence, my insistence on the attention to be given to the actual human situation within the socio-cultural context. After all, is it not true that an inculturated theology is the result of *culturally defined and culturally embodied theological responses to the situation*?

The previous discussion above presupposes, to be sure, that culture is self-rejuvenating and is as dynamic as its creators. Social change should not be considered as necessarily incompatible with the indigenous culture or that a culture is unable to deal adequately with social change. A historical analysis of a given culture easily reveals how much change it had already undergone earlier. So doing theology as inculturation is not just a matter of looking at the way the culture is developing; it is cooperation with and involvement in cultural development.

A SCHEMATIC DESCRIPTION OF DOING THEOLOGY AS INCULTURATION

We have stated methodologically that theology begins with the issues, questions and concerns of people. Moreover, in this reflection on the actual human situation in the light of the Gospel, we are emphasizing the use of the positive resources of the culture *to interpret both the situation and the Faith Tradition*. Let me now schematically lay out the methodological procedure I am elaborating here. I stress the *schematic* character of the following description of procedure in order to highlight the possibilities inherent in it. It is not intended to give a true-to-life picture, as it were, of how the method actually functions.[20] It is only in the actual doing of theology itself, which requires careful analysis of both culture and Tradition, especially Scripture, that better clarity and fuller understanding come, and this within the practice of the faith itself by the community.

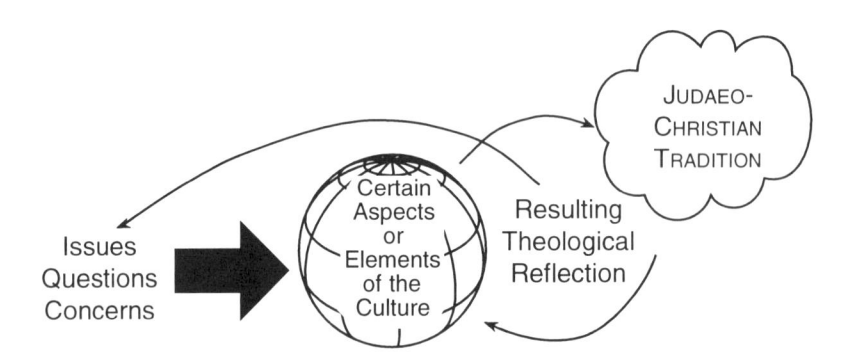

```
                                                      _____
                                                     /         \
                                                    | JUDAEO-   |
                                                    | CHRISTIAN |
                                                    | TRADITION |
                          _____                    _____/
                         / Certain \
                        / Aspects   \    Resulting
    Issues     ➡       |    or      |   Theological
   Questions           \ Elements   /    Reflection
   Concerns             \ of the   /
                         \ Culture/
                          _____/
```

In the first stage the situation we are confronted with (issues, questions and concerns) brings to our attention what theology should be about. A respectful stance towards the culture sensitizes us to the positive resources and potential of the culture. This leads us to discover or focus on those aspects or elements of the indigenous culture which have or can have a bearing on the situation. Obviously, some form of cultural analysis at this stage is essential. I emphasize the culture of the local people because it is possible to use a foreign culture to interact with the Judaeo-Christian Tradition, something that people who have been trained in Western thought and ways may be prone to do.

The second stage is the actual respectful and critical correlating of the cultural aspects in question with the Judaeo-Christian Tradition. Using the relevant cultural aspects as interpretative elements (hence, using the culture as *source*), we are able to discern and discover the riches and strengths of the Judaeo-Christian Tradition in relation to our context. The discovery, then, of cultural resources leads to a second discovery which is that of the relevance of the Faith Tradition in the here and now. There is no need to elaborate here the important links which people will discover between their culture and Scripture in a process like this. In this cultural interpretation of the Tradition the meaning of the Gospel in the understanding of people is deepened.

For instance, in a context of widespread suffering in the Philippines, the cultural aspiration for well-being, *ginhawa*, guides Filipinos to discover that the breadth, the depth and the height of the gift of salvation as envisioned by our Faith Tradition encompasses much more than just salvation of the soul; that well-being from God is at least earthly well-being.[21] If one were to restrict oneself to the traditional institutional language of Catholicism (i.e. neo-scholastic) for this reality of salvation and ignore the potential of the culture, then the relevant aspects of the Tradition may not be retrieved.

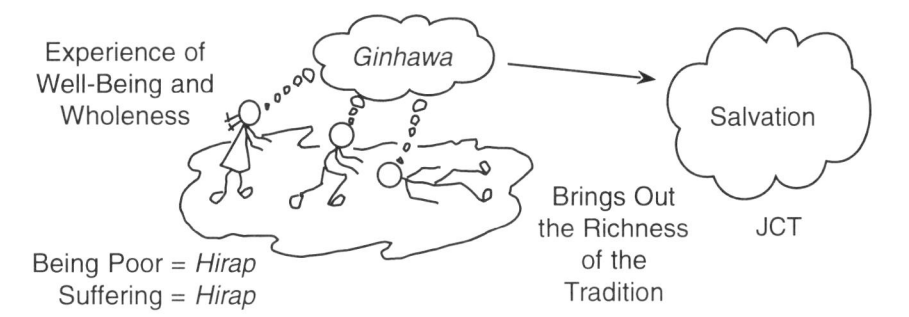

[Diagram: Stick figures with thought bubble "Ginhawa" → "Salvation" (JCT). Labels: "Experience of Well-Being and Wholeness", "Being Poor = Hirap / Suffering = Hirap", "Brings Out the Richness of the Tradition"]

Using the culture as source does not only allow us to discover the riches and strengths of this Tradition. It also takes a critical posture towards that Tradition. It gives us also, within the same process, the capacity to discern and challenge the limitations or weaknesses of the present cultural and historical embodiments of this Tradition. One sees, therefore, that in this interaction, change is not only on the side of the culture nor criticism only from the side of Tradition.

Starting, for example, from the Filipino understanding of a person or a human being—which is either a description of a whole human person from the perspective of inner reality, the "within" (*loob*), or from the perspective of the body and its relatedness to others and the world (*katawan*)[22]—one is led to question the seeming definitiveness of the Graeco-Roman categories of body-soul to describe a human being, categories which wreaked havoc on Christian theology and spirituality, as we well know. We are aware that the dichotomy between body and soul, especially in the areas of spirituality and ethics, has rendered the Tradition about being human misleading. So the culture can serve as a corrective to the Tradition too.

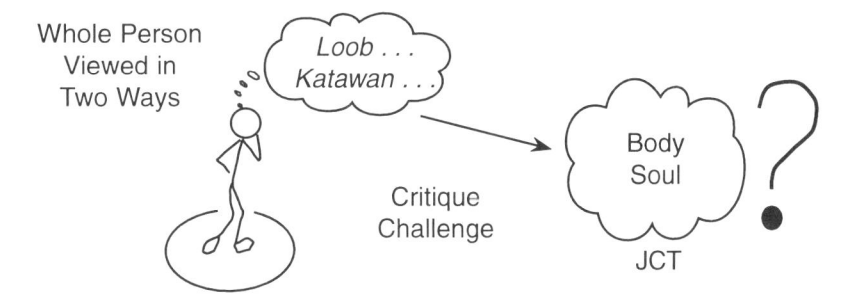

[Diagram: Stick figure with thought bubble "Loob... Katawan..." → "Body Soul" (JCT)?. Labels: "Whole Person Viewed in Two Ways", "Critique Challenge"]

The second stage does not end with the utilization of the culture as source. Culture, too, is the "target" of the respectful and critical posture of the Tradition when this Tradition is used as source to interpret the relevant cultural aspects. This Tradition, which is a Tradition of experiences of a God who cares for people, must be appropriated culturally, but that can only be done through continuous interaction with the culture itself. By using the Tradition, then, as the source of interpretative elements to throw light on the cultural aspects in question, the method enables us to discern and discover the riches and strengths of the culture. This is certainly a way of enhancing the cultural identity of a people.

To illustrate the point: A better understanding of the resurrection in the Tradition has opened up a wonderful possiblity for Filipinos to have a better grasp of this reality in a context where there is rampant "trampling down" on human dignity and honor, especially in the economic, social and political areas of life—exploitation, oppression and brutal silencing of voices of protest.[23] To be more specific, biblical research has made us aware that there are ways of speaking of what happened to Jesus after his death other than the use of the imagery of raising from the dead (resurrection). These alternative ways of understanding the event are the *Parousia* (The Lord is coming), the *Ascension* (going to the Father) and the *Exaltation-Vindication* (sitting at the right hand of the Father), all of which are present in our Tradition. While there is no doubt that the imagery of the Resurrection has become the one most commonly used to refer to the event and the experience, we should bear in mind the legitimacy and usefulness of the other images as well.

It is the interpretation of the Resurrection as *Exaltation-Vindication* which directs attention to a cultural value of immense importance to Filipinos: "*Pagbabangong-dangal*," literally the lifting up or raising up of one's dignity and honor. Why is this so? If one analyzes the Exaltation-Vindication of Jesus against his humiliating and shameful death and what that implied at the time, i.e., rejection and failure, then one sees the resurrection of Jesus by the Father as the restoration of his dignity and honor. The resurrection means that Jesus' claim, his faith in God's closeness, the way he lived his life and met his death were confirmed. With his proclamation and his whole behavior he was right. Jesus' assumption into God's glory means God's acknowledgement of him to whom the world denied acknowledgement. So the shame and dishonor were taken away. Jesus—his person, message, behavior and commitment—was vindicated by way of exaltation: "He sits at the right hand of the Father." Through the resources of the Tradition, therefore, our attention is called to the value of *pagbabangong-dangal*.

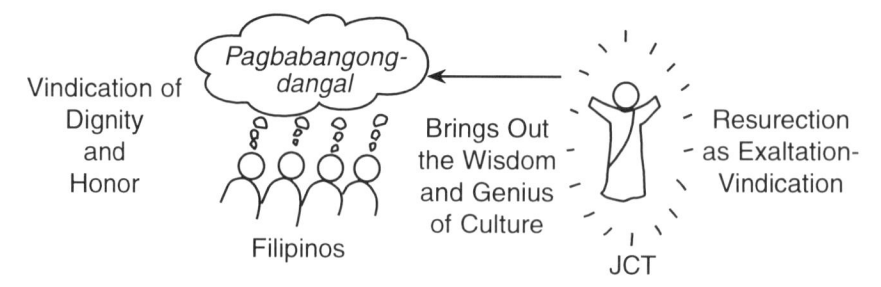

With certain clarifications, *pagbabangong-dangal*, first of all, provides us Filipinos with a culturally intelligible theological language with which to make sense of the resurrection in the present context of rampant desecration of human dignity and honor, at times with brutal and senseless force. It makes us understand that whenever a person's dignity and honor are restored, vindicated and uplifted in one way or another, the resurrection is experienced. Surely, it is experienced when people are willing to stand up, like Jesus, for the common humanity which they share with others, even if it means risking their lives. By the inspiration of the Tradition, then, not only is a positive cultural value promoted, it also shows how the Gospel can be expressed, thought of and lived in cultural terms.

So Tradition enables the rediscovery and recovery of the cultural wisdom and genius of a people. It does not only do that; it also aids us in discerning and challenging the limitations and weaknesses of our present culture vis-à-vis human well-being. It also serves a critical function towards the culture in the same way that culture maintains a critical posture towards the particular embodiment of the Tradition. And it should not be surprising if the Tradition alerts us to aspects of the culture which have become ideological.

A good illustration of this is the realization in our Tradition that God's will for us is our total well-being and not what brings harm and destruction to us. The Tradition captures this insight and conviction in the Gospel of John where Jesus says, "I have come to bring life, life in its fullness" (Jn. 10:10). This point serves as a critical challenge to that negative aspect of the Filipino culture which contends that anything that happens, whether good or evil, comes from the hand of God.[24] For many sincere Filipino Christians capricious fate is nothing other than the will of God. It is not difficult to perceive how a belief like this can legitimate widespread poverty in the Philippines which is really caused by unjust and exploitative relationships and structures. But God is pure goodness; no evil comes from Him. Thus the Tradition not only exposes this negative element of the culture but purifies it as well. It serves as a corrective to the culture.

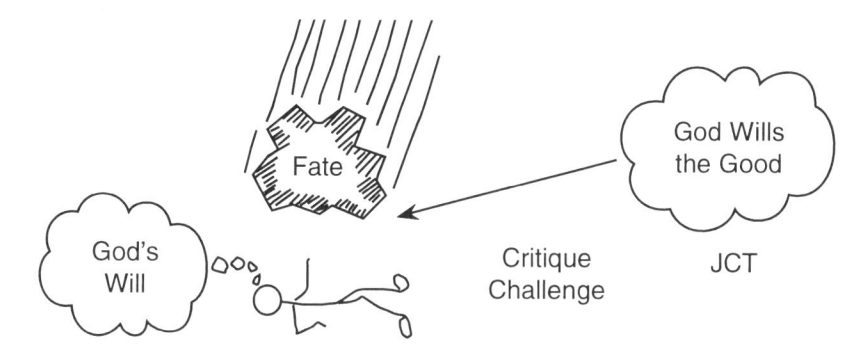

We can see from this that when there is a conflict between the Judaeo-Christian Tradition and the culture, not only is there a need for recognizing the disharmony and inconsistency between the two, but also for an unbiased decision as to which pole should undergo change or purification. "The correlations will ordinarily prove 'mutually critical'," notes David Tracy, "a phrase introduced to remind theologians that prior to the actual analysis there is no way of predicting what concrete kind of correlation is needed in this particular instance."[25] We cannot unilaterally solve the clash by imposing the Tradition on the culture, because the Tradition as we have seen earlier is never without a particular cultural and historical form and expression through which the Tradition is accessible. If we do, we are in fact denying the dialectical relationship between the two poles. We must realize that the interaction can at times be a critical confrontation.

The third stage is actually the tentative result of the interaction between the two poles in their relevant aspects. At this stage we have a culturally intelligible theological interpretation which addresses the issues that triggered off the theological process in the first place. This is a tentative theological reflection because no one can, first of all, claim to a definitive answer. Secondly, constant interaction with the situation necessitates an on-going reflection as well. The theological process is, to be sure, a continuous one. Even this tentative result could easily be the achievement of many already dynamic interactions between the two poles.

Moreover, the theological reflection that arises from the interaction is intended and, hopefully, able to have an impact on the actual situation. It may be good to remind ourselves again at this juncture that the task and responsibility for inculturation is not shouldered by theology alone. The praxis and liturgical life of the local Church are involved in this enterprise, too. But theology contributes definitely to this undertaking by way of interpretation of both the situation and Faith Tradition in relationship to one another.

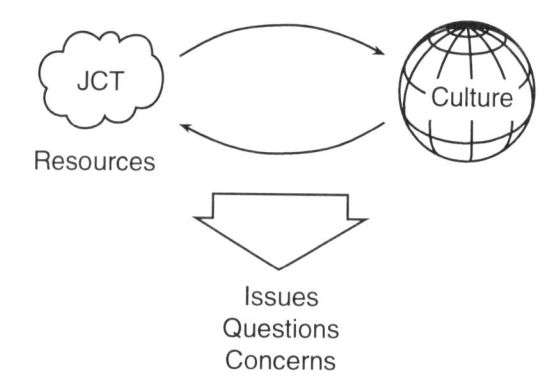

JCT Resources ⇄ Culture

⬇

Issues
Questions
Concerns

Finally, this stage of the process shows us that the interaction between the two poles enables the resulting theology to utilize the resources and potential of both the Judaeo-Christian Tradition and the culture in responding to the imperatives arising from the situation by throwing light on it and critically confronting it.

I hope that the foregoing exposition has made somewhat clear how doing theology in a specific socio-cultural setting contributes to the inculturation of the Gospel and of the local Church. Within the basic process of theologizing, i.e., the mutually respectful and critical interaction between the culture and the Faith Tradition, we emphasized the contribution of a specific theological method towards the achievement of cultural identity in contemporary society among the peoples of Asia. It was the intent of the method to bring the doer of theology to appreciative awareness of, and to utilize the positive resources offered by not only the cultural wisdom and genius of a people but also the Judaeo-Christian Tradition. May it serve as an invitation to do theology that is culturally meaningful and situationally relevant.

NOTES

1. *Collectanea* I (1907), 130-41, as cited by L.J. Luzbetak in "Adaptation, Missionary," *New Catholic Encyclopedia* I (New York: McGraw-Hill Book Company, 1967), p. 121.

2. See Patrick O'Connor, "The Bishops' Synod and Indigenization," *Worldmission* XXVI:4 (Winter, 1975-76), p. 4. For a list of the most important themes discussed in the

Synod, see "Topics Specially Discussed in the Synod," *Teaching All Nations* XII: 1 & 2 (1975), 9-14.

3. "Statements and Recommendations of the First Plenary Assembly of the Federation of the Asian Bishops' Conferences, Taipei, Taiwan" (mimeographed).

4. Pedro de Achutegui, S.J., ed., *Asian Colloquium on Ministries in the Church* (Quezon City: Loyola School of Theology, 1977), p. 27.

5. As cited in Gerald Anderson, ed., *Asian Voices in Christian Theology* (Maryknoll: Orbis Books, 1976), p. 5.

6. Ibid., pp. 5-6.

7. Cf. José M. de Mesa and Lode Wostyn, CICM, *Doing Theology: Basic Realities and Processes* (Quezon City: Maryhill School of Theology, 1982).

8. Gerald Arbuckle, "Inculturation, Community and Conversion," *Review for Religious* XLIV:6 (November-December, 1985), 837-38.

9. Kosuke Koyama, *Waterbuffalo Theology* (Maryknoll: Orbis, 1974, rev. ed. 1999), p. 3.

10. *The Visit of His Holiness Pope Paul VI to the Philippines and the Asian Bishops' Meeting* (Philippines: The Catholic Bishops' Conference of the Philippines, 1971), p. 236.

11. "Our contemporary world of experience must be reflected in theology but not necessarily in the form of a comprehensive economic, political, sociological or philosophic analysis, but rather as a recurrent theme touching upon our contemporary experience and sense of life and current concern." Hans Küng, "Toward a New Consensus in Catholic (And Ecumenical) Theology," *Journal of Ecumenical Studies* XVII:1 (Winter, 1980), 15.

12. Cf. Robert Schreiter, *Constructing Local Theologies* (Maryknoll: Orbis, 1985), p. 23.

13. Ibid., pp. 32-33.

14. Achutegui, *op. cit.*, p. 22.

15. See Miguel A. Bernad, *The Christianization of the Philippines: Problems and Perspectives* (Manila: The Filipiniana Book Guild, 1972), pp. 162-70, especially p. 168.

16. Cf. Q. García and J. Arcilla, "Acts of the Conference of the Bishops of the Philippines held in Manila under the Presidency of the Most Reverend Apostolic Delegate, Monsignor Placide de la Chapelle—1900," *Philippiniana Sacra* IX: 26 (1974), 315-17.

17. See E. Schillebeeckx, *Interim Report on the Books "Jesus" and "Christ"* (New York: Crossroad, 1981), p. 3.

18. Cf. J.J. Mueller, S.J., *Faith and Appreciative Awareness* (Washington, D.C.: American University, 1981), p. 135.

19. Horacio de la Costa, S.J., "The Missionary Apostolate in East and Southeast Asia," *Studies in the International Apostolate of Jesuits* I:2 (September, 1972), 122.

20. Schreiter uses the idea of a "map" to describe a theological process. See, *op. cit.*, chapter two.

21. José M. de Mesa, "The *Ginhawa* which Jesus Brings," *Witness* II:3 (Third Quarter, 1982), 45-66.

22. José M. de Mesa, "Understanding God's, *Kagandahang-loob*," *Witness* I:1 (First Quarter, 1981), 4-13; Patricia Martinez, "*Katawan* as the Basis of Solidarity and Relationships: A Proposed Dynamic Equivalent of *Soma*," Unpublished Master's thesis. Maryhill School of Theology, 1982.

23. José M. de Mesa, "The Resurrection in the Filipino Context" (unpublished article).

24. José M. de Mesa, *And God Said, "Bahala Na!": The Theme of Providence in the Lowland Filipino Context*, Maryhill Studies 2 (Quezon City: Maryhill School of Theology, 1979), pp. 81-188; *Isang Maiksing Katesismo Para sa Mga Bata: A Study in Indigenous Catechesis* (Quezon City: CSP Bookshop, 1984).

25. David Tracy, "'Project X': Restrospect and Prospect," *Concilium* 170 (10/1983), 15.

10

Called to One Hope: The Gospel in Diverse Cultures

Musimbi R.A. Kanyoro*

In this major plenary address to the 1996 WCC-CWME Conference at Salvador de Bahia, a Kenyan Lutheran female theologian deals not only with the major conference theme of "the gospel in diverse cultures" but also with a wide range of mission challenges for the twenty-first century. At the time of the conference Dr. Kanyoro served as executive secretary for the Women in Church and Society desk of the Lutheran World Federation. She is now the General Secretary of the World YWCA, Geneva, Switzerland.

The theme of this conference is "Called to One Hope—The Gospel in Diverse Cultures." The theme chosen for this year's World AIDS Day is "One Hope, One World." Even though the offices of the World Council of Churches and World Health Organization are close to each other in Geneva, I am quite sure that there was no consultation on this matter. Yet this coincidence can remind us of the inclusive nature of hope. The longing for "one hope" is not just a religious matter within the Christian community, but something with significant implications for all people everywhere. "Called to one hope" reminds us that, whatever our agenda, we cannot pursue it apart from the values that make common life possible.

This conference is set within the broader context of dialogue and discussion which has popularly come to be termed "gospel and culture." Culture is not a marginal issue appended to gospel, but touches the core of the church's identity and mission. Culture calls us to accept diversity, while gospel calls us to affirm unity—and both of these are essential for dialogue. "One hope" and "diverse cultures" is a natural combination of two realities that cannot be separated, for indeed people can express or live out their hope only within the context of the culture that shapes them.

---

* From *Called to One Hope: The Gospel in Diverse Cultures*, ed. Christopher Duraisingh (Geneva: WCC, 1998), pp. 96 - 110. Dr. Kanyoro has also co-edited, with Mercy Amba Oduyoye, *The Will to Arise: Women, Culture and Tradition in Africa* (Maryknoll, NY: Orbis Books, 1992).

Yet this theme with its two attractive parts puts me in the position of the proverbial African hyena, who was following the enticing and mouth-watering aroma[1] of barbecuing meat when suddenly he came to a fork in the path. Unsure which direction would lead him to the meat, he put his legs astride the two paths and tried to walk along both. Alas! the poor hyena split in the middle and died. I will let myself be educated by this proverbial wisdom from my roots and will walk on one path at a time: I shall look at the two parts of the theme separately, and then, begging permission from the wisdom of my community, invert the fork and look at the meeting-point of the paths. In that section, I will map out what I see as the challenges for mission in the coming millennium.

CALLED TO ONE HOPE

The word "hope" is ambiguous. In many languages it refers both to *the activity of hoping* and *that which is hoped for*. Thus, hope is a word which on the one hand sets off the flashing amber lights warning us, "Beware, barriers ahead!," but on the other hand encourages us with assurance not to give up. In hoping, we have permission to keep going on, and to insist and persist despite all odds. The Old Testament scholar Walter Brueggemann clearly captures this journey of hope when he says, "Hope is the refusal to accept the reading of reality which is the majority opinion, and one does that only at great political and existential risk."[2]

I came to this conference to ask you to risk disbelieving what you see, to be defiant and rebellious, because hope calls for resistance—active resistance to the void of hopelessness that is defining our world. Thus hope is not merely an intellectual frame of mind. Hope is to be lived out. To hope for justice and peace is to work for the elimination of injustice and to be a peacemaker. To hope for democracy means to practise being democratic in our personal relationships. To hope for wholeness means to face our own lack of wholeness with courage and to be prepared to go through the pain of self-examination which leads to change. Change is, more often than not, a painful metamorphosis.

Hope is a central theme of the Bible and a major tenet of the Christian faith. For Christians, hope is *an expectation linked to faith*. We do not hope for what we have, but rather what we long for. Paul writing to the assembly in Rome says: "Now hope that is seen is not hope. For who hopes for what is seen? But if we hope for what we do not see, we wait for it with patience" (Rom. 8:24).

Christian hope is *radical* in nature, for it is grounded in God's act of raising Jesus from the dead and thus "making all things new" (Rev. 21:5). Resurrection for Christians is victory over any death-dealing possibility. It is a victory of the cross. In his *Theology of Hope*, German theologian Jürgen Moltmann states: "Hope is the distinctive contribution of Christian faith to our world in the midst of the ambiguous and even hopeless circumstances that plague human existence."[3] I really like this statement, but I cannot fail to ask what exactly it means. Can Christians claim to be the only vendors of hope?

I am raised in Lutheran theology and therefore sincerely proclaim again and again that Christian hope is linked to *grace*. It is by grace that we have this privilege to proclaim Christ incarnate as the hope of all creation and of the church. In this sense none may claim that they and only they deserve to hope.

Christian hope moves us to *a new order of priorities*. There is no greater witness to hope than Jesus of Nazareth. He was not silent about his mission to preach the good news to the poor, to release those who were captives and to give health to those who were ill (Luke 4:18-19). As he visited the towns and villages and saw with his own eyes the poverty, the inequality, the religious and economic oppression, the unemployment, the depression, the mental and physical illness and the cultural uncleanness facing the people (Matt. 9:35-38), his heart was filled with pity. In his witness Jesus told the people, "The time is fulfilled, and the kingdom of God has come near; repent, and believe in the good news" (Mark 1:15).

Christian hope invites *praxis*. Through his message about the reign of God, Jesus challenged his followers to be his witnesses, to have a new vision of what life is about, to live by new values and to enter into new relationships with each other as brothers and sisters in Christ, thus helping to transform the world through acts of love and service. The church, as the community of faith entrusted with communicating the gospel, is called to be a sign of the promised reign of God which is present wherever the liberating, saving and transforming power of Christ is incarnate. This is the hope that gathers us here as people from different cultures, yet committed to the gospel of Jesus Christ incarnate. In this conference we must dream God's dream that all people may have life and have it abundantly. It is not enough that some die and others just survive. It is our thoughts, actions and attitudes that make the difference.

From a faith perspective, this means engaging hour by hour with life in such a way that our deeds express that for which we hope, even while acknowledging the reality of disappointment, frustration, anger, brokenness and even despair. The challenge before us is *to dare to hope* as we dialogue together and find so much that is contradictory to hope. In daring we must wrestle with that which seeks to deny us hope and to disempower us. As we meet in Brazil, we would do well to listen to the words of the former Roman Catholic bishop of Recife, Dom Helder Câmara:

> We must have no illusions. We must not be naive. If we listen to the voice of God, we make our choice, get out of ourselves and fight non-violently for a better world. We must not expect to find it easy; we shall not walk on roses, people will not throng to hear us and applaud, and we shall not always be aware of divine protection. If we are to be pilgrims of justice and peace, we must expect the desert.

HOPE IN A WORLD OF HOPELESSNESS

Our times are ripe for flirting with hopelessness. Cast your mind's eye over the news of the world or of your own community during the past few weeks. Think and explore with me for just one second! Our collective memory by now will have gathered a world of enormous problems. There is a kind of pessimism in the air which can afflict anyone concerned about hope. For the masses, traumatized by war, violence, poverty, insecurity, hunger or disease, the very mention of "hope" is ominous and deadly.

I embody some of the contradictions and dilemmas that speak the language of hopelessness. For I stand here not just as an individual but as one connected to a people. I embody a continent whose cultural and spiritual history in regard to mission and evangelization has left its people insecure and unsure. Yet we are also a continent that has been hospitable to all kinds of religions and religious beliefs. We have welcomed all our guests, to the point where the song of the guest has become the household song. For all these centuries of embracing Christianity, whatever has come out of Africa has not been seen to be appropriate in the missiological discussions about God.

As I prepared this presentation, war was looming in central Africa. Pictures of weeping women and children with small bundles on their heads, moving to unknown destinations, flooded the media as I struggled with "one hope . . . in diverse cultures." Reality seems to mock conversations about hope. It is not easy to grasp the full range of problems of faith that this kind of destabilization inflicts on the church and society. I bring the vulnerability of my continent to this gathering. According to our cultures and traditions, we are living with the curse of the blood of our massacred brothers and sisters, the children of the land of Africa. Our rivers and lakes are marked with that blood. The mass graves and the roaming spirits of the unburied dead have polluted the land, pointing to sins of omission and commission. What can we do to capture and celebrate a unity of purpose in the linguistic, ethnic, spiritual and cultural diversity that is our heritage, when in fact all our energy is spent on senseless wars that have left us hopelessly uprooted in a continent which has the largest population of refugees and displaced people in the world.

And so I ask, where shall we turn for hope? To African cultures? No, we have erred so much that we would never have enough animals to sacrifice for our atonement. In the face of all this humiliation, we must try to hear and face God's question to Cain: "What have you done? Listen; your brother's blood is crying out to me from the ground!" (Gen. 4:10). But "the neighbour" is also called to wear sackcloth and to lament. Where were you when all this was happening? What did you do? What is happening where *you* are? The neighbour too is guilty. What is happening today on our continent is rooted in histories which were exacerbated by our Western neighbours. The ethnic wars and violence in Africa are in a way present to a fair degree in all parts of the world. The current language of globalization should also be addressing the globalization of injustice and disrespect to life and to creation. It is at this moment of facing our own death in a world cluttered with death that we come face to face with the question of Christ crucified; it is through him alone that we are enabled to be free and to regain our dignity, and through him that we are made a people called to the ministry of reconciliation (2 Cor. 5:18-20).

This context prompts the question of whether the church offers *something new, different, helpful and hopeful* to lead people to rediscover the God-experience in lives which are governed by the question, "My God, my God, why have you forsaken me?" The question of what it means to be church in societies experiencing crisis looms large in any discussion of mission and evangelism today. An experience of faith that holds itself aloof from people seeking to escape marginalization poses a serious risk to the future of the church and the church of the future. The witness of the church will not be credible unless we who claim to be church take into account the traumatic situation of millions of people living in perilous conditions in many parts of the world. What meaning can mission have in churches that seek to witness to Christ without sharing the people's battles with the forces of oppression which assault their dignity? Is this not the time for the church to reclaim the language and practice of being a conscience of society? If the church does not, who will speak in God's name against the injustice, hatred, oppression, discrimination and greed of our time? Who will bring God back to the people? We cannot avoid seeking answers to the question, "Does the church make a difference?"

Over these past months as I read and prayerfully considered what I might say at this conference, what kept me awake was not the big debates regarding the major issues confronting our world, but rather people for whom Christ died. I was kept awake by the pain in families as marriages break up, jobs become harder to come by and food and shelter—once thought to be a basic need—become in reality luxuries affordable only to some people. I was kept awake by children. Children crying out for love, reaching out in vain, and turning to the streets, to crime, to prostitution, to death. Children in hospitals, in prisons, on the front line of wars—children who have never been given the chance to be children. Children orphaned by AIDS and wars. Children abused by adults and turned into commodities by society. Children whom we would rather not see because they upset our neat, comfortable lives. And I pondered, what does mission have to say about these little ones whom Christ welcomed: "Let the little children come to me . . .; for it is to such as these that the kingdom of God belongs" (Mark 10:14)?

For several years now the media have been drawing attention to the plight of children in our host country, Brazil. We have heard of children killed in the streets on "clean-up" missions, children who have become commodities for the trade in human organs. Just a few days after an international conference on children was held in Sweden (August 1996), we read of the horrendous rape and killing of two Belgian girls in the prime of their youth, and of the many other Belgian children who are still missing. The reaction of some people in Europe made it clear that this was the first time that crimes against children had become real to them.

Why have the thousands of Brazilian street children, Liberian child-soldiers or Filipino child prostitutes not elicited an equal reaction of shock? The international trafficking in women and children, from Asia in particular but now from Eastern Europe as well, has not been high on the agenda of the churches, even though activist groups have been speaking against it for more than two decades. Does the world react differently to the sufferings of people of different cultures and different economic possibilities? Is *one hope* possible for people of diverse cultures?

I table these issues because I am convinced that our times call us to maturity and honesty in dialogue. Dialogue is a conversation that entails two-way communication. Only when there is mutuality in our relating will we be able to wrestle with the realities of our diversity and still hold onto hope.

Brazil is a fitting venue for this world mission conference on the gospel-cultures dialogue because it enables us to learn something about mission from the realities of people in this country of so much diversity. To speak of children makes Bahia and Brazil a relevant place to meet. Yet it is also here that we might begin to raise our voices on culture and difference. This is the place to focus on the issue of race relations. What does it mean to be black in this country? What does it mean to be a descendant of a continent so far away and to live here with a history of slave trade? This is a place that presents the meeting of cultures and religions. Expectantly, we must be curious about what we will learn from the Afro-Brazilian religious expression called Candomblé. In what ways does it inspire hope? What can we take home with us from Brazil?

And so I turn to my next path in the forked road of the proverbial African hyena.

THE GOSPEL IN DIVERSE CULTURES

Gospel and culture has been an issue of concern for the church since the beginning. Already in the book of Acts we read about conflicts in the early church over worship, table fellowship, circumcision, the Holy Spirit, gospel and government.

Yet in missiological discussion a kind of dualistic thinking developed in which culture was for a long time simply seen as a concern of the South. Discussions about inculturation, indigenization and contextualization, wherever they took place, were aimed mainly at addressing issues and theologies of the former missionized churches. It is interesting for those of us who come from these churches to see the issues of culture now being brought to the forefront of global church discussion. Not only are we reminded of the various condemnations of our cultures throughout history which stripped us of our very identity, but we vividly remember the WCC seventh assembly in Canberra (1991), where the keynote address[4] of Prof. Chung Hyun Kyung of Korea sparked controversy. Truly speaking, how do we define syncretism today? Is this perhaps a word that has served its purpose and is no longer useful for the Christian church? Is there any confession that can claim to be free from syncretism?

Neither gospel nor culture is good news until it liberates. That is to say, there is no gospel or culture that is automatically liberating. All hearing of the gospel in any culture is situation-variable. Gospel always comes with culture. We must always ask, is it good news for others? For whom is the gospel good news? For whom is this culture good news? My putting of gospel and culture on the same level could be provocative and will surely make many uneasy. In reality I am appealing to missiologists and evangelists to consider the intercultural dimension of evangelization. We must exercise the hermeneutical function of theology when we are invited to speak about gospel and culture.

"Gospel" and "culture" are not abstract terms but are descriptions of realities. Within these words are people with faces, people who bleed when pricked and laugh when tickled. Participation in culture is so natural and ubiquitous that most people take culture for granted and do not reflect critically on it. To me, mission means giving gospel and culture a human face. Mission is unwrapping the gospel packaged in theological words and concepts and making it relevant to human beings for whom Christ gave his life on the cross. The communication of the gospel happens only through culture—language, structures, art, music, dance and other expressions which influence the relationships between people and with God. If that culture is not liberating neither will the gospel that it interprets be liberating.

I grew up in a village in Africa. When I think of culture I think of a little animal we call the *ekogongolo*, which is often found in fresh moist soil. When touched, it coils into a harmless small spiral. Under normal conditions it can move either way without turning itself. Culture has this kind of double mobility. In some instances culture is the badge, or even the "creed," for community identity—for culture defines who we are and gives us security as a community. In other instances culture is used to make distinctions between different people in the community and to assign roles, functions and practices (some of which can be oppressive).

When we speak of dialogue in cultural matters, the issue is not just to become accepting of the diversity of cultures, but rather to find ways by which we can work creatively with cultures and traditions so that they can be liberating. For nearly ten years I have been involved in reading the Bible with groups of rural women in Africa. I began to write about my accumulated experiences about three years ago in an analysis which I have come to call "cultural hermeneutics."[5] I came into that work after realizing that under the rubric of accepting cultures—our own and that of others—we risk tolerating unjust behaviour.

For generations, African women have unquestioningly obeyed all that society prescribes for them in the name of culture. Child marriages, female circumcision and the rites of passage from birth to death, whether useful or harmful, are imposed on African women simply because it is "our culture." This might be taken to mean that what is culture is natural, good and unavoidable. Culture has silenced many women in Africa. It has hindered them from experiencing Jesus' liberating promise of abundant life for all (John 10:10). Cultural hermeneutics seeks to demystify the abstractness of "culture" by calling for analysis of and reflection on culture and its effects on people.[6]

African women (whose voices are only now beginning to surface) are calling the churches to go beyond a theology of inculturation and place cultures themselves under scrutiny, in order to determine whether they promote justice, life, peace and liberation or whether they diminish and dehumanize people. Cultural hermeneutics is therefore the analysis and interpretation of cultural practices with a view to discerning their liberative and oppressive aspects. African women do cultural hermeneutics by telling stories of our own experience and explaining how we read and understand the scriptures within our cultural setting. By telling our stories and reviving those of our foremothers, we will be able to unearth those elements of our culture that were holistic and bring them back into the church. We will be able to unmask those aspects of our culture that are harmful and bring them to the public as collective sins for which the society, the church and especially we as women must make confession and receive forgiveness. For me, that is renewal in the power of the Holy Spirit, renewal for the whole church in Africa. Women in other parts of the world[7] have also identified cultural hermeneutics as an urgent need in their own contexts.

Doing cultural hermeneutics is not easy. It requires, on the one hand, questioning and examining age-old beliefs and practices and, on the other, finding possibilities to affirm and reclaim those aspects of culture that are good but have been discarded. The missionary, anthropological and colonial era condemned the cultures of many of their subjects. The formerly colonized world has responded by glorifying culture, and the skin of both colonizer and colonized is still too raw to accommodate criticism. Critiquing other people's cultures is a very sensitive matter at this point in history. The former colonizers have shifted their attitudes, so that they too either over-glorify the cultures they once criticized, or stand aloof even in the face of injustice because "it is their culture." The tension is now how to take part in analyzing cultures—our own and other people's—objectively. Can people cross boundaries and speak about the ills in other people's cultures without being seen as neo-colonialists? How can dialogue take place in our world today when we have become so "sensitive" to each other that we can no longer draw a line between the needed and the unjust critique? I consider this the most difficult issue facing intercultural hermeneutics. We are trapped in emotions and subjectivity and sometimes this is counterproductive.

MISSION CHALLENGES FOR THE 21ST CENTURY

Let me return now to the meeting-point of our two paths—"one hope" and "diverse cultures"—and suggest six areas of mission which I consider urgent for the 21st century:

- mission involves helping people to read the Bible for themselves;
- mission involves celebrating difference and diversity;
- mission involves developing new models of partnership;
- mission involves listening to the new voices from struggling communities;
- mission involves addressing new issues of our time and age;
- mission involves listening to the small voices of hope from the seemingly weak.

READING THE BIBLE

Reading the Bible on one's own creates the possibility of a sincere response to the message of the Bible. Many people, even churchgoers, are biblically illiterate, because the tradition of reading the Bible in the family and in one's private life has greatly diminished. The Bible as a book of faith has become distant, and while many people know about it, few *know* it. It is urgent that the Bible be returned to its central place in the lives of Christians. Churches must work together with ecumenical bodies for this mission. The Bible societies, which seem to be almost marginalized in the ecumenical movement, should be given their rightful place of leadership because they publish the most important resource for churches, for mission and for all Christians' spiritual growth. Here we have lessons to learn from the Bible itself. Recall the Ethiopian finance minister who upon reading the scriptures for himself asked Philip for baptism (Acts 8:26-40). I also would like to lift up the work of the so-called evangelical churches or the base communities in Latin America where people have been transformed by gathering and reading the Bible together. Women's prayer groups and Bible study groups have from time immemorial been witnesses to the importance of the Bible in the daily lives of Christians.

CELEBRATING DIFFERENCE AND DIVERSITY

Our times compel us to accommodate contradictions and diversities on the one hand, and uniformity and globalization on the other. In this context the question posed by African American womanist theologian Katie Cannon is appropriate: "Can we be different, but not alienated?"[8] Mission today requires a painful and heart-searching effort to walk with people in "difference." If we want to build strong and faithful relationships throughout the world we must deepen our trust of one another and develop a healthy approach to diversity reflected in styles of worship and relationships of race, gender, generation. Healthy diversity builds upon trust and a common vision for the good of the whole community.

Mission today must face the challenge of being hospitable to those who question the exclusive jargon and way of presenting what appears to Christians as the ultimate truth. The institutional church must come to terms with the challenge of what to do with our faith that is built on the "foundation" (or is it the *myth*?) of certainty. How will the mission and evangelism of the church of today and the next millennium appropriate the knowledge gained by working with other faiths? The San Antonio world mission conference humbly stated, "Since God's mystery in Christ surpasses our understanding and since our knowledge of God's saving power is imperfect, we Christians are called to be witnesses to others, not judges of them."[9]

While we carry this affirmation into the 21st century, we cannot say that it ends the daunting questions of how to be faithful in presenting the message of Christ in a pluralist society and in a world of cultural diversity. We have to be clear that our certainty is not to be equated with security, but rather is dependent on the faithfulness of God. It is a spiritual certainty which we can express only through an attitude of love towards other people as enjoined by the Christian faith. Our worship and actions of faith must reflect that we are at every moment in the presence of the living God.

DEVELOPING NEW MODELS OF PARTNERSHIP

In our globalized world, mission too must be seen as a global phenomenon. The mission of the church today begs for new models of partnership that promote mutual and reciprocal learning among people globally. Missiological reflection still takes place mostly in the North, and the persons who teach in these institutions are rather homogeneous. The decision-making boards of church mission departments and missionary societies are still predominantly male. Whenever I visit missiology departments and mission boards in connection with my responsibilities with the Lutheran World Federation, I am delighted to meet the "experts" (who are mostly former missionaries to the South), but wonder whether this does not have the unintended consequence of maintaining Western intellectual dominance (or possibly intellectual myopia). Churches in the North and South have to work together to find forms of theological and ministerial formation that promote and encourage mutual learning and healthy partnership.

To foster sustainable new models of partnership, the former missionizing countries need to rethink their superiority complex, and the former missionalized countries must squarely face and overcome their inferiority complex. Only then can the present monologue be turned into a dialogue on what it would take to be partners in mission. Let me speak to the inferiority of the South and challenge my brothers and sisters from the North equally to make yourselves vulnerable by addressing your superiority complex. We have been and are still angry about being dominated by the North. It would be naive simply to dismiss the past, but it would do us no good to continue this litany until doomsday. Having awakened from the slumber of considering Europe and North America as the cradle of world civilization, we must now ask ourselves what we are to do with this knowledge. How do we assist former missionaries and colonial masters to look at the world with different eyes? I am convinced that mission today calls people of the former mission fields into more responsibility than we seem to understand. We have gone through a period of justified resistance. In the Bangkok world mission conference in 1973 we said: "We refuse to serve simply as raw material which others use for their salvation."[10] At one time this frankness was shocking to traditional missionary agencies and churches in Europe and North America, who were not prepared for the new consciousness of the South and its articulate voicing of this rejection. I believe there is more openness to change now. I see signs of willingness on both sides—but also regret that the inferiority complex of the South is fuelled by poverty in terms of material goods, money and power.

LISTENING TO NEW VOICES FROM STRUGGLING COMMUNITIES

For many years the ecumenical agenda has been influenced by the desire to promote the unity of the church, to such an extent that it sometimes sacrifices the integrity of the groups within it. Today these groups question an ecumenical agenda that does not take a decisive option for their needs. The voices of the marginalized, seeking to move their concerns to the centre of ecumenical debate, will increasingly define ecumenical formation. The solidarity groups, bound together by race, ethnicity, gender, various orientations of opinions and practices on (for example) environmental concerns, indigenous issues and human rights interests, require fundamental changes in the powers, procedures and forms of being "ecumenical" as well as being "church." Do these voices not mirror the signs of the reign of God?

To take but one illustration: women in many parts of the world are calling the churches to be accountable with regard to the attitudes to women reflected in their theology, liturgy and worship, structures, history and access to ministry and leadership. The struggle for the acceptance of women is at the same time a struggle for the trustworthiness of the church's proclamation (Gal. 3:28). Can the church take an issue like violence against women and develop programmes around it to help the society to change? Can the church give hope without first being renewed itself?

ADDRESSING NEW ISSUES OF OUR TIME AND AGE

One of the most visible challenges to Christianity today is posed by urbanization and the secularization of societies. People in the cities of the South and North alike are adopting similar globalized cultural behaviour conditioned by the constraints of their context. They are striving to make sense out of their lives amidst so many contemporary struggles. The majority have no church background and are unfamiliar with the message of the gospel, and so will not listen to the message of the church unless the church itself is significantly different and has something particular to offer. If Christianity is to make sense to them, it will have to be what Paul described as "all things to all people."[11] In the church we speak the language of Hallelujah and Amen, but we must remember that today our world also speaks of Coca-Cola and Toyota.

Another urgent issue of our time is how to do mission in a divided world among divided people. How will the church of today and the next millennium package and market the gospel of one hope in the face of globalization and rapid transformation of a world catalyzed by information technology, the never-ending gap between rich and poor, urban and rural, those advocating ethnic unity and those seeking national unity, men and women, youth and adults?

DRAWING HOPE FROM THE "WEAK"

I believe that people from the South, through their experience of suffering and longing for God, have a chance to share their hope with the world. It is Africa that prompts me in this belief. In Africa we know death, humiliation, what it means to be down. Yet it is precisely at such times, when we search for God in the midst of the rubble, that we are called by the Christian faith to embrace *hope*. Economic and political issues challenge the self-understanding of Christians as an ecclesial community and have consequences for their understanding of the role of the church in the wider human community. However, the church's mission comprises more than ecclesial and social issues. The church is about God and the love of God, which is not limited to those who do good and live rightly but which invites and begs us daily to turn to God who first loved us (1 John 4:19) and to rejoice in hope. There is some of that rejoicing among the people of Africa. The churches are full and people sing and dance to the message of the gospel. Let the picture of Archbishop Tutu dancing during the days of apartheid tell the story of African hope.

The hope of the church is a *spiritual* hope based on God's love. The certainty of the Christian faith is grounded not in religion but in the everlasting God of love. Those who are at their weakest depend upon this God of hope, who loves and forgives.

The hunger for faith and for spirituality in Africa never ceases to surprise both the guests and the hosts on that continent, whether in times of death or in times of celebration. It is precisely this search for God, even now when things are bleak, that makes my region a continent of great hope. For us in Africa, this is *a time to hope*. In our diverse cultures, we hope because God promises liberation from all that oppresses us. Hope with us, by embracing the theme of this conference, "Called to One Hope—The Gospel in Diverse Cultures."

NOTES

1. In the past few months, I have been thoroughly enticed by the aromas of what has been written and spoken in preparation for this conference. The WCC-stimulated gospel and cultures studies which have been published in (to date) 15 pamphlets, together with the numerous reflections that have appeared since January 1995 in the *International Review of Mission*, have been the major source of that enticing sweet aroma, pulling me in different directions. Knowingly or unknowingly I certainly draw from these materials, and therefore I offer public acknowledgment of and gratitude to the authors of the various pamphlets and articles, and to the WCC's Programme Unit II for having made these resources available to me.

2. Walter Brueggemann, *The Prophetic Imagination*, Philadelphia, Fortress, 1978, p. 67.

3. *Hope for the Church: Moltmann in Dialogue with Theology*, Nashville, Abingdon, 1979, p. 10.

4. Chung Hyun Kyung, "Come Holy Spirit—Renew the Whole Creation," in *Signs of the Spirit: Official Report, Seventh Assembly*, ed. Michael Kinnamon, Geneva, WCC Publications, 1991, pp. 34-37.

5. See, for example, Musimbi Kanyoro, "Cultural Hermeneutics: An African Contribution," in *Women's Visions: Theological Reflection, Celebration, Action*, ed. Ofelia Ortega, Geneva, WCC Publications, 1995, pp. 18-25.

6. In 1989, a group of women theologians met in Accra, Ghana, to create the Circle of Concerned African Women Theologians. The theme of the convocation was "Arise, daughter." There we arose and began writing our first continental volume, *The Will to Arise: Women, Culture and Tradition in Africa* (Mercy Amba Oduyoye and Musimbi R.A. Kanyoro, eds. Maryknoll, NY, Orbis, 1992). We have never returned to slumber. We are writing, speaking, preaching, meeting to reject dehumanization. We have now produced more than ten books, most of which focus on the need to liberate women from oppressive aspects of culture.

7. Mercy Amba Oduyoye has done perhaps the most extensive work on cultural hermeneutics, although she has never named it such. Her *Daughters of Anowa* (Maryknoll, NY, Orbis, 1995) is the most complete work produced to date. Elsa Támez, Letty Russell and Mary John Mananzan all speak to the need for cultural hermeneutics in *Women Resisting Violence: Spirituality for Life*, Mary John Mananzan et al., eds. Maryknoll, NY, Orbis, 1996.

8. This is the title of an exchange of letters between Katie Cannon (African American womanist theologian) and Carter Heyward (American feminist theologian) published in *Feminist Theological Ethics*, Lois K. Daly, ed., Louisville, KY, Westminster John Knox, 1994.

9. *The San Antonio Report*, Frederick R. Wilson, ed., Geneva, WCC Publications, 1990, p. 32.

10. Bangkok World Mission Conference, 1972-73. Many third-world forums and writings are even more outspoken today than they were in the 1970s.

11. See 1 Corinthians 9:19-23, where Paul argues that he became like every other person in order to be able to be a blessing to them. Jesus was accused of eating with tax collectors and sinners. He neither avoided nor condemned those who were different from him. What better model for Christians could there be than Jesus the Christ!

11

Translatability and the Cultural Incarnations of the Faith

*Kwame Bediako**

In this essay, Ghanaian Evangelical theologian Kwame Bediako argues that "translatability" and not "indigenization" is the proper way to conceive the relation between Christian faith and local culture. While the latter term implies that Christianity is a foreign "western" religion that needs to be "transplanted" in new soil, the former implies a basic openness of the Christian gospel to all cultural expressions. " . . . universality, translatability, incarnation and indigeneity belong in a continuum and are integral to the warp and woof of the Christian religion. It is only by a serious misconception then that we call it a Western religion."

TRANSLATABILITY AS UNIVERSALITY

Andrew Walls has taught us to recognise the Christian religion as "culturally infinitely translatable."[1] From this perspective it becomes possible to see Christianity's various cycles of expansion into different cultural contexts in its history as so many cultural manifestations or incarnations of the faith. Each incarnation has been different and yet each has managed to preserve elements which unite them all as sharing in a common reality, elements like worship of the God of Israel, attribution of ultimate significance to Jesus Christ, a sense of belonging to a people of God extending beyond the local context and in the midst of whom God's activity is recognised, reading of common Scriptures, and sacramental use of bread and wine and water.[2]

Translatability is also another way of saying universality. Hence the translatability of the Christian religion signifies its fundamental relevance and accessibil-

---

* From *Christianity in Africa: The Renewal of a Non-Western Religion* (Edinburgh: Edinburgh University Press; Maryknoll, NY: Orbis Books, 1995). Kwame Bediako is director of the Akrofi-Christaller Memorial Centre in Ghana, and Visiting Lecturer in African Theology at the Centre for the Study of Christianity in the Non-Western World, New College, University of Edinburgh, Scotland.

146

ity to persons in any culture within which the Christian faith is transmitted and assimilated. Nowhere is this character of Christianity more evident than in the Christian view of Scripture. Unlike, say, Islam, in which the effectual hearing of the Word of Allah occurs essentially only through the medium of the Arabic language, Christian doctrine rejects the notion of a special, sacred language for its Scriptures and makes God speak in the vernacular so that "all of us hear . . . in our own languages . . . the wonders of God."[3] Accordingly, the Bible translated into whatever language remains essentially and substantially what it is believed to be in its original autographs.

But behind the Christian doctrine of the substantial equality of the Scriptures in all languages, there lies the even profounder doctrine of the Incarnation, by which the fullest divine communication has reached beyond the forms of human words into the human form itself. "The Word [of God] became flesh and dwelt among us."[4] Translatability, therefore, may be said to be in-built into the nature of the Christian religion and capable of subverting any cultural possessiveness of the Faith in the process of its transmission.

I do not intend to pursue these ideas in the manner of a theoretical discussion, but rather to show how, in our post-missionary setting, such considerations truly come into their own, and also to point out how it is only by an adequate and firm grasp of this principle of the translatability of the Christian religion that we can appreciate the true character of continuing Christian witness and enhance the genuine development of new indigenous traditions of Christian thought. The discussion will relate mostly to a body of literature and developments in the African field.

NON-WESTERN CHRISTIANITY AND WESTERN VALUE-SETTING— THE SEVENTH INTERNATIONAL AFRICAN SEMINAR

It is appropriate to begin this discussion by recalling an event which indicates the extent to which Western value-setting for Christianity was still exerting an impact on the interpretation of non-Western Christianity even in the post-missionary era, and was therefore having a distorting effect on indigenous developments in Christian thought. The principle of translatability is not necessarily one which is most readily recognised in the process of the transmission of Christianity.

In April 1965, an international gathering of academics and scholars representing various intellectual disciplines with interest in the missionary transmission of Christianity in Africa met at the University of Ghana, Legon, near Accra, under the auspices of the International African Institute, to discuss and assess the place of Christianity in sub-Saharan Africa. The proceedings of that seminar, edited by Christian Baëta of Ghana, were published under the title *Christianity in Tropical Africa*.[5] When one reads the papers presented and the account of the discussions, one gets a distinct impression that the gathering took a positive but not triumphalist view of the fortunes of Christianity on the African continent. Clearly, not all issues were considered to have been resolved, yet *Christianity in Tropical Africa* gives every indication that there was a feeling that the Christian presence in Africa represented the most significant spread and advance of the Faith in history since the penetration of the early Roman Empire and of Europe. The phenomenon of

Christianity in Africa was therefore an important subject to study. An observation by Baëta sums up the mood of the gathering and the state of understanding reached: "Intangible in many of its aspects, the Christian presence has been and remains, in the African scene, a massive and unavoidable fact and factor."[6] Africa seemed to be a success story of the missionary endeavour. Adrian Hastings, writing in the 1970s and looking back to the two previous decades, could comment: "Certainly, if one looked around Africa in 1950, the achievement of the missionary enterprise could not but appear considerable."[7] And yet it also seems that there was some measure of surprise, with not a little perplexity, at this rich African harvest. In the mind of the missionary movement, there had been a general hesitancy about ascribing to Africa's pre-Christian religious traditions and socio-cultural forms of life any substantial theological status. Not many had been convinced that African societies gave evidence of any "preparation for Christianity." Furthermore, the entanglement of the missionary histories of African peoples with European colonial ventures served to complicate the outcome all the more. How successfully could the one be dissociated from the other?

On the specifically religious plane, it was not the great and high religious cultures of Asia—on which considerable missionary resources and personnel had been expended—but the "animistic" world of Africa, to use the language of the Edinburgh World Missionary Conference of 1910,[8] which now became the test case of the missionary enterprise, and probably of Christianity generally, in the new era that was beginning.

One area of the discussions at the Accra seminar in which this perplexity seemed particularly acute was that relating to African conversion. The seminar seemed to give a variety of interpretations of the "massive and unavoidable fact and factor of the Christian presence" in Africa. The explanations ranged from those which were broadly sociological and political to those which sought to be specifically religious. The British theologian, F. B. Welbourn who had worked in Uganda, for example, wondered whether a missionary (Protestant) preaching of salvation from the standpoint of guilt could be understood by traditional African societies which, in his view, were conditioned more by a shame-culture.[9] He saw conversion to Christianity in Uganda as providing a "phantasy structure" for an African identity within the new political structure that was emerging.[10] On the other hand, the Kenyan theologian, John Mbiti, then working in Makerere University College, Kampala, Uganda, called for greater attention to be given to religious considerations in their own terms, and asked whether sociological or political considerations alone provided an adequate explanation of the facts. Mbiti cited the testimonies of converts who gave as reasons for their conversion a positive demonstration of love by missionaries and the impact of some Christian doctrines, particularly the resurrection and the nature of the Christian afterlife. "Did they not have an inner religiosity which found fulfilment in Christianity?"[11] Perhaps it is not surprising that the need was felt for a study comparable to the work of Arthur Darby Nock on conversion in the Hellenistic world of the early Roman Empire, another time and place which recorded a massive response to Christianity as it crossed cultural frontiers.[12] The feeling was that "the spread of Christianity in Africa is a topic of far greater importance in Christian history than is generally recognised,"[13] that there was a need to explore "fundamental questions," and that at issue was really the question of Christian identity, a study of which was made even more urgent by the wind of political nationalism then sweeping across the continent:

> The search must continue for an identity which ensures to all African Christians . . . a satisfying self-consciousness and dignity in social and interracial relations. If the definition of this identity has so far been predominantly in nationalistic terms, . . . this must be supplemented by the reflection that a Christian comes from God and goes to God; [his citizenship is in heaven, i.e. his total and final value system extend well beyond those of his own culture]. Full realisation of the potentialities of genuine Christian culture within the African context will involve both the working out of a clear Christian mind regarding this context and an equally clear African mind concerning Christian values and ideas.[14]

The Accra seminar of 1965 is important for an understanding of what was happening to Christianity in Africa, at least in the minds of its most influential scholars, interpreters and advocates, at the critical time of the heyday of African nationalism, and also in the period when African Christian intellectuals were themselves beginning to make serious efforts to come to terms with the Christian presence in African life.

The seminar is also important in a rather disturbing way, in that, in at least some of its aspects, it is a pointer to the hurdles which still had to be overcome, if the Christian religion in Africa was to be seen as a truly African experience and reality. For despite the recognition in some of the papers presented, that there was a valid African contribution,[15] an appreciation of the full dimensions of their contribution was only just beginning to be recognised. It still seemed as if the whole matter of the planting of Christianity in Africa was little more than the religious equivalent of the political and cultural impact of the West. The difficulties in the interpretation of African conversion are an indicator of the inhibiting effects of such a frame of reference.

Furthermore, African independent churches had become a significant element of the Christian presence on the continent. Yet despite George Shepperson's argument in his paper, "Ethiopianism: past and present" that these African initiatives in Christianity had a "rightful place in the history of the Church"[16] and David Barrett's analysis from 200 different societies across Africa, showing that independency was "playing an increasing part in the expansion of Christianity in Africa,"[17] the seminar's treatment of the phenomenon of the independent churches was less than positive, seeing them rather as "separatist" movements. Academic orthodoxy was still far from recognising that it was the independent churches which were in fact indicating the trend and direction of African Christianity. In a later trenchant criticism of the seminar on this point, two African historians with an interest in African Christian history have asked why the convenors failed to "invite participation by these African Churches, or to recognise their existence as propagators of Christianity in Africa."[18]

A FALSE START FOR AFRICAN THEOLOGY?—
THE INDIGENISATION CRUSADE OF IDOWU

Perhaps it was the whole conception of the nature of African church history which was the problem in 1965. In some "polemical thoughts on African Church History," Paul Jenkins wrote a few years ago: "An African church history that begins with missionary institutions—and especially one that begins with missionary initiatives—is almost bound to stress the foreign nature of the faith and its practices."[19] This was the dominant frame of reference for understanding Christianity in Africa at the time, as can be seen in the early direction that the then emergent movement of African theology took. This direction reveals the skewing effect of that frame of reference on the development of theological thought and agenda.

All who were concerned with the fortunes of Christianity in Africa at the time naturally felt the urgency to demonstrate the African credentials of the faith but, understandably, it was African Christian scholars and churchmen themselves upon whom that burden fell most heavily. Apart from Christian Baëta, there were three other African churchmen and theological academics who presented papers at the Accra seminar, and who were destined to become influential in the growth of African theology in the subsequent decades. These were Bolaji Idowu (of Nigeria), John Mbiti (of Kenya) and Vincent Mulago (as he was then called) of Zaire. Idowu's paper, under the title "The Predicament of the Church in Africa," presented a disturbing picture of the church in Africa as "still dependent, . . . looking to missionaries from outside for manpower and material resources, dependent in its theology, its liturgy and its church discipline, in fact in its whole expression of the Christian life."[20] For Idowu, "the Church in Africa came into being with prefabricated theology, liturgies and traditions."[21] Mbiti presented a paper on "Ways and Means of Communicating the Gospel" to ensure effectiveness and relevance,[22] whilst Mulago, in his paper entitled "Christianity and African Culture: the African Contribution to Theology,"[23] made a case for an African theology which would make use of African categories of experience and thought.

This is, perhaps, not the place for a detailed exposition of those papers. All these men were, however, testifying to what they, together with others, perceived to be the "predicament of the church," to use Idowu's language, and were also showing an awareness of the intense pressure which this perceived predicament was exerting upon African churchmen, compelling them to find (one might even say, almost invent) a theological identity, a theological idiom and a Christian *modus vivendi* that would be more appropriate to the African context and reality. They seemed united in the concern that the "massive and unavoidable fact and factor" of the Christian presence still needed deeper rooting in the African scene, at least to the extent that it should cease to be and be seen as a foreign plant, and to become instead, a home-grown and indigenous reality.

Not surprisingly, therefore, in the subsequent few years, the major concern became the "indigenisation"—of Christianity, church and theology. Idowu quickly earned a status as a "doyen" among African theologians, certainly in the West

African region, and took up the challenge of indigenisation in a spirited publication of 1965, *Towards an Indigenous Church*,[24] though some of the material had been developed for three radio talks as far back as 1961, on the "problem of indigenisation of the Church in Nigeria." This was probably the first and clearest statement by a leading African theologian, setting forth specific proposals that an African Church might consider in order to transform itself into an authentic African Christian community, if it found itself "heavily tinged with Western culture." For Idowu, Christianity was in Africa, but not of Africa . . . not yet. In other words, for Idowu, the "foreignness" of Christianity in Africa was a fundamental *datum* and the starting point of the discussion. Indigenisation was as much about discarding "foreignness" as it was about rooting the faith in local realities. Accordingly Idowu specified five areas which, in his view, needed attention:

1. the Bible in Nigerian languages,
2. the language of evangelisation,
3. theology,
4. liturgy,
5. dress and vestments.

It may seem odd that for all his insistence on the church in Nigeria bearing "the stamp of originality," Idowu decided that ministers' vestments was one area in which "the Church in Nigeria must preserve something as token of her being part and presence of the Universal Church." On the other hand, it could also be argued that Idowu was seeking a far more fundamental indigenisation than merely external features. Whatever the merits of Idowu's arguments, the reason for replacing, in his words, "the European complexion of the Church" with an indigenous complexion was that "Christian Nigerians cease to see Jesus Christ as an imported divinity from a European pantheon" and that they come to see Him as "God's Messiah to Nigerians, their own personal Saviour and Lord."[25]

The really important question to ask for our present purposes is why this spirited apologia for indigenisation has not been followed through in the theological and intellectual career of Idowu; why, eight years later, in his *African Traditional Religion—A Definition*, Idowu concluded that:

> African traditional religion is *the* religion practised by the majority of Africans, nakedly [i.e. overtly] in most cases, but also in some cases under the veneers supplied by Westernism and Arabism.[26]

Why, when Idowu quoted the Biblical text of *1 John* 3:2: "It does not yet appear what we shall be," did he apply it not to the church in Nigeria, but to the prospect of African traditional religion? The task of vindicating and establishing "a satisfying African self-consciousness and dignity" which in *Towards an Indigenous Church* was laid upon the Christian church, later came to be confidently entrusted to the old traditional religion, now revitalised with its "God-given heritage and indigenous spiritual treasures."[27] Through the years, it seems, Idowu remained haunted by the "foreignness" of Christianity, and having started from that foreignness, was never able to arrive at indigeneity.

TRANSLATABILITY SEEN IN MBITI'S WRITINGS

Like Idowu, Mbiti was early to deplore the lack of sufficient and positive engagement by Western missions with African cultural and religious values. He saw the result of this in an African church which had "come of age *evangelistically*, but not *theologically*": "a church without theology, without theologians and without theological concern," as he was writing in 1967 and also in 1969.[28]

Mbiti, however, soon came to make a distinction between "Christianity" which "results from the encounter of the Gospel with any given local society" and so is always indigenous and culture-bound, on the one hand, and the Gospel, which is "God-given, eternal and does not change" on the other. In 1970 he wrote: "We can add nothing to the Gospel, for this is an eternal gift of God; but Christianity is always a beggar seeking food and drink, cover and shelter from the cultures it encounters in its never-ending journeys and wanderings."[29] Mbiti had already given an indication of this trend of thought in his paper at the Accra seminar of 1965, when he stated: "We cannot artificially create an 'African theology' or even plan it; it must evolve spontaneously as the Church teaches and lives *her* Faith and in response to the extremely complex situation in Africa."[30] But the definitive break came later, when Mbiti rejected the very idea of the quest for indigenisation of Christianity or of theology in Africa. In a response to a study of his theology by John Kinney,[31] Mbiti wrote:

> To speak of "indigenising Christianity" is to give the impression that Christianity is a ready-made commodity which has to be transplanted to a local area. Of course, this has been the assumption followed by many missionaries and local theologians. I do not accept it any more.[32]

It may be of interest also to compare the attitudes of our two representative thinkers to the African independent churches. Idowu found no place for them in his drive for indigenisation. He saw them instead as "syncretistic sects which have spread all over the country like the seed of contagion . . ., the product of syncretising Christianity with some dominant practices of the national cults." He saw no positive contribution coming through the ministries of these churches:

> The end product of this syncretism is a church whose characteristics are frothy, ecstatic ritual, seeing of visions and dreaming of dreams, making predications and prescriptions, mass hysteria which gives birth to babbling of incoherent things as symptoms of possession by the Spirit. All these naturally make them popular with the mass who like neglected hungry sheep flock where they find promises of nourishment.[33]

Mbiti, on the other hand, though not an uncritical admirer of the independents, nevertheless saw in them an African Christian consciousness and experience having its own integrity. They represented not only a massive rejection of imported forms of the Christian life; they also bore witness to the fact that "African peoples have taken seriously to Christianity." Through them and their distinctive styles of ministry and community, God was speaking to the world church and to the world. Mbiti looked forward to a time when they would not be "as far apart from the historical churches as they are at present."[34]

For Mbiti, therefore, the Gospel is genuinely at home in Africa, is capable of being apprehended by Africans at the specific level of their religious experience and in fact has been so received through the missionary transmission of it. The Western missionary enterprise, from this perspective, has a place within a religious history which properly belongs to African tradition. Since God is One, Mbiti maintains, "God, the Father of our Lord Jesus Christ is the same God who has been known and worshipped in various ways within the religious life of African peoples" and who therefore, was "not a stranger in Africa prior to the coming of missionaries." They did not bring God; rather God brought them, so that by the proclamation of the Gospel through the missionary activity, Jesus Christ might be known, for "without Him [Jesus Christ] the meaning of our religiosity is incomplete."

> The Gospel enabled people to utter the name of Jesus Christ . . . that final and completing element that crowns their traditional religiosity and brings its flickering light to full brilliance.[35]

By this approach, Mbiti in effect "exorcises" the "Westernism" and "foreignness" in the Western transmission of the Gospel, and internalises whatever was of the Gospel. By the same process, he affirms the missionary endeavour, but without making the missionary central; for the whole operation began with God and was carried through by God. The encounter was, at its deepest levels, not the meeting of Western ideas and African traditions; rather it was the meeting of African man in his religiosity with Jesus Christ, whose "presence in the world is not a historical [i.e., chronological] but a geographical presence in the world made by Him and through Him."[36]

The theological principle we see operating in Mbiti's thought is that of translatability—the capacity of the essential impulses of the Christian religion to be transmitted and assimilated in a different culture so that these impulses create dynamically equivalent responses in the course of such a transmission. Given this principle, it is possible to say that the earlier concern to seek an "indigenisation" of Christianity in Africa, as though one were dealing with an essentially "Western" and "foreign" religion was, in effect, misguided because the task was conceived as the correlation of two entities thought to be unrelated. Such an effort was bound to lead to a dead end, as we have noted in Idowu's case, precisely because it fastened too intently on the "foreignness" of the Western modes of the transmission of the Faith, and correspondingly paid too little attention to actual achievement "on the ground." The achievement meant here is not to be measured in terms of Western missionary transmission, but rather by African assimilation of the Faith. Evangelisation is not simply the "communication of foreign ideas to passive recipients who have to swallow every bit whether or not they approve,"[37] it was therefore misguided to assume that African converts to Christianity assimilated the missionary message in Western terms rather than in terms of their own African religious understanding and background.

TRANSLATABILITY AND AN APPROPRIATE
HISTORICAL FRAMEWORK

Since the subject of Western missions will continue to provide part, at least, of our understanding of Christianity in the non-Western world, it is important that we pursue the question of an appropriate frame of reference for appreciating their role from the perspective of the principle of the translatability of the Christian religion. A most stimulating contribution to the subject has been made by Lamin Sanneh.[38] Since Sanneh's treatment is important to the present discussion, I shall summarise its salient points.

Sanneh states his concern as follows: "The subject of Western missions needs to be unhinged from the narrow colonial context and placed in the much wider setting of African culture, including the religious background of African societies."[39] For Sanneh this is crucial because it is what African converts did (and do) with the Gospel received through the Western missionary transmission which really counts, certainly more than the mere transmission itself. He asks: "The question with which we are faced fundamentally is this: Of the two processes at work, the historical transmission and the indigenous assimilation, which one is more significant?"[40] Sanneh has no doubt, and he expects his readers to agree with him, that "without hesitation it is the latter. For it is within that that the historical process itself becomes meaningful."

To put this shift of emphasis firmly into the context of the assimilation of the missionary message, Sanneh adds the crucial role that Bible translation has played in Western missions. For Sanneh, the importance of Bible translation and its priority in missionary work are an indication that "God was not disdainful of Africans as to be incommunicable in their languages."[41] This carried two far-reaching consequences for how one may view the African cultural world. First: "This imbued local cultures with eternal significance and endowed African languages with a transcendent range." And second, it also "presumed that the God of the Bible had preceded the missionary into the receptor-culture—so the missionary needs to discover Him in the new culture." Therefore, according to Sanneh: "It is the hidden reality of this divine presence that both validates external mission and requires translation as a *sine qua non* of witness."[42] Through the very process of Scripture translation, "the central categories of Christian theology—God, creation, Jesus Christ, history—are transposed into their local equivalents, suggesting that Christianity had been adequately anticipated."[43] But, as we noted earlier, Sanneh is concerned to show not only that the crucial factors involved in the Gospel communication do not require the Western missionary transmitter to be at the centre of the picture, but also that African pre-Christian religions have had a theological significance in the whole process. The centrality of Scripture translation points to the significance of local religions for providing the idiom for Christian apprehension:

> The enterprise of Scriptural translation, with its far-reaching assumptions about traditional religious categories and ideas as a valid carriage for the revelation and divine initiative that precedes and anticipates historical mission, concedes the salvific value of local religions.[44]

Accordingly, the popular notion of Christianity as "the white man's religion" or Western religion, is effectively set aside, for African Christianity is no less Christian for being mediated through African languages, whilst Western Christianity does not enshrine universal standards. On the contrary, the very possibility of Scripture translation, as well as the elements that come into play through it, demonstrate that an African "incarnation" of the Faith is valid too:

> Translation assumed that the abstract Word of God would find its true destiny when embodied in concrete local idiom, lending credence to the theological insight that the Word of God had always carried the burden of the incarnation, and that its historical manifestation in Jesus Christ concentrated and made visible a process that is occurring throughout history.[45]

Sanneh's description of this whole process is the comprehensive term, *Missio Dei*, encompassing the divine initiative through the pre-Christian tradition, the historical missionary transmission and the indigenous assimilation:

> *Missio Dei* sustained traditional religious enterprise by bringing about a convergence with Christianity . . . so that *Missio Dei* activated by the stimulus of historical contact with the West, has fused with local religious enterprise and acquired a concrete reality.[46]

But the "concrete reality" is a local reality, achieved by indigenous assimilation and African religious agency through the critical role of the Scriptures in African languages. Observing this phenomenon at its highest in the independent churches—the "African Charismatics" as he calls them—Sanneh finds the evidence to vindicate the claim that "local adaptation held incomparably greater prospects for the future of the religion in Africa than external agency did."[47]

Then Sanneh finally comes full circle: once we have subordinated Western missionary transmission to local assimilation and adaptation under African agency, then "we cannot continue to appropriate Christianity as an ideological theme and annex it as a subplot to the history of Western imperialism."[48] If we wish to maintain the principle of the translatability of the Christian religion as well as the proper religious perspective on the process of its transmission, then we must admit that Sanneh is right.

A large portion of Sanneh's argument is also that "the historical experience of Africa is a demonstration of the salvific value of religion,"[49] by which he means African primal religions. One would wish that he pursued the question as to why his statement could not be made equally with regard to areas which are "highly Islamised." The phenomenological relationship of primal religions to the Christian religion may need to be taken seriously here too.[50]

But the major contribution which Sanneh's article makes is the historical frame of reference that it gives for understanding issues which lie beyond the missionary enterprise itself. By placing the whole exercise of missionary transmission and indigenous assimilation under the overarching concept of *Missio Dei*, Sanneh shifts the discussion away from considerations of the impact of the West upon the non-Western world. The Christian religion is rescued from a Western possessiveness of it, whilst at the same time the true proportions of the missionary endeavour are seen for what they really were, that is, the extent to which it stimulated the emergence of a genuine indigenous Christian tradition in terms of *Missio Dei* in the local setting; a fresh cultural incarnation of the Faith.

If it is translatability which produces indigeneity, then a truly indigenous church should also be a translating church, reaching continually to the heart of the culture of its context and incarnating the translating Word. For the Word who took flesh and dwelt among us, not only exegetes (and so translates) God (*John* 1:18), but also exegetes the human predicament (*John* 4:29), bringing the two together in a mutually intelligible communication. This makes it all the more important to pay attention to what happens at the level of indigenous assimilation. To agree with another of Paul Jenkins's "polemical thoughts" on African Church history:

> African Church history must be concerned with the free dialogue that is already taking place between questions and problems as formulated in the different traditional cultures and the answers and solutions latent in the Christian message.[51]

It is by doing this that we come to recognise the extent of indigenisation that is already present in the very process of indigenous assimilation. Sustained by *Missio Dei*, the indigenous and translating church becomes a catalyst for newer assimilations, hence further manifestations and incarnations of the Faith.

Accordingly, translatability is the only true basis and starting point for seeking indigeneity. From this perspective, however, indigeneity does not lie at the *end* of a quest. Rather it is presumed within the very translatability of the Christian religion. Indigeneity is as much a matter of recognition within the Gospel as it is an achievement of actual Christian witness. Thus, universality, translatability, incarnation and indigeneity belong in a continuum and are integral to the warp and woof of the Christian religion. It is only by a serious misconception then that we can call it a Western religion.

There is an interesting comment by E. A. Ayandele (the Nigerian historian) reported by Walbert Buhlmann in his book, *The Coming of the Third Church*.[52] At the first international congress of the International Association for Mission Studies held in Driebergen, The Netherlands, in 1972, after many Western scholars had expressed views which he considered too critical of the missionary enterprise from the West, Ayandele intervened: "Even if *you* came to us within the framework of colonialism, and did not preach the Gospel in all its purity, that has not prevented *us* from receiving the Gospel and genuinely living it."[53] For Ayandele and others like him, Christianity had already become disentangled from any Western possessiveness of it; it is a non-Western religion.

NOTES AND REFERENCES

1. Andrew F. Walls, "The Gospel as Prisoner and Liberator of Culture," *Faith and Thought*, 108 (1-2), 1981, pp. 39-52; also in *Missionalia*, vol. 10, no. 3, November 1982, pp. 93-105; also in this volume, pp. 17-28.

2. Andrew F. Walls, "Christian Tradition in Today's World," in F. D. Whaling (ed.), *Religion in Today's World*, Edinburgh: T. and T. Clark, 1987, pp. 76-109.

3. *Acts of the Apostles* 2:11.

4. *John* 1:14.

5. C. G. Baëta (ed.), *Christianity in Tropical Africa* (Studies presented and discussed at the seventh International African Seminar, University of Ghana, April 1965), London: Oxford University Press, 1968.

6. Ibid., p. xii.

7. Adrian Hastings, *A History of African Christianity 1950-75*, Cambridge: Cambridge University Press, 1979, p. 43.

8. C. G. Baëta (ed.), *Christianity in Tropical Africa*, p. 129. At the Accra seminar too it was stated that Africa has never had a general high culture of its own. See also *World Missionary Conference 1910: Report of Commission IV - The Missionary Message in Relation to Non-Christian Religions*, Edinburgh and London: Oliphant Anderson and Ferrier, 1910, p. 24.

9. Ibid., pp. 182-99.

10. Ibid., p. 125.

11. Ibid., p. 126.

12. Ibid., p. 3. (See also A.D. Nock, *Conversion: The Old and the New in Religions from Alexander to Augustine*, Oxford: Clarenden Press, 1933.)

13. Ibid., p. 123.

14. Ibid., pp. 129-30.

15. For example, Richard Gray, "Problems of Historical Perspective: the Planting of Christianity in Africa in the 19th and 20th Centuries," in Baëta, *Christianity in Tropical Africa*, pp. 18-30.

16. C. G. Baëta (ed.), *Christianity in Tropical Africa*, p. 363.

17. Ibid., p. 284.

18. Ade Ajayi and E. A. Ayandele, "Writing African Church History" in P. Beyerhaus and C. Hallencreutz (eds), *The Church Crossing Frontiers—Essays on the Nature of Mission* (in honour of Bengt Sundkler), Gleerup: Studia Missionalia Upsaliensa XI, 1969, pp. 90-108.

19. Paul Jenkins, "The Roots of African Church History: Some Polemical Thoughts," *International Bulletin of Missionary Research*, vol. 10, no. 2, April 1986, pp. 67-71.

20. C. G. Baëta (ed.), *Christianity in Tropical Africa*, p. 353.

21. Ibid., p. 426.

22. Ibid., pp. 329-50.

23. Ibid., pp. 308-28.

24. Bolaji Idowu, *Towards an Indigenous Church*, London: Oxford University Press, 1965.

25. Ibid., pp. 22-4, 49.

26. Bolaji Idowu, *African Traditional Religion—A Definition*, London: SCM Press and Maryknoll, N.Y.: Orbis Books, 1973, p. 208.

27. Ibid., p. 205.

28. John Mbiti, "Some African Concepts of Christology," in G. F. Vicedom (ed.), *Christ and the Younger Churches*, London: SPCK, 1972, pp. 51-62; published earlier in German in P. Beyerhaus et al., *Theologische Stimmen aus Afrika, Asien und Lateinamerika III*, München, 1968; also *African Religions and Philosophy*, London: Heinemann, 1969, pp. 232 and 233.

29. John Mbiti, "Christianity and Traditional Religions in Africa," *International Review of Mission*, vol. 59, no. 236, October 1970, p. 438.

30. C. G. Baëta (ed.), *Christianity in Tropical Africa*, p. 332.

31. John Kinney, "The Theology of John Mbiti—His Sources, Norms and Method," *Occasional Bulletin of Missionary Research*, vol. 3, no. 2, April 1979, pp. 65-7.

32. John Mbiti, "Response to the Article of John Kinney," *Occasional Bulletin of Missionary Research*, vol. 3, no. 2, April 1979, p. 68.

33. Bolaji Idowu, *Olódùmarè—God in Yoruba Belief*, London: Longman, 1962, pp. 211-12.

34. John Mbiti, "The Future of Christianity in Africa 1970-2000," *Communio Viatorum* XIII, nos. 1-2, 1970, pp. 34f.

35. John Mbiti, "Response to the Article of John Kinney," p. 68.

36. Loc. cit.

37. Ajayi and Ayandele, "Writing African Church History," p. 91.

38. Lamin Sanneh, "The Horizontal and the Vertical in Mission: An African Perspective," *International Bulletin of Missionary Research*, vol. 7, no. 4, October 1983, pp. 165-71.

39. Ibid., p. 165.

40. Ibid., p. 166.

41. Loc. cit.

42. Loc. cit.

43. Loc. cit.

44. Ibid., p. 170.

45. Loc. cit.

46. Loc. cit.

47. Loc. cit.

48. Loc. cit.

49. Loc. cit.

50. Sanneh has since developed this theme more fully in his *Translating the Message—The Missionary Impact on Culture*, Maryknoll, N.Y.: Orbis Books, 1989.

51. Paul Jenkins, "The Roots of African Church History," p. 68.

52. Walbert Buhlmann, *The Coming of the Third Church* (English translation), Slough: St. Paul Publication, 1976. (First published in German as *Es kommt die dritte Kirche—Eine Analyse der kirchlichen Gegenwart und Zukunft*, 1974.)

53. Ibid., p. 171.

12

Evangelization and Inculturation

Concepts, Options, Perspectives

Paulo Suess*

In this essay, Paulo Suess first surveys various concepts of culture, and judges that the most adequate concept is one that understands culture as a human ecosystem. Suess then reflects on several options available which attempt to express the relationship between Christian faith and local, Latin American culture. Rather than a strict separation between the two, or a facile identification, the notion of inculturation—based on an analogy with God's incarnation in Jesus—is chosen as the best expression available today, and one that accords particularly well with Christian tradition. Inculturation, finally, is understood from the perspective of evangelization. Evangelization must be inculturated, that is, it must be holistic and integral, focused on local identity, and open to other local expressions and churches throughout the globe.

The peoples of Latin America live in the context of a double-sided reality: the situation of social misery and the the situation of multicultural and multi-ethnic richness. The hunger of the *poor* and the aggression against Latin American "otherness" both threaten the very existence of peoples, civilizations and individual lives. The social question of the *poor* is at the same time a cultural issue for "otherness." Both—social reality and multicultural and multi-ethnic reality—can be neither confused nor separated. Latin Americans are not simply *poor*; their problems are much more extensive. Poverty, as a result of structural lopsidedness on the socio-economic plane, is a social pathology to be combatted. *"Otherness"*—i.e., Latin American

---

* Taken from *Evangelizar desde los proyectos historicos de los otros: Diez ensayos de misionología* (Quito, Ecuador: Abya-Yala, 1995). Translated by Stephen B. Bevans. Paulo Suess, born in Germany, has lived in Brazil for thirty years, where he works with indigenous peoples and teaches missiology at the Faculty of Nossa Senhora da Asuncao in São Paulo. He is vice president of the International Association of Mission Studies (IAMS) and a contributing editor of *Mission Studies*.

indigenous culture—represents a richness that needs to be defended; it is a source of resistance in the face of reductionism of systemic, institutional and rationalistic technocracy and utilitarianism.

The practice of inculturation radicalizes the question of liberation. The evangelical perspective of the *poor* does not come from material possessions, but from the joy of living with dignity, confident that they know who they really are. Participative equality and universal solidarity seek both to overcome the socio-economic imbalances that generate poverty and misery and to call for the recognition of the irreducible "otherness" of Latin America's cultures.

In the context of this article, our concern is not with Latin American cultural subjects as such, independent of their social condition, but with Latin Americans in their "otherness" in so far as they are *poor*. The category of indigeneity adds something essential to the notion of "being poor"; it adds a cultural factor which confers identity and situates the poor in geographic space and historical time. In the history of humanity, indigeneity is prior to poverty, but in the history of the individual and of social groups, both can coincide. Poverty and its extreme form, misery, are a consequence of cultural destruction.

THE CONSTRUCTION OF THE CONCEPT OF "CULTURE"

The contemporary world presents us with very different concepts of culture, and the polysemy resulting from this is evident in theological texts and ecclesial documents as well. A definition of culture provides a device by which we are to be able to discuss and compare aspects of reality. A definition is like a perspective, the limits of which need to be acknowledged beforehand.

This essay argues for the continuity and viability of the historical "project"[1] of Latin America's cultural "otherness." One must, therefore, provide a concept of "culture" which enables the multicultural reality of the continent to be expressed, and which links this cultural reality to the socio-religious and historical reality of the Latin American peoples. Starting from this position we will outline the concepts of "culture" which social scientists use today, and then propose a concept of "culture" which will not contradict the vision of the gospel, nor the historical project of human beings.

FULFILLMENT OF THE HUMAN SPIRIT

A current "idealist" position sees culture as the *great fulfillment of the human spirit* (art, literature, education, religion). The "world of culture," consequently, is the world of artists and intellectuals. Simple people would have little culture, or none at all. In this perspective, for example, *Gaudium et Spes* declares that "the benefits of culture ought to be and actually can be extended to everyone" (GS 9; see also GS 60) and the Conclusions of the Medellín Conference point to an "enormous" number of people who are marginalized in terms of culture, those who are illiterate (Education 3). Reducing culture to the specific activities of the Ministry of Culture, inculturation would be converted into an ecclesial presence concerned with "educational work," or connected to the elites of the "world of culture."

UNIVERSAL VALUES

Other authors endow culture with universal values. They speak of the "culture of peace," "culture of love," "culture of solidarity," "culture of work," "democratic culture," etc. In these cases the concept of culture is understood as a common denominator to emphasize values that are apparently common among many people. Cultures, however, and their value systems, symbolic expressions, beliefs, social organization and material production are not reducible to universal values of some kind of "metaculture." What is specifically human—culture—is not reducible to a kind of universal morality. The particular project with its "local values" is always prior to a global project. Universal values emerge from values that are locally cultivated.

To endow "culture" with universal values is to speak analogically. As in a laboratory one can create a "culture" of bacteria to manufacture a vaccine, one can also imagine the creation of universal values for the good not only of a specific group of people but also for all of humanity. "Inculturation" in this context of "meta-culture," with its universal values, would mean the dissemination of those values and/or their revitalization for all peoples. Concretely, however, these meta-cultures do not exist, nor do peoples exist who might be considered the subjects of such metacultures. The analogous concept of cultures generates also a practical analogy of inculturation. Strictly speaking, it is a contradiction to speak of "inculturation in the metaculture." The universal dimension of inculturation is in the muliplicity of inculturations that one can experience.

ANTI-VALUES

In the context of the paradigm of the "evangelization of cultures" in recent ecclesial documents, culture appears in a negative light, branded as the "culture of consumerism," "culture of hedonism," and even as the "culture of death."[2] By describing cultures positively or negatively, as universal values or anti-values, the concept of culture loses its analytic ability. So as not to compromise the "taking on of culture" in the following of Jesus it is necessary to keep the concept of culture for the positive historical aspects of the life of each social group. The anti-values can be analyzed under the rubric of "structures" or "powers of death," as the meeting at Santo Domingo has done (SD 13, 243).[3] But in a so-called "culture of death," inculturation would seem to have no place.

SUPERSTRUCTURE

Another train of thought, of Marxist inspiration, treated culture until recently as a superstructure or ideology. Consequently, the spiritual plane and the world of ideas were considered a "reflection" or "ideological interpretation" of the material plane (infra-structure). In this perspective, the economic plane ultimately determines the cultural plane. Consequently, the culture of a people can—by reflecting these underlying, i.e., economic, relationships—cover up or even justify the social relations which cause oppression. Where culture is considered ideology, what is evident is a deep distrust of cultures and a desire to change them. At this level, inculturation is untenable, because it would represent the "assumption of an ideology." Evangelization would involve a permanent intervention in the culture of peoples and social groups in order to reveal its alienation, an alienation that originates in economic causes.

CULTURE AS A DIVISION OF SOCIAL REALITY

Following the thought of Max Weber, many social scientists today treat culture as a sector or "department" of social reality. Like Weber, they divide reality into spheres: political, economic and cultural. This division of social reality is not satisfactory, however, because it does not explain how culture involves the economic-material sphere and the political organization and expression of every people. The political and economic spheres are also, as specifically human organizations, cultural manifestations. Without realizing the cultural dimension of the political and economic spheres it is impossible to understand or have any profound influence on those dimensions of the social life of a particular group of people. Inculturation in this understanding of social reality as compartmentalized would mean the assumption of only one sector of society to the exclusion of the political and economic spheres from the inculturating perspective of the gospel.

CIVILIZING PROGRESS

Certain authors understand culture as *civilizing progress*. In this way culture is seen principally from the perspective of material and technological progress which these authors judge to be the best from each *civilization*. The reduction of culture to technology and buildings (temples, pyramids, airplanes, etc.) provides a way of making the ethnocentric distinction between "superior" and "inferior" cultures, or between "high civilizations" and "primitive cultures." The underlying ideology of this notion, one that would link "culture" together with "civilizing progress," is a kind of "social Darwinism" (*evolutionismo*). In this evolutionistic vision of progress, the "primitive cultures" generally have "modern culture"—or the culture of the outsider—as a goal. In this context evangelization prides itself on its works of civilization and often turns into a "civilizing mission." Inculturation as Christian presence to stimulate or critique material and technological progress would not correspond to the specific task of the churches to engage the historical projects of peoples.

Vatican II distinguishes culture from civilization: culture, linked to the particular territory of a people or social group, is different from civilization that emerges from the multiple contributions of various peoples. The latter can serve as a common treasure. In this perspective *Gaudium et Spes* interprets civilization as a treasure that is contributed to by the experiences of all cultures. The contacts among nations and social groups "opens more widely to all the treasures of different cultures. Thus, little by little, a more universal form of human culture is developing, one which will promote and express the unity of the human race to the degree that it preserves the particular features of the different cultures" (GS 54).

CULTURE AS SACRIFICE

Sigmund Freud, however, who in several of his works treats the issue of culture and civilization, does *not* distinguish culture from civilization. He explicitly declares: "I scorn to distinguish between culture and civilization"[4] Culture/civilization is "the whole sum of the achievements and regulations which distinguish our lives from those of our animal ancestors, and which serves two purposes, namely, to protect men against nature and to adjust their mutual relations."[5] Freud treats religion independently from culture by considering it a collective illusion ("mass delirium"[6]). Also according to Freud, through culture humanity achieves almost everything that it has dreamt of and men and women themselves virtually become gods.[7]

Human life, especially cultural existence, only becomes possible when the power of the individual is substituted for the power of a community. This is the decisive step for civilization. Its essence consists in the fact that the members of the community sacrifice their instincts and abandon any possibility of brute force. The motivating force of all human activities is utility and pleasure.[8] The cultural process causes modifications in the instinctive dispositions of human beings. Some of the instincts of the individual are suppressed for the sake of civilization. Others are induced to displace the conditions of their satisfaction. The "Discontent in Civilization" is due to the "sublimations" and "sacrifices" demanded of each individual so that any aggressivity (barbarity) would be kept in check for the sake of communal life and communal justice. Such "cultural frustration," according to Freud, dominates social relationships. It is the cause of all hostility, and every civilization fights against it. The regression of the instincts is always possible: religion can turn into religious fanaticism (fundamentalism), individual rights can be repressed by depersonalizing forces of mass collectivism; the civilizing covenant (which sees all peoples as equals) can be broken by racism, by nationalism, or by class interests. There is no remedy for such destructive drives except constant education. "The anti-religious alarm can free people from the tutelage of the church, but it can generate a sense of being orphaned which puts them at risk of new tutelages like those offered by the Führer."[9] The program of happiness that civilization offers is not realizable, but we cannot abandon our efforts for its realization.[10]

This anti-barbarian and sacrificial banner of civilization has always found a strong support in Christianity, but it is also an ambivalent one, like the notion of civilization itself. It is easy to demonstrate the historical ambivalence of "mission as bringing civilization." It cannot suspend its collaboration in the common civilizing task of the "reduction of aggession," and, at the same time, it cannot fulfill this task without being in dialogical structures, stripped of all hierarchical power and without any social and theological clout. The inculturation which makes a contribution to the construction of the identity of human communities can offer a substantial contribution to the struggle against collective regression.

MODERNITY

Modernity is a civilization and as such a "common fund" maintained by the secular contributions of many peoples. Many social groups are served by this "common fund," and, usually, those who borrow from it pay high interest rates and those who contribute to it pay high prices. Fewer and fewer people are able to steer clear of modernity's influence. But although it has conquered a large part of humanity, it does not have citizens of specific land and history. In order to be a universal civilization, it distinguishes itself from any one culture.

Modernity, with its all-encompassing and homogenizing aspects, has made great conquests, but at the same time it represents a radical threat to the identity of many peoples and their cultures. The perspective of emergence of a "global village" does not announce the substitution of cultural plurality for one civilization with small regional or folkloric variations. "Humanity is forever involved in two conflicting currents," notes Levi-Strauss in *Race and History*, "the one tending towards unification, and the other towards the maintenance or restoration of diversity."[11] Modernity generates cultural elements, structures, values and behaviors, all of which influence local cultures and press upon them historic changes, without making modernity itself *their own* culture or basis of their identity.

POP CULTURE

"Pop culture" (or global "hyperculture") is a product of modernity. In contrast to *popular* cultures whose subjects are particular peoples, pop culture deprives a people of its subjectivity. Pop culture stimulates passive consumerism, and does not bestow identity on peoples or social groups. By means of its homogenizing force, pop culture makes the shape of all civilizations the same, without itself being—because of its passive consumerism—a real civilization. Pop culture is not really a culture, but a commodity. As a purveyor of commodities, pop culture on the one hand stimulates desire, constantly trying to seduce and alienate. On the other hand, people can adapt this pop culture and its commodities to their own cultural universe and give it meanings and functions compatible with their own particular culture. Neither television as such, nor the tractor—although they can represent great challenges—will necessarily destroy traditional culture.

CULTURE AS A HUMAN ECOSYSTEM

In the final analysis, what is culture? The Conclusions of the Puebla Conference (# 386), following the definition of *Gaudium et Spes*, presents a concept of "culture" which can serve as a point of departure for the construction of a paradigm for inculturation:

> The term "culture" means the specific way in which human beings belonging to a given people cultivate their relationship with nature, with each other, and with God in order to arrive at "an authentic and full humanity." It is the

shared lifestyle that characterizes different peoples around the earth, and so we can speak about "a plurality of cultures" (GS 53; EN 20).[12]

This notion of culture designates the specific difference of each group or people—i.e., their identity. All that is human is culturally determined:

- material construction and the transformation of nature, so that the world will be made more habitable and land more arable (the adaptive system);
- social conventions, the way of doing politics, the proper structures for the exercise of power, defense against enemies and structures of parenthood (the associative system);
- worldviews, expressed in religion, philosophy and ideology, and in education and art (the interpretive system).

Various peoples and social groups construct, by means of their cultural activities, a second-level environment, a *human ecosystem*.

Culture is both an inheritance and a collective task. In such a historical ecosystem, the subsystems (the adaptive, associative and interpretive systems) and the different levels of human reality (the real, the symbolic, the cognitive, the imaginative and the affective) are all interrelated and interdependent, each with the others. Cultural changes and the very intention of inculturation are slow processes which interact within a complex network of systems and levels, seen as normative for the individual and collective socialization of various protagonists and social groups.

Culture as historical construction of life means a permanent resistance against individual brute force, and against suffering and death. Each group or people establishes a consensus about "who takes part in this struggle" for life, and a consensus as well about a particular "quality of life." Above all, culture as the specific "space" of all that is human is the "space" of identity and difference, the "space" in which particular ways of living life are chosen.

As "spaces" of identity and life, of transformation (through technology) and creativity (through art), of filial relationship with God and brotherly/sisterly relationship with fellow human beings and with nature, cultures are constructed on the axes of *gratitude* (play, leisure, festivity), of *production* (work, cause-and-effect, cost-and-benefits) and of *resistance* to the forces which threaten life (enemies, supernatural and natural forces, hunger). The first is the dimension of ritual and celebration, by which peoples commemorate the past, celebrate the present and anticipate the utopian hope of a "land without evils." The second is the dimension of human work. The third, the dimension of struggle and resistance, is nourished by the first and the second dimensions of culture. In any case, cultures are historical constructions of work and leisure, struggle and contemplation. The broken arrow does not impede the dance, nor does it block out remembrance. The exuberance of play, of gratitude and of remembering can be as important as a battle that is won or lost. Gratitude which breaks the vicious circle of cause-and-effect or cost-and-benefit represents a radical critique of the domination of human relations by relationships determined by profit. But culture properly speaking is also the domain of production. The *production, gratitude and resistance* of cultures play a major role in the process of evangelization.

OPTIONS IN THE RELATIONSHIP OF GOSPEL AND CULTURE

Gospel and culture are complementary aspects of living life, and yet each is distinct from the other. For various reasons, the false understanding of the relationship between gospel and culture can make culture seem incomprehensible, irreconcilable or irrelevant to the gospel. Whether we speak of distance or even a split between gospel and culture, or whether we speak of identification of one with the other, such ways of speaking threaten the specific goals and contributions of each. The relationship between gospel and culture might be thought of in terms of four alternatives: separation, identification, acculturation, and inculturation.

SEPARATION

Zeal for the ontological purity of the gospel can create a separation between a seemingly model culture at the beginning of the process of evangelization and the concrete cultures of today. This separation enters into conflict with the very mystery of the Incarnation. To maintain the distance between a "pure gospel" and the "historical situation of peoples," the church would encourage the "split between the gospel and culture" (EN 20) which *Evangelii Nuntiandi* laments. An ontologically perfect gospel, but socio-culturally and historically remote from people, would become an irrelevant gospel and dead letter.

The gospel proclaimed out of a seemingly model culture, historically, was often a gospel tainted with a hegemonic culture belonging to a group that imposed *its* culture on the church as *the* culture of the gospel. Although admitting a seemingly "model culture," it never actually represented the gospel in its original form, but only one cultural tradition. The inevitable historical conditionedness of any gospel expression does not permit access to a kind of pre-cultural gospel. A pre-cultural gospel would necessarily eliminate the mystery of the Incarnation. The gospel is always known from the perspective of its first translations and inculturations. In contrast with a static, monocultural inculturation, the origins of Christianity represent a multicultural inculturation in every time and situation, the best possible approximation among peoples and social groups to the mystery of God. The multiplicity and diversity of "cultural illuminations" of the gospel permits a permanent purification of the evangelizing process and strengthens fidelity to the *missio Dei*. "Gospel energy" requires many cultural lamps in order to fulfill its mission to be the light of the world.

The gospel and, consequently, an evangelization, that would define themselves abstractly as "life projects," without identifying their preference for the poor, could be coopted by the dominant class and *its* "life project." This would transform the gospel into an ideology. Cultures are not exempt from divisions and stratifications of social classes. In fact, such ideologization or identification of the gospel with the interests of the dominant class actually took place, for example, in the defense of slavery as a work of divine providence for the salvation of Black people. Those who owned slaves certainly benefited materially from this so-called spiritual kind of reasoning. Moreover, a preferential option *only* for the poor or *only* for indigenous peoples will not suffice. Both options need to be linked together to form one option which considers the social sphere as an integral part of the culture of social groups.

IDENTIFICATION

The opposite of the separation between gospel and culture, a notion based on identification of the gospel with a particular model culture, is the identification of the gospel with *all* cultures. The separation between gospel and cultures lamented by *Evangelii Nuntiandi* was caused by the identification of the gospel with the culture of a particular epoch and/or social class. The gospel became, in this case, a type of civilization of a privileged class, educated in Latin and Greek philosophy. The identification of two objects results in one of them losing its particularity or identity. In this identification the gospel would become culture and would lose the specificity of its mission. With this the "order of grace" would be exchanged for the "order of nature."

An electric light bulb is lit not only by electric power, but also by the existence of "tension" and "resistance" between two poles. In the evangelizing process there occurs a mutual exchange of energies between gospel and culture. The exchange of energies needs the difference and proximity of both poles, in this case, the specific difference of the gospel over against culture, and, at the same time, the close connection between them both. With the identification of both poles, one disappears and the light is snuffed out. In the identification of gospel with cultures, there would be no gospel to give light to the world. The gospel would become culture. In the identification of the missionary with the "other" or with the neighbor, there would be no more "others" or neighbors. The missionary would lose his or her identity *as* missionary. The love of neighbor and solidarity with the other would turn into mere love of oneself. The introduction of the gospel into cultures calls for a presence of solidarity and love, but a presence that is also objective and critical. With such presence and with such a radical stance, missionaries will not lose their identity; on the contrary, they will encounter their integrity and identity as they encounter themselves renewed in the transparency and integrity of the *missio Dei*, God's "project" that has the power to transfigure their lives.

Only those are evangelizers who, in the process of insertion and inculturation, come close to the poor and indigenous peoples and are in solidarity with them, yet still maintain their *own* otherness and identity. The brotherhood and sisterhood in Christ strengthens the identity and otherness of peoples—whether social groups or individuals; at the same time however, it seeks to destroy the social inequity which corrodes that relationship. We can become brothers and sisters and remain "other." But we cannot become brothers and sisters if we continue being oppressors of the oppressed. Socio-political inequality will destroy any hopes raised by our community. Cultural diversity, however, will only enrich it.

Identification of gospel and the world's cultures can develop from either direction: identification with the culture of those being evangelized, or identification of those evangelized with the culture of the evangelizers. In the course of history, the identification was made in terms of a privileged proximity to European culture. In his diary entry of October 11, 1492, Christopher Columbus says of the original inhabitants of the Americas that "they should be good servants and of quick intelligence, since I see that they very soon say all that is said to them, and I believe that they would easily be made Christians."[13] For a long time there prevailed in evangelization the ideal of identifying with the missionaries, and there prevailed as well the idea of "imitation" rather than authentic discipleship.

In the relation between gospel and cultures it is helpful to return to the categories of the Council of Chalcedon (451), which defined the relation between the divine nature and human nature of the incarnate *Logos* as unconfused, immutable, undivided and inseparable (DS 302). The Puebla Conference speaks of a link between gospel and cultures and warns against their identification:

> When the church, the People of God, announces the Gospel and peoples accept it in faith, it becomes incarnate among them and assumes their cultures. This gives rise, not to an identification between the two, but to a close bond between them.[14]

ACCULTURATION

Rejecting both the separation and the identification of gospel and culture, one can conceive of the relation between both in a kind of middle path. This would be the proposal of aculturation between gospel and culture. Acculturation, in fact, does happen. However, in a society in which social relations are lopsided, the process of acculturation is always lopsided as well, and this is especially incompatible with the notion of the brotherhood/sisterhood that is proper to the gospel, and with the imperatives involved in the following of Jesus.

From the perspective of the incarnation and the following of Jesus, acculturation would be the "assumption" of a middle path. The culture of the "other," however, cannot be assumed in any half-way measures, with the representative of the dominant culture making a few concessions regarding folklore. Indigenous rites and paraphernalia integrated into Roman liturgies are only signs of a vertical acculturation, and not of an inculturated evangelization.

INCULTURATION

The analogy between incarnation and Christian presence in the socio-cultural and historical context of peoples—*Lumen Gentium* (8) speaks of an "excellent analogy"—has called forth the emergence in theological and pastoral reflection of the paradigm of inculturation.[15] Incarnation seeks a radical and critical relationship between gospel and culture. This relationship is a presupposition for the communication of the Good News of the love of God in the world's many different cultures. In inculturation are intertwined goal and method, the universality of salvation with the particularity of the here and now. The universal "will promote and express the unity of the human race to the degree that it preserves the particular features of the different cultures" (GS 54). The goal of inculturation is liberation and the way of liberation is inculturation.[16] The Second Vatican Council suggested the prioritization of values and goals, and admitted a "hierarchy of truths" (UR 11) and a "lawful diversity" (GS 92). The principle of ecumenical dialogue is also valid in inculturation: unity in what is necessary (in what is signified), freedom in things which do not pertain to the substance of the faith (particular ways of signifying), and charity in all things (see GS 92, UR 4 and 11).

By analogy, if we can say "to assume, without destroying," we can also say "inculturation without identification." Inculturation as socio-cultural solidarity cannot be confused with the identification of the evangelizer or the gospel with the "other" or with other cultures. By not identifying itself with any culture and inculturating itself in all cultures, the gospel and those who preach it respect otherness and preserve the identity of both the gospel message and the cultures in which the gospel is preached. Inculturation seeks a respectful relationship to cultural otherness, but one that is critical in the face of sin and in solidarity with those who suffer. Taking on a culture is to seek integral redemption:[17] *incarnatus est proper nostram salutem*. In inculturated evangelization the church demonstrates that it is not indifferent to what is different, but is consecrated to difference by the incarnation of the Word and through the animation of the Spirit.

RESPONSES OF TRADITION

The social misery in which the great majority of Latin Americans live and the diversity and complexity of Latin American cultures represent the great challenges of a New Evangelization. There is a split between the gospel transmitted in monocultural garb and the great diversity of Latin American cultures. The New Evangelization has been proposed to establish a point of contact between gospel and culture; it is an attempt to heal the wounds caused by the original Christianization of Latin America in an evangelization carried out in the context of the colonial system.

Vatican II makes a great effort to open a dialogue with the new reality presented by the modern world. The world recognizes the legitimacy of different cultures, religions and ideologies. It is a world that, theoretically at least, does not accept the hegemony of any human group over another. Vatican II recognizes as legitimate "the independence which culture claims for itself" (GS 56), and recovers the traditions of Christianity which permit otherness to be seen in a positive light. The conciliar texts remind the universal church of phrases from the early days of Christianity. All the authors that it cites, with the exception of Eusebius, are from the pre-Constantinian era: Justin Martyr (+ c. 165), Irenaeus of Lyons (+202), Clement of Alexandria (+ before 215), and Eusebius of Caesarea (+ 329), who in the defense of paganism, justified the pagan past of the emperor Constantine, to whom he was devoted.

ANIMA NATURALITER CHRISTIANA

In his treatise *De Testimonio Animae*, Tertullian develops a phrase of his *Apologeticum* (c. 17) affirming that the life of pagans demonstrates a common

Christian root for all of humanity. In the encyclical *Evangelii Praecones* of 1951, Pius XII takes up once more the paradigm of Tertullian: "human nature . . . has in itself something that is naturally Christian" (57). The church does not permit "that the Gospel on being introduced to any new land destroy or extinguish whatever its people possess that is naturally good, just or beautiful. For the Church . . . does not act like one who recklessly cuts down and uproots a thriving forest. . . ." (56). In view of the "natural goodness" of peoples, the missionary's task is not to "transplant European civilization and culture, and no other, to foreign soil . . . ."; rather, it is "to teach and form" people "so that they are ready to accept willingly and in a practical manner the principles of Christian life and morality; principles, I might add, that fit into any culture . . . ." (60).[18] Vatican II does not cite Tertullian's phrase "the soul is naturally Christian" explicitly, but the spirit of the Council—for example that of *Gaudium et Spes*—is profoundly permeated by this optimistic vision of the world. The thesis of Karl Rahner that each human person is a potential "anonymous Christian" is also inspired by Tertullian.

PREPARATIO EVANGELICA

The history and cultures of peoples represent, as Eusebius of Caesarea says, a preparation for the gospel. *Lumen Gentium* 16 takes Eusebius' idea up once again. Referring to non-Christians, it says that "whatever goodness or truth is found among them is looked upon by the Church as a preparation for the gospel." *Evangelii Nuntiandi* reprises the text of *Lumen Gentium* in 1975, acknowledging that there exist "vast groups of people" who practice non-Christian religions, and that these religions constitute a true "preparation for the Gospel" (53). Along the same line, but perhaps more restricted, *Ad Gentes* bases itself on Irenaeus and Clement of Alexandria to affirm that the "religious endeavors" of peoples "can sometimes serve as a guidance course toward the true God, or as a preparation for the gospel" (3).

SEMINA VERBI

In the same vein as the notion of "preparatio evangelica" is the phrase "semina Verbi" or "seeds of the Word." This Word, universally active, has already been present in cultures and religious traditions. "Gladly and reverently," says *Ad Gentes* 11 without mentioning the patristic source, Christians will discover "the seeds of the Word which lie hidden in them."

Evangelii Nuntiandi, in the admission that non-Christian religions "are all impregnated with innumerable 'seeds of the word'" (53), makes reference to the writings of Justin Martyr and Clement of Alexandria. At Vatican II, *Lumen Gentium* had previously said that through the work of the church, "whatever good is in the minds and hearts of women and men, whatever good lies latent in the religious practices and cultures of diverse peoples, is not only saved from destruction but also healed, ennobled, and perfected unto the glory of God, the confusion of the devil, and the happiness of humanity" (17).

Citing Irenaeus, *Gaudium et Spes* says in summary that "under the impulse of grace, men and women are disposed to acknowledge the Word of God. Before He became flesh in order to save all things and to sum them up in Himself, "He was in the world" already as "the true light that enlightens every human being" (Jn. 1:9-10) (GS 57). And Puebla says clearly that "the work of the Church is not a process of destruction; rather, it is a process of consolidating and fortifying those values, a contribution to the 'seeds of the Word' present in cultures . . . ." (401).[19]

INSERTION

In the reality of the non-Christian world, positively regarded as "preparation for the gospel" and empowered by the "seeds of the Word," the church desires to insert itself without any preconditions. Already before the coming of the "Incarnate Son," God "has spoken to the culture proper to different ages" (GS 58). Vatican II's decree *Ad Gentes* is very clear: "In order to be able to offer all of them the mystery of salvation and the life brought by God, the Church must become part of all these groups for the same motive which led Christ to bind Himself, in virtue of his Incarnation, to the definite social and cultural conditions of those human beings among whom He dwelt" (10; see also 22).

Gaudium et Spes sees as reality that which continues to exist as an imperative for the future. The church, "from the beginning of her history, . . . has learned to express the message of Christ with the help of the ideas and terminology of various peoples, and has tried to clarify it with the wisdom of the philosophers, too. Her purpose has been to adapt the gospel to the grasp of all as well as to the needs of the learned, insofar as such was appropriate. Indeed, this accommodated preaching of the revealed Word ought to remain the law of all evangelization" (44). Under the banner of *insertion*, many communities have been inspired to change, as much in their lifestyles as in their presence-in-solidarity with people who are socially oppressed and culturally marginalized.

ASSUMPTION

As *Gaudium et Spes* points out, Christian presence in the world is, following the example of Jesus, a respectful presence, universal and salvific: ". . . by His incarnation the Son of God has united Himself in some fashion with every human being. He worked with human hands, He thought with a human mind, acted by human choice, and loved with a human heart." Jesus, who took on human nature without that nature being overcome, "truly has been made one of us, like us in all things except sin" (22).

Lumen Gentium speaks of an "excellent analogy" between the mystery of the incarnate Word and the church's assumption of earthly reality (8). *Assumption* is the condition for the possibility of *redemption*. "The sainted Fathers of the Church firmly proclaim," *Ad Gentes* reminds us, "that what was not taken up by Christ was not healed" (3). Puebla's Final Document (# 400) explains this relation between incarnation and assumption for the context of Latin America. In fact, the word "to assume" could even be considered the document's key word.[20]

PERSPECTIVES: INCULTURATION AND ARTICULATION

The new directions of evangelization can be understood in terms of two poles: "inculturation" and "articulation." The first seeks the de-centering of the Christian message from European tutelage, and looks for the incarnation of the gospel within the variety of human cultural contexts; the second looks for the unity between human hopes and a Kingdom-oriented faith. It might seem difficult at times, however, to discover, above all in the large cities, the cultures of marginal groups, particularly since the sense of their own cultures has been destroyed. How do we encounter the culture of migrants, of those without land and without homes? Do those who live in the slums of large cities have history and culture?

One of the first tasks of evangelizers is to take a historical-cultural inventory of those with whom they work. Where have they come from? On what do they live? And how? Where do they sleep? How can they be mobilized? How do they spend their leisure time? What are their dreams? What kind of entertainment do they enjoy? What is the relationship between parents, children and neighbors? Whom do they call upon when they experience life's hardships? In whom do they confide? What are their reasons for living? Out of these questions emerge the profile of their "second level environment,"—their culture—which enables them to resist suffering and live with hope. From these questions emerge elements by which their lives can be situated in the context of the history of salvation; from them as well emerge signs that can be employed in the celebration of the mysteries of the faith and ways by which the good news can be announced and the bad news *de*nounced. The historical memory of each people and its cultural inventory are the *materia prima* of evangelization. The goal of inculturated evangelization is a balanced relationship between dialogue as the presupposition of the proclamation of the good news and the celebration of the mysteries. The practice of inculturation will have the effect of allowing there to emerge a new relationship between the particular church and the church universal, between the unity of the faith and the diversity of manifestations of that faith.

Evangelization that takes its starting point from culture does not mean a Christianity lived in isolation. The attention of the evangelizer to the particular and specific will not lose the vision of liberation on a wider scale. The liberation of the local depends on understanding and connecting with the larger political scene. Authentic local dialogue is conditioned by the balance between the local and the global.

Taking as a starting point the *integral* (all human efforts), *specific* (regional identity) and *global* (all human groups) aspects of culture, the evangelization of the Latin American peoples which takes culture as its point of departure must also be integral, specific and global. The art of this evangelization will consist in the construction of common meanings that depart from material conditions, signs and a supremely diversified imagination. Neither signs nor unified products of the imagination that are globally supervised will guarantee the unity of the faith. The unity of the faith and of the struggle for life can only be the result of the articulation of differing experiences, ideas and methods, and done without the hegemony of a group that is more numerous or more "authentic" than the rest. Cultural difference is the indicator of cultural identity. Evangelization looks for a "new world," renewed by the Holy Spirit, the "Father of the poor" and "giver of abundant gifts."[21] The Holy Spirit is the principal agent of mission (RM 21). A world filled with the polyphony of all languages, races and nations can turn back the cacophonous, postmodern confusion of Babel. The diversity of gifts from "one and the same Spirit" (1 Cor. 12:11) cries out for the diversification of ministries, services and signs. The Spirit cries, at the same time, for just social structures in which all can actively participate.

The construction and strength of unity, as much in the arena of political struggle as on the field of evangelization, always depends on the articulation of "human regions" which have a clearly defined identity. To evangelize a people means to collaborate in strengthening their identity and to believe in a specific future. Only social groups with established identities will be able to provide the "clearings" in which dialogue with the gospel is possible. To construct unity without insisting on identity, especially in the context of specific cultural differences, is to build a house on sand. The processes of assimilation, which are processes that erode cultural specificity, call for the forces of cultural specificity and incarnation/inculturation. Cultural changes are historical facts. Often, however, peoples and social groups lose control when such changes are imposed upon them. Changes that occur without people's consent always possess a traumatic aspect to them. The suffering and cultural traumas cause difficulties not only for the political orgainization of social groups, but also for the task of evangelization.

Neither the urgency of people living in misery nor the lack of personnel—both results of an authoritarian and patriarchal monoculture—justify wagering on universal formulas to communicate the good news on a grand scale. Those called to the "common priesthood of all the baptized," must be accompanied by new structures and practices of participation. To evangelize today, in Latin America, means to open spaces so that the poor, the cultural "others," can evangelize themselves and be evangelized from the point of departure of their cultures and histories. The gospel denounces all that has destroyed the identity of peoples; at the same time it acts as a force of corrosion upon the monotony of conformity, of goods, and of language. To follow the incarnate and crucified Word in solidarity with women and men is to experience the paschal mystery of God in the diversity of the Spirit. In the proximity with the poor in all processes of inculturated evangelization "we shall see face to face" (1 Cor 13:12) our crucified Lord.

NOTES

1. The Spanish word "proyecto"—translated here as "project"—is notoriously difficult to translate into English. The idea behind the word is something like "vision," "agenda," "task," and even "mission." It has been translated in various ways throughout this essay (Trans.).

2. See Documentos da CNBB (n. 45). *Diretrizes gerais da ação pastoral da Igreja no Brasil (1991-1994)*. São Paulo, Ed. Paulinas. 1991. See also the Conclusions of the Santo Domingo conference, #9, 26, 219, 235. In Alfred T. Hennelly, SJ, ed., *Santo Domingo and Beyond* (Maryknoll, NY: Orbis Books, 1993).

3. See Hennelly, ed., pp. 75-76; 138-39.

4. Freud treats the question of culture especially in *The Future of an Illusion* (1927) and in *Civilization and Its Discontents* (1930). Both are found in James Strachey, trans. and ed., *The Standard Edition of the Complete Works of Sigmund Freud*, Vol. XXI (1927-1931) (London: The Hogarth Press and The Institute of Psycho-Analysis, 1961). The quotation is from *The Future of an Illusion*, p. 6.

5. *Civilization and Its Discontents*, p. 89; *The Future of an Illusion*, pp. 5-6.

6. *Civilization and Its Discontents*, p. 85.

7. See *Ibid.*, p. 91.

8. See *Ibid.*, pp. 86-98.

9. Sergio Paulo Rouanet, *Mal-estar na modernidad* (São Paulo: Companhia das Letras, 1993), p. 117.

10. See *Civilization and Its Discontents*, p. 83.

11. Claude Levi-Strauss, *Race & History* (Paris: UNESCO, 1952), p. 49.

12. "Evangelization in Latin America's Future." Final Document of the Third General Conference of the Latin American Episcopate, Puebla de los Angeles, Mexico. In John Eagleson and Philip Sharper, eds., *Puebla and Beyond* (Maryknoll, NY: Orbis Books, 1979), p. 176.

13. Christopher Columbus, *The Journal of Christopher Columbus*, Cecil Jane, trans. (London: Anthony Blond, 1968), p. 24.

14. Puebla, Final Document, # 400. In Eagleson and Sharper, eds., p. 179.

15. Santo Domingo, "Message," # 30, 243. In Hennelly, ed., pp. 67 and 138-139.

16. *Ibid.* #243, p. 139.

17. Puebla, # 400. In Eagleson and Sharper, eds., p. 179.

18. Pius XII, *Evangelii Praecones*. In Claudia Carlen, ed., *The Papal Encyclicals 1939-1958* (Raleigh, NC: McGrath Publishing Company, A Consortium Book, 1981), pp. 189-202.

19. Puebla, Final Document. In Eagleson and Sharper, eds., p. 179.

20. *Ibid.* See also the following phrases in the document: "The Son of God assumes everything human and everything created, re-establishing communion between his Father and human beings" (# 188, p. 146); "The Spirit, who filled the whole earth, was also present in all that was good in pre-Columbian cultures" (# 201, p. 149); " 'what is not assumed is not redeemed' " (# 400, p. 179); "Evangelization will be a work of pastoral pedagogy in which the Catholicism of the common people is assumed, purified, completed, and made dynamic by the Gospel" (# 457, p. 187); "Once again the Church is faced with stark alternatives: what it does not assume in Christ is not redeemed, and it becomes a new idol replete with all the old malicious cunning" (#469, p. 188).

21. The references are to verses from the Sequence sung on the feast of Pentecost, "Veni, Sancte Spiritus:" "veni, Pater pauperum / veni, dator munerum."

Part II

DOCUMENTATION

13

Nairobi Statement on Worship and Culture

Nairobi, 1996

Lutheran World Federation*

S. Anita Stauffer first introduces the "Nairobi Statement," putting it in the context of several other Lutheran World Federation (LWF) consultations of worship and culture. The statement then follows, pointing out four dimensions of how Lutheran worship and local cultures need to interact. First, worship has a transcultural *dimension, because there are certain aspects of worship which will be present in every cultural context. Secondly, worship is* contextual *in that various elements of local cultures can be employed to root worship in particular contexts. Worship, thirdly, has a* counter-cultural *dimension since Christian values inevitably challenge local values that are shot through with human sinfulness. Finally, worship is* cross-cultural; *communities of different cultural backgrounds can learn from and be enriched by each other's cultural expressions, thus strengthening the* communio *of the entire church.*

Introduction by S. Anita Stauffer

How can worship—liturgy, preaching, hymns and other music, and the spatial environment for worship—be both Christian and local in the diversity of the world's cultures? How can the gospel take root in local cultures so that the people in those places can worship meaningfully and thereby themselves be more deeply rooted in the gospel? How can preaching make use of diverse local images and styles of communication? In what ways can the worship space of a church building make use of

---

* From *International Review of Mission*, LXXXV, 337 (1996). S. Anita Stauffer, a pastor of the Evangelical Lutheran Church in America, is study secretary for Worship and Congregational Life, Department for Theology and Studies, Lutheran World Federation, Geneva, Switzerland.

the local aesthetic system, put to the service of the gospel? How can both the music and the texts of hymns reflect the local context? All of these are questions of the contextualization of worship.

At the same time, how can the worship life of a local congregation witness to the gospel by rejecting or transforming those elements of the culture that are in opposition to it? How, for example, in the current North American culture of consumerism and entertainment, can congregations learn the many significant differences between passively being entertained and actively participating in corporate worship? Or how can African congregations make use of some indigenous musical instruments while avoiding or transforming the "pagan" understandings that have prevented generations of African Christians from using them? In what ways can local cultural elements be reinterpreted or transformed for use in Christian worship? All of these are questions of the counter-cultural in worship.

The questions of the contextual and the counter-cultural are all complex, indeed, more complex than they seem at first glance. Even more complicated is the matter of balance between the two in any given local place in the world.

In an attempt to explore such questions, in 1992 the worship office of the Lutheran World Federation's (LWF) Department for Theology and Studies began a long-term study of the relationships between Christian worship and the world's cultures. It is of necessity an interdisciplinary effort, for worship includes (as indicated above) not only liturgy and preaching, but also their musical and architectural/ artistic settings—and of course, matters of cultural anthropology are also inherently involved in any such study. In a way, the LWF worship and culture study has paralleled the WCC gospel and culture study, by focusing on congregational worship life (even though that topic cannot be considered without attention to the larger gospel/culture issues). And while the LWF study has concentrated on worship in Lutheran congregations around the world, it has from the beginning had strong ecumenical involvement, and has increasingly recognized the shared ecumenical core of word and sacrament. Thus, the study has also paralleled recent and current work in worship by the WCC Unit I: Unity and Renewal—Ecclesial Unity: Faith and Order Stream.[1]

The LWF established an ongoing international study team, comprised of about twenty-five scholars and church leaders from around the world, including three ecumenical participants (Anglican, Roman Catholic, and Methodist). Phase I involved two global consultations, the first (in Cartigny, Switzerland, October 1993) to explore the biblical and historical foundations of the topic, and the second (in Hong Kong, March 1994) to begin to explore some of the contemporary issues.[2] The first of these two consultations resulted in the Cartigny Statement on Worship and Culture: Biblical and Historical Foundations. That statement, along with the papers and reports from these two consultations, were published in 1994 as *Worship and Culture in Dialogue*.[3] This book served as the foundation of phase II of the study, which involved regional and subregional research around the world (using a wide variety of methodologies, as determined regionally). The reports of that research, in turn, provided the "grist" for phase III—when the study team gathered again (in Nairobi, Kenya, January 1996) to analyze and synthesize the reports, to consider in some detail both the contextualization of the eucharist and the ways in which the eucharist is inherently counter-cultural, and to plan for implementation in LWF member churches of study findings thus far. This implementation will comprise phase IV of the study. The reports and papers of the Nairobi consultation have appeared in 1996 in a new volume in the LWF Studies series, *Christian Worship: Unity in Cultural Diversity*. It is hoped that a further consultation of the study team can be held in 1998 to consider further elements of the topic.

However, even with all this effort, all these meetings, all these papers, only the surface has been skimmed. Raising consciousness takes time; making liturgical changes requires persistent but gentle pastoral and episcopal leadership. Further scholarship and training are required, and have been especially requested by churches in the developing world. It is hoped that the LWF Study on Worship and Culture will make a significant contribution to international ecumenical efforts in the area, but at the same time it is recognized that such efforts must continue over the long term. Indeed, both because of the nature of Christian worship as participatory (i.e., constantly involving new generations) and because cultures constantly evolve, efforts at contextualization can never end. At the same time, recognition of the meaning of the ecumenical core of Christian worship must ever deepen, that we may all be one, so that the world can know Christ (John 17).

The Nairobi Statement, which follows, is a summary document of the study conclusions at present. It follows logically and builds on the 1993 Cartigny Statement, which said:

> ... the Christian assembly for worship, with its music and its spatial environment, stands at the intersection of Christian faith and cultural patterns. Out of this complex interplay of Christianity and culture, three areas for consideration readily become apparent—the cultural, the countercultural, and the transcultural ... (3.2.).
>
> ... the task of relating worship and culture is ultimately concerned with finding the balance between relevance and authenticity, between particularity and universality, while avoiding eclecticism and/or syncretism (3.6.).
>
> An examination of the tradition, from the Biblical witness, the early Church, and the Lutheran Reformation, reveals the core of Christian worship to be Word, Baptism, and Eucharist. The pattern, or *ordo*, of entry into the community is teaching and baptismal bath. The pattern of the weekly gathering of the community on the Lord's Day is the celebration centered around the Word and eucharistic meal. These core elements are clearly evident in the historical witnesses of the Christian worship tradition. Further, it is evident that the purpose of this pattern of worship is to receive and faithfully to proclaim the gospel of Jesus Christ (3.7.).
>
> One helpful model, then, which is evident throughout the history of the Church, is found where the worshiping community is able to receive and use the important elements of the culture (and thus be localized in a particular context), while at the same time critically shaping these elements so that they may bear witness to the gospel of Christ who transcends and transforms all

cultures (and thus be rooted in the universal Christian tradition). "See, I am making all things new" (Revelation 21:5; NRSV) (3.8.).[4]

The Nairobi Statement further refines, in a brief summary way, some of the key intersections between Christian worship and the world's diverse local cultures, and suggests both methodologies and criteria for contextualization. Elaboration of the background and content of this statement appear in the Lutheran World Federation's new volume, *Christian Worship: Unity in Cultural Diversity.*

NOTES

1. See, for example, *So We Believe, So We Pray: Towards Koinonia in Worship* (Faith and Order Paper No. 171), edited by Thomas F. Best and Dagmar Heller. Geneva: World Council of Churches, 1995. Further background on the LWF study is contained in the present author's brief article, "Worship and Culture," pages 65-67 of that volume.
2. For an "interim" report and reflections up to this point, see this author's "Culture and Christian Worship in Intersection," in *IRM*, vol. LXXXIV, nos 332/333, January/April 1995, pp. 65-76.
3. Geneva: Lutheran World Federation, 1994; hence, *WCD*. Complete translations in Spanish and French, and a partial translation in German, also exist. For a recent review of this volume, see *IRM* vol. LXXXIV, no. 334, July 1995, pp. 317-19.
4. *WCD*, pp. 132-34.

The Statement

CONTEMPORARY CHALLENGES AND OPPORTUNITIES

This statement is from the third international consultation of the Lutheran World Federation's study team on worship and culture, held in Nairobi, Kenya, in January 1996. The members of the study team represent five continents of the world and have worked together with enthusiasm for three years thus far. The initial consultation, in October 1993 in Cartigny, Switzerland, focused on the biblical and historical foundations of the relationship between Christian worship and culture, and resulted in the "Cartigny Statement on Worship and Culture: Biblical and Historical Foundations." (This Nairobi Statement builds upon the Cartigny Statement; in no sense does it replace it.)

The second consultation, in March 1994 in Hong Kong, explored contemporary issues and questions of the relationships between the world's cultures and Christian liturgy, church music, and church architecture and art. The papers of the first two consultations were published as *Worship and Culture in Dialogue.*[1] In 1994-1995, the study team conducted regional research, and prepared reports on that research. Phase IV of the study commenced in Nairobi and will continue with seminars and other means to implement the learnings of the study, as LWF member churches decide is helpful. The study team considers this project to be essential to the renewal and mission of the church around the world.[2]

1. INTRODUCTION

1.1. Worship is the heart and pulse of the Christian Church. In worship we celebrate together God's gracious gifts of creation and salvation, and are strengthened to live in response to God's grace. Worship always involves actions, not merely words. To consider worship is to consider music, art, and architecture, as well as liturgy and preaching.

1.2. The reality that Christian worship is always celebrated in a given local cultural setting draws our attention to the dynamics between worship and the world's many local cultures.

1.3. Christian worship relates dynamically to culture in at least four ways. First, it is *transcultural,* the same substance for everyone everywhere, beyond culture. Second, it is *contextual,* varying according to the local situation (both nature and culture). Third, it is *counter-cultural,* challenging what is contrary to the Gospel in a given culture. Fourth, it is *cross-cultural,* making possible sharing between different local cultures. In all four dynamics, there are helpful principles which can be identified.

2. WORSHIP AS TRANSCULTURAL

2.1. The resurrected Christ whom we worship, and through whom by the power of the Holy Spirit we know the grace of the Triune God, transcends and indeed is beyond all cultures. In the mystery of his resurrection is the source of the transcultural nature of Christian worship. Baptism and Eucharist, the sacraments of Christ's death and resurrection, were given by God for all the world. There is one Bible, translated into many tongues, and biblical preaching of Christ's death and resurrection has been sent into all the world. The fundamental shape of the principal Sunday act of Christian worship, the Eucharist or Holy Communion, is shared across cultures: the people gather, the Word of God is proclaimed, the people intercede for the needs of the Church and the world, the eucharistic meal is shared, and the people are sent out into the world for mission. The great narratives of Christ's birth, death, resurrection, and sending of the Spirit, and our Baptism into him, provide the central meanings of the transcultural times of the church's year: especially Lent/Easter/Pentecost, and, to a lesser extent, Advent/Christmas/Epiphany. The ways in which the shapes of the Sunday Eucharist and the church year are expressed vary by culture, but their meanings and fundamental structure are shared around the globe. There is one Lord, one faith, one Baptism, one Eucharist.

2.2. Several specific elements of Christian liturgy are also transcultural, for example, readings from the Bible (although of course the translations vary), the ecumenical creeds and the Our Father, and Baptism in water in the Triune Name.

2.3. The use of this shared core liturgical structure and these shared liturgical elements in local congregational worship—as well as the shared act of people assembling together, and the shared provision of diverse leadership in that assembly (although the space for the assembly and the manner of the leadership vary)—are expressions of Christian unity across time, space, culture, and confession. The recovery in each congregation of the clear centrality of these transcultural and ecumenical elements renews the sense of this Christian unity and gives all churches a solid basis for authentic contextualization.

3. WORSHIP AS CONTEXTUAL

3.1. Jesus whom we worship was born into a specific culture of the world. In the mystery of his incarnation are the model and the mandate for the contextualization of Christian worship. God can be and is encountered in the local cultures of our world. A given culture's values and patterns, insofar as they are consonant with the values of the Gospel, can be used to express the meaning and purpose of Christian worship. Contextualization is a necessary task for the Church's mission in the world, so that the Gospel can be ever more deeply rooted in diverse local cultures.

3.2. Among the various methods of contextualization, that of dynamic equivalence is particularly useful. It involves re-expressing components of Christian worship with something from a local culture that has an equal meaning, value, and function. Dynamic equivalence goes far beyond mere translation; it involves understanding the fundamental meanings both of elements of worship and of the local culture, and enabling the meanings and actions of worship to be "encoded" and re-expressed in the language of local culture.

3.3. In applying the method of dynamic equivalence, the following procedure may be followed. First, the liturgical *ordo* (basic shape) should be examined with regard to its theology, history, basic elements, and cultural backgrounds. Second, those elements of the *ordo* that can be subjected to dynamic equivalence without prejudice to their meaning should be determined. Third, those components of culture that are able to re-express the Gospel and the liturgical *ordo* in an adequate manner should be studied. Fourth, the spiritual and pastoral benefits our people will derive from the changes should be considered.

3.4. Local churches might also consider the method of creative assimilation. This consists of adding pertinent components of local culture to the liturgical *ordo* in order to enrich its original core. The baptismal *ordo* of "washing with water and the Word," for example, was gradually elaborated by the assimilation of such cultural practices as the giving of white vestments and lighted candles to the neophytes of ancient mystery religions.[3] Unlike dynamic equivalence, creative assimilation enriches the liturgical *ordo*—not by culturally re-expressing its elements, but by adding to it new elements from local culture.

3.5. In contextualization the fundamental values and meanings of both Christianity and of local cultures must be respected.

3.6. An important criterion for dynamic equivalence and creative assimilation is that sound or accepted liturgical traditions are preserved in order to keep unity with the universal Church's tradition of worship, while progress inspired by pastoral needs is encouraged. On the side of culture, it is understood that not everything can be integrated with Christian worship, but only those elements that are connatural to (that is, of the same nature as) the liturgical *ordo*. Elements borrowed from local culture should always undergo critique and purification, which can be achieved through the use of biblical typology.

4. WORSHIP AS COUNTER-CULTURAL

4.1. Jesus Christ came to transform all people and all cultures, and calls us not to conform to the world, but to be transformed with it (Romans 12:2). In the mystery of his passage from death to eternal life is the model for transformation, and thus for the counter-cultural nature of Christian worship. Some components of every culture in the world are sinful, dehumanizing, and contradictory to the values of the Gospel. From the perspective of the Gospel, they need critique and transformation. Contextualization of Christian faith and worship necessarily involves challenging of all types of oppression and social injustice wherever they exist in earthly cultures.

4.2. It also involves the transformation of cultural patterns that idolize the self or the local group at the expense of a wider humanity, or that give central place to the acquisition of wealth at the expense of the care of the earth and its poor. The tools of the counter-cultural in Christian worship may also include the deliberate maintenance or recovery of patterns of action that differ intentionally from prevailing cultural models. These patterns may arise from a recovered sense of Christian history, or from the wisdom of other cultures.

5. WORSHIP AS CROSS-CULTURAL

5.1. Jesus came to be the Savior of all people. He welcomes the treasures of earthly cultures into the city of God. By virtue of Baptism, there is one Church; and one means of living in faithful response to Baptism is to manifest ever more deeply the unity of the Church. The sharing of hymns and art and other elements of worship across cultural barriers helps enrich the whole church and strengthen the sense of the *communio* of the Church. This sharing can be ecumenical as well as cross-cultural, as a witness to the unity of the Church and the oneness of Baptism. Cross-cultural sharing is possible for every church, but is especially needed in multicultural congregations and member churches.

5.2. Care should be taken that the music, art, architecture, gestures and postures, and other elements of different cultures are understood and respected when they are used by churches elsewhere in the world. The criteria for contextualization (above, sections 3.5 and 3.6) should be observed.

6. CHALLENGE TO THE CHURCHES

6.1. We call on all member churches of the Lutheran World Federation to undertake more efforts related to the transcultural, contextual, counter-cultural, and cross-cultural nature of Christian worship. We call on all member churches to recover the centrality of Baptism, Scripture with preaching, and the every-Sunday celebration of the Lord's Supper—the principal transcultural elements of Christian worship and the signs of Christian unity—as the strong center of all congregational life and mission, and as the authentic basis for contextualization. We call on all churches to give serious attention to exploring the local or contextual elements of liturgy, language, posture and gesture, hymnody and other music and musical instruments, and art and architecture for Christian worship—so that their worship may be more truly rooted in the local culture. We call those churches now carrying out missionary efforts to encourage such contextual awareness among themselves and also among the partners and recipients of their ministries. We call on all member churches to give serious attention to the transcultural nature of worship and possibilities for cross-cultural sharing. And we call on all churches to consider the training and ordination of ministers of Word and Sacrament, because each local community has the right to receive weekly the means of grace.

6.2. We call on the Lutheran World Federation to make an intentional and substantial effort to provide scholarships for persons from the developing world to study worship, church music, and church architecture, toward the eventual goal that enhanced theological training in their churches can be led by local teachers.

6.3. Further, we call on the Lutheran World Federation to continue its efforts related to worship and culture into the next millennium. The tasks are not quickly accomplished; the work calls for ongoing depth-level research and pastoral encouragement. The Worship and Culture Study, begun in 1992 and continuing in and past the 1997 LWF Assembly, is a significant and important beginning, but the task calls for unending efforts. Giving priority to this task is essential for evangelization of the world.

Lutheran World Federation, 1996

NOTES

1. Geneva Lutheran World Federation, 1994. Also published are complete translations in French and Spanish, and a partial translation in German. The Nairobi papers will be published in a second volume in 1996.

2. Parallel to the LWF Worship and Culture Study has been work by the WCC Commission on Faith and Order [now known as WCC Unit 1, Unity and Renewal—Ecclesial Unity: Faith and Order Stream], on the relationship between worship and church unity. A part of that work has necessarily examined contextual questions, as well as questions of the essential shape or *ordo* of Christian worship. Work of the two projects has been mutually informative. See WCC Faith and Order's "Ditchingham Report," reprinted in Thomas F. Best and Dagmar Heller, eds., *So We Believe, So We Pray: Towards Koinonia in Worship*, Faith and Order Paper No. 171 (Geneva: WCC, 1995); and "Concerning Celebrations of the Eucharist in Ecumenical Contexts: A Proposal from a Group Meeting at Bossey," in *Ecumenical Review*, vol. 47, no. 3, July 1995, pp. 387-91.

3. *Worship and Culture in Dialogue*, pp. 39-56.

14

On Intercultural Hermeneutics

Jerusalem, 5-12 December 1995

World Council of Churches*

The following is a statement prepared by a group of theologians on intercultural hermeneutics and communication. The group met three times as part of the World Council of Churches' study process on gospel and cultures. Recognizing both the difficulty and the necessity of communicating the gospel across cultures, the document proposes two notions—"contextuality" and "catholicity"—as particularly helpful in this regard. When faith is contextual, "there is a recognition that the gospel speaks to Christians in their language, connects with their symbols, addresses their needs and awakens their creative energies." Such contextuality, however, "must enter into a process of giving and receiving with the church as a whole, both around the world and through history." Thus the notion of catholicity *is of equal importance to that of contextuality. Both notions are sustained by the theological and spiritual conviction that any intercultural communication occurs "under the power of the Holy Spirit," and by the development of skills and capacities of patient listening and frank critique. "The search for integrated Christian lives and communities must be carried out with diligence and vigilance, in openness to the Holy Spirit and in readiness to be corrected by the wider Christian community."*

Christians cannot think about the gospel apart from its engagement with culture, for the gospel directly engages the lived experience of those whom it addresses. It speaks a word of power and hope to the broken and oppressed, the diseased and the poor. It brings life within the context of the lives of its hearers. This was Jesus' message in his inaugural sermon: that the Spirit of the Lord had anointed him to bring good news to the poor, to proclaim release to the captives, recovery of sight to the blind and freedom to the oppressed (Luke 4:18).

---

* Taken from *International Review of Mission*, LXXXV, 337 (1996).

The account of the miracle of hearing at Pentecost—which mentions three times that the listeners heard the message "in their own languages" (Acts 2:6,8,11)—illustrates how the gospel engages each human culture by coming to it in familiar language, in terms that connect with the everyday life, memory and conceptual world of that particular people. In today's rapidly changing world, however, a variety of factors complicate the issue of communicating the gospel in different cultural situations:

- The gospel is being witnessed to in many more cultures than ever before.
- These many cultures are coming into closer contact with one another. Multicultural societies are emerging on an unprecedented scale, heightening questions of cultural identity and creating conflicts among cultures.
- Many people whose cultural identity had not previously been challenged find themselves in a minority when they become migrants or refugees. Others find their culture suppressed when their country is occupied by a stronger military power.
- Fierce religio-ethnic struggles create narrow ethnocentrisms, often leading to hatred and violence. In many places cultures are maintained and legitimated along ethnic lines. We witness also the fact that class, race, gender and other interests shape and reshape cultures.
- Cultures that had been brutally suppressed, sometimes even in the name of the gospel, are rediscovering their voice and renewing their resistance against their oppressors.
- Many cultures struggle to maintain their traditional way of life against encroaching secularization and corrosive globalization.

On top of the narrow nationalisms and xenophobia of our day, the fundamentalisms of various kinds and the relentless advance of "modernization," the shadow of human-created threats to the survival of the earth fosters cultural ferment and turmoil. Communities do not share a common world or a common way of communicating with one another. This creates uncertainty, fear, avoidance of encounter and often conflict and violence. Intercultural encounter is an opportunity for revealing the hidden treasures of the gospel, but it has always been a challenge, and never more than in the present. Communication within communities is difficult enough. What can we learn about how to communicate the gospel across cultural boundaries?

GOSPEL, CULTURE AND THEIR ENCOUNTER

In order to address this question we should clarify our use of several terms that will arise often in the discussion. The first is "gospel." This term is sometimes used to indicate apostolic faith as a whole, sometimes to indicate the basic Christian proclamation (*kerygma*), sometimes to accent the significance of the Christian message as *good* news. We will emphasize primarily the kerygmatic understanding of "gospel," but in a way which also acknowledges the importance of its being received as *good news* and its place within the larger complex of apostolic faith as a whole.

At the simplest level, the Christian understanding speaks of the gospel as the story of God's self-giving and transforming love, especially the life, death and resurrection of Jesus Christ, witnessed by the apostles and proclaimed in the New Testament as the revelation of God's saving purpose for the world. Over the centuries, the church has confessed that this central gospel story of Jesus is the decisive point within a larger story which spans the whole Bible and encompasses all of creation and history. It identifies this story as the source of its own identity.

The New Testament portrays the gospel as a particular story, enacted by God in history through Jesus Christ, the incarnate Son of God, in the power of the Holy Spirit. Already in the New Testament, this story is told in many different ways, for the gospel is not good news unless it engages the culture of its hearers in a way which takes seriously that culture's identity and integrity.

The first four books of the apostolic canon of the New Testament contain four different versions of the story. Their titles imply that there is *one* gospel, related *according to* four different writers (see Luke 1:1-4). Elsewhere in the New Testament the same story is remembered and expanded on in sermons, creeds, teaching, hymns and poetry. In church history, the story continued to be told in diverse ways using fresh concepts, vocabulary and images to speak to new people.

Whenever the Scriptures are translated into a new language, the gospel assumes a new cultural form. Even so, the church believes that what is being remembered, interpreted and lived in these many different ways is still the same story, the same gospel. But discerning this "sameness" is difficult, for there is no "pure" gospel that can be understood apart from the various forms in which it is embodied in culture and language.

Culture is a complex reality, comprising vast interlocking symbol systems and a wide variety of practices, structures and systems of power relationships. Only within the context of these symbols, practices and relationships can the gospel be understood, for culture is not merely *addressed by* the gospel—it is the instrument by which the gospel makes its address.

The church confesses that the gospel is no ordinary story, but one which discloses a whole new understanding of the triune God, of Christians themselves and of the world. When the gospel story genuinely engages the context of the lived experience of people—addressing them in cultural forms accessible to them—it brings about transformation. To recognize the truth of the gospel and to trust and obey the God revealed in it is to discern God's presence and activity in powerful ways that can transform all of life. Material goods may be shared, oppressive structures overturned, power found in weakness, sins forgiven and wrongs set right (cf. Acts 4:32).

The gospel story is only one of the stories that shape the identity of Christians and teach us how to live in the world. These many stories convey the society and culture which form us and the history that shapes our memory. While culture shares in the brokenness of human life, it also reflects the creative activity of the Holy Spirit. The inherent worth of every culture must be affirmed; and compassion and justice require giving particular value and respect to cultures which are under threat due to oppression and injustice. Even before the gospel is heard in a culture, the

Spirit of God is at work in its stories, seeking opportunities through them to draw all things toward the reality of God's power and presence revealed in the gospel. In addressing a culture, the gospel engages its stories, illuminating some more deeply, reinterpreting others, challenging or rejecting still others, always deepening the meaning and significance of the culture in its light. The converse is also true. Although some cultural forms may hinder the gospel, stories from diverse cultural settings also help to convey the meaning of the gospel and to illumine its truth and depth more completely.

RESPONDING TO THE CHALLENGE OF DIVERSITY

This complex and multi-layered interaction between the gospel and culture— between the story of the gospel and the many other stories of the human family— produces a wide range of diversities as the gospel moves across different cultural landscapes. Sometimes the transformations effected by the gospel and the forms in which it is expressed seem so varied that Christians wonder if they in fact share the same central story. Already in the New Testament we find the early church having difficulty keeping up with the Spirit as the gospel crosses cultural boundaries and elicits new cultural forms of appropriation (Acts 10, 15).

It is not always easy to tell when diversity is healthy and when it is not. The transformations brought about by the gospel in the church are always in process, never complete; and some diversities arise from resistance to the gospel or failure to move with the leading of God's Spirit. Several basic and inter-related questions are thus raised for the unity and mission of the church: How can we recognize that we share the same story when it can be *told* in so many different ways? How can we recognize that we share the same story when it can be *appropriated* in so many different ways? How can we distinguish between *authentic* and *inauthentic* ways of telling and living out the gospel?

As the gospel is announced and lived out in more diverse languages and contexts, these questions become more and more difficult to answer. This is especially so in a time like our own, when the centres of spiritual vitality in the whole church are shifting to new places. Some Christians in older centres of power, especially in the North, find it unsettling when people in other contexts—in the South and among minorities and other excluded groups—insist on their right to speak and respond to the Christian story in ways integral to their own contexts and different from those dictated by historically dominant cultures and churches.

These Christians have found that when the Christian story was told to them by dominant cultures, the effect has often been a *suppression* rather than a *transformation* and *renewal* of their own stories, for when churches try to announce the transforming power of the gospel without being transformed by it themselves, oppression results. In such contexts the gospel must also be heard as a word of judgment which demands that justice be done.

The solution to the churches' difficulties with recognizing in each other their common faith therefore cannot be arbitrarily restricting the ways of telling and living out the gospel. Indeed, our response to diversity must begin by recognizing it not as a problem but as a gift for the church. These diversities are a stimulus and aid disclosing more deeply the inexhaustible mystery and power of the gospel. As the church explores them, it discerns the richness of the gospel more profoundly and learns to respond more fully to its implications for all of life. They may also help specific churches to discover their own need for further transformation and how their own responses to the gospel have suppressed some of its transforming elements.

But these diversities must also be welcomed as gifts to the church because the church *needs* diversity. We need each other especially when we are different from each other. The Apostle Paul compares the differentiation that is critical to the proper functioning of the human body to that within the church. Diversity within and among local churches protects them from their blind spots, broadens their vision and deepens their awareness of God's reconciling work throughout the cosmos. When churches from different cultures encounter each other in real communion, the resulting experience of the fullness of Christ transcends the experience of any church by itself; and the mutual assistance and shared mission they render offer a sign of God's reconciling purpose for all humanity in a world where the powerful often suppress diversity by destroying the culture of the weaker.

One way of responding to this diversity is through an *interconfessional* analysis of Christian differences: how do differing Christian confessions or traditions reflect the same or compatible Christian understandings? Here we propose another approach: an *intercultural* analysis of Christian differences: how can differences in cultural expression of Christian faith be understood and interpreted?

CONTEXTUALITY AND CATHOLICITY

In attempting theologically to interpret the diversity we have been describing, we have found the terms "contextuality" and "catholicity" particularly helpful.

The *contextuality* of the church's faith is reflected in the diverse ways in which the gospel story is told and lived out in various contexts. It appears whenever the gospel works like salt and leaven, not overwhelming a context, but permeating and enlivening it in distinctive ways. When the church's faith is genuinely contextual, the shame and stigma imposed on oppressed people begins to be lifted. They find a new dignity as they see not only their own lives but also their culture in God's redeeming light. When faith is contextual, there is a recognition that the gospel speaks to Christians in their language, connects with their symbols, addresses their needs and awakens their creative energies.

But this contextuality must enter into a process of giving and receiving with the church as a whole, both around the world and throughout history, so that the fullness of Christ's life comes to more complete expression and the whole church is drawn towards its divinely appointed goal. The *catholicity* of the church (from the Greek *kata holon*, "according to the whole") is "the quality by which the church expresses the fullness, the integrity, and the totality of life in Christ" ("The Holy Spirit and the Catholicity of the Church," WCC Fourth Assembly, Uppsala, 1968). It grows by drawing on a common ecclesial experience and by a lifestyle of collegiality and conciliarity among churches, a companionship characterized by mutual learning from and accountability to the same gospel. Catholicity is a gift the church has received; even more importantly, it is an eschatological work of the Spirit for which the church continually hopes, prays and works.

At the root of genuine catholicity is the participation of the local in the global and of the global in the local. Catholicity is not the destruction or overwhelming of the local; it is the local in communion. When the gospel shared by all Christians plays a central role in the life of the local Christian community, the local reality is part of the global reality of the gospel. Similarly, when the local fellowship understands that gospel within the context of the whole Bible and Christian tradition, it draws on the rich fund of ecclesial experience stored up throughout the history of the people of God. Catholicity grows from the commitment of local churches to communion, both with other churches in the present and with the church throughout the ages. Catholicity means that the life of the local church shares the fullness of Christ's life and bears the fruit of the Spirit for the transformation of the world. It leads to cooperation in works of justice and righteousness, in which local efforts are joined with others in the movement towards the reign of God.

If the church's life is to be healthy, it must be characterized by a dynamic interaction between catholicity and contextuality. Otherwise the identity of the gospel as transforming story is compromised. If catholicity is emphasized at the expense of contextuality, the gospel may not fully connect with the life of the people and may cease to be good news. If contextuality is emphasized at the expense of catholicity, division and instability may undermine the gospel's expression of God's reconciling purpose for the world as a whole.

Of course, merely making the distinction between contextuality and catholicity does not resolve the differences to which we have pointed. Churches differ in their understandings of the normativity of the Bible and the Christian tradition and over the proper way to interpret the gospel, the Bible and Christian tradition. They differ over what is universal and what is particular or contingent in Christian faith. They differ about whether to start with the gospel or with culture in relating the two and whether certain cultural categories are compatible with the gospel. Grappling with such questions interculturally is precisely what the interaction between catholicity and contextuality is all about. Hence we believe that the most productive way to address such issues is not to abandon the catholicity-contextuality framework, but rather to deepen the process of dialogue between and among cultures. To this challenge we now turn.

CULTIVATING INTERCULTURAL COMMUNICATION

To communicate the gospel between cultures we need to cultivate two kinds of awareness. The first is theological and spiritual; the second focuses on skills and capacities.

Any communication and reception of the gospel, within cultures or between them, occurs under the power of the Holy Spirit. The Spirit opens the word of God for us, illumines our minds and gives us understanding. Through the discernment that follows, we come to see how the word of God leads us forward, drawing us into community which transcends our human limitations and liberates us from all that oppresses human possibility. The Spirit opens to communities in both cultures the inexhaustible treasure of the gospel which is being witnessed to and received. Through this experience the gifts of the Holy Spirit prepare us for communicating between different cultures by creating an atmosphere of hospitality in which trust and respect for the foundations of any intercultural communication can be nurtured and developed, pointing to the unity we share as being created by the same God who calls us into a communion that will lead to fulfilment in the reign of God.

Trust and respect in turn engender the patience and commitment to persevere in the often difficult task of communicating between different cultures, humbly acknowledging our mistakes and generously forgiving those of our partners. These gifts of trust, respect, humility and generosity are not given once for all, but must be received again and again as we journey towards ever greater communion. Fixing our eye on that destination gives us the confidence we need to acknowledge and embrace the differences which are an inevitable and irreducible part of intercultural encounter. In this interplay of communion and difference, we recognize a communication which is now necessarily incomplete but looks forward to its final destiny at the banquet table of heaven.

The theological and spiritual awareness that sustains our commitment to stay with the struggle to communicate in difficult and conflictive situations also urges us to learn more about how to communicate across cultural boundaries. We shall look here at two of these skills for communicating across cultural boundaries: active speaking and listening, and honest recognition of power relationships.

Intercultural communication is essentially a conversation in which both parties try to communicate to each other what is important to them. Thus it requires that both try to speak and both try to listen. Each of these is an active role: speaking requires deciding how to communicate so that the other might better understand; listening requires patient and attentive engagement both to the speaker and to our own memory and knowledge.

But the goals of listening and speaking in such communication are not quite the same. Those who speak are trying to communicate a message or experience to listeners who live in a different cultural world. They are concerned that the listeners receive that message or experience in the way it was intended to be understood—in other words, with its *integrity*.

Listeners surely want to understand the message in its integrity as well, but if it is to be meaningful to them they must understand it in relation to their own experience. Consequently, they try to relate this new knowledge to what they already know. That may relocate or change the message in a way unintended or even undesired by the speakers; and the greater the difference between the world of the speakers and the world of the hearers, the greater the likelihood of such unintended change.

In the case of intercultural communication of something so precious as the gospel, speakers often express their concern that their message has lost its intended integrity and been understood in an incorrect way in terms of "syncretism." In fact, what is happening in such cases is more complex than what is called syncretism. Speakers are rightly concerned about integrity. Listeners are rightly seeking meaning that makes sense within their identity. But rather than jumping to the conclusion that listeners have distorted their message and breaking off the communication (which is what usually happens when someone mentions syncretism), speakers should recognize such misunderstanding not as the end of the process but as the beginning of genuine intercultural communication.

Speakers become aware that in communicating their message they have presumed too many things, leaving them unsaid or otherwise unexpressed. Listeners in turn become aware by the speakers' reaction that they have not understood, but may not know what they should do next. The next step is not to break off the conversation out of fear or anger or a feeling of helplessness. Instead, based on the theology and spirituality of intercultural communication outlined above, both partners must commit themselves to being listeners *and* speakers in a process that recognizes differences and deepens communion. Listeners become speakers and speakers become listeners until meaning is conveyed successfully for both parties: that is, speakers are satisfied that their meaning has been conveyed, and hearers make sense of that meaning in their cultural world.

When such intercultural communication is achieved, the original speakers discover new and previously unrealized aspects of their message. The original listeners also gain a new awareness of their own world. Both are enriched by the experience of opening to the world of the other, but both are also challenged. The truth of the communication, therefore, is not to be judged only by the speaker who originated the message. It is both parties, in intense and ongoing dialogue, who come to discover together the truth which is greater than either of their original conceptions.

When the message thus conveyed is the gospel story as it has become intertwined with their own cultural stories, the intercultural encounter becomes a special moment of grace, revealing new possibilities of communion and a freedom from older, narrow views. Intercultural communication of the gospel is thus not a one-time encounter between speakers and listeners, but an ongoing and intense interaction in which all are deepened in a discipleship of God's good news for the world.

This interaction is ongoing especially because intercultural encounters nearly always involve an unequal distribution of power. Intercultural communication can never act as though power does not play a role in its processes. Although we strive to experience and build communion in the Holy Spirit, we are communities with histories—often with one another, and too often marked by memories of pain, suffering and oppression. These histories necessarily affect how we interact now, sowing mistrust and lack of respect. As a result, we are fearful of new contact. Angry over past injustice and unable to put it out of our minds, we avoid encounter in order to protect ourselves.

Because power is often misused in intercultural encounters to dominate, oppress and humiliate, the ground must often be cleared before communication can take place. Those who have been oppressors in the past cannot presume that their actions are forgotten in a new encounter. They must learn to listen and to repent. Those who have been oppressed must struggle, with God's help, to come to a place where communication can again be taken up.

Intercultural communication requires mutual accountability. This accountability begins in a sincere respect for each other's culture and produces growing trust between them. On this respect and trust a commitment to continuing dialogue can be built, even when that dialogue becomes difficult and must struggle with past abuses of power. Out of the sharing of stories—one's own story and the gospel story—a communion can be realized that looks toward its fulfilment in God's promised reign.

GOSPEL CRITERIA

One feature of intercultural communication needs the particular attention of any Christian community: the authenticity of the faith that is communicated. How do we know that what we have communicated interculturally is truly the gospel of Jesus Christ? Communicating with a theological and spiritual awareness that promotes trust, respect and commitment to dialogue and a mastery of the skills of intercultural communication are necessary conditions for a genuine communication of the gospel across cultural divides, but they cannot of themselves guarantee it.

To these must be added other criteria rooted in the gospel itself and in the two millennia of Christian experience of living out that gospel. Given the complexity of communication today, no single criterion, used alone, is adequate to ensure that the gospel is truly communicated in an intercultural situation. These criteria are suggested by accumulated Christian experience. Each has received different interpretations in different churches at different times, but they can nevertheless be seen as principles for adducing Christian identity.

The first criterion is that whatever is proposed must be *according to the Scriptures*, that is, in harmony with the confession of the triune God, salvation through Christ and the final destiny of humanity and creation as witnessed to in the Scriptures and the testimony of the undivided church of the first centuries.

The second criterion is that of *praxis*: how that which is proposed resonates with the praise of God in the liturgy and in the action by which Christians commit themselves to the furtherance of God's reign and its justice.

The third criterion is that of commitment to seek the truth within the communion of the church and the upbuilding of the church in a peaceable, nondominating way: accepting prophetic critique from others and in turn exercising a prophetic critique of other communities of faith for the sake of the truth. In this regard, special regard is given to the critique from communities of the poor and oppressed.

In such a way we ensure, through mutual accountability, the faithfulness of which we are capable until all things have been revealed to us in the fullness of Christ.

LEARNING FROM OUR FAILURES

Although the goal of fullness in Christ is clear, it is not easy to reach. Human sinfulness often prevents a fruitful encounter between gospel and culture, whether because of lack of communication skills and sensitivity, one-sided understanding of the Scriptures or imbalance in power relations between churches. From the many examples of this, we have chosen to highlight two: racism and sexism. In what follows, we explore how the struggles of the churches in these areas illumine the dynamics of intercultural communication.

Racism or racist elements have been prevalent in several societies and cultures in the world. While all these cultures have shown an attitude of superiority towards people with darker skin, the violence connected with racist attitudes has varied. One of the most destructive kinds of racism was developed in Western Europe, and reached its peak in the late 19th and early 20th centuries. It was both violent and expansionist, and it was formed in a society where the majority of the inhabitants were Christians. This Western racism remains an unresolved problem for the churches. Why did the gospel challenge antisemitism (which had a long history in Christianity, but became an intra-European kind of racism in the 19th century) and colonial expansion only to a very limited extent? Why, instead, were biblical passages, including parts of the gospel narratives (for example, John 8:12-39), employed to defend and encourage such practices? The racism which found its final form in South African apartheid used two texts in particular: Genesis 9:25-27 (Ham being identified with the Africans south of Sahara) and Genesis 11:1-9 (the story of the tower of Babel).

Such interpretations of the biblical message have brought pain to innumerable people and have made the name of Christ hated by many who have suffered at the hands of Christians. The churches have too often been silent when Christians have justified oppression by using arguments from the Bible. A careful study of the abuse of biblical texts to defend inhuman practices is urgently needed. It must be conducted from the perspective of those who have experienced the consequences of such abusive readings of the Bible.

Just as the churches often have accepted interpretations of the scriptures which legitimize exploitation, subjugation and sometimes even systematic extermination of entire peoples, so also the Bible has also been read to condone and support practices which keep women exploited and subjugated (for example, Gen. 3:16, 1 Tim. 2:12-15). Sometimes destructive cultural traditions have been preserved in the Christian community, sometimes oppressive customs have been introduced in the name of the Christian faith. A Christian anthropology affirms that both women and men are created in the image and likeness of God. Any practices in the churches which are not in accord with this must be rectified.

Sexism will not be easily eradicated. Even if all churches were to denounce sexism as evil, not all would agree that what is practised in their particular tradition should be called sexism. What is sexism to some is considered by others to be the order of creation; what some find offensive others accept as a cultural custom. The churches need to develop criteria for discerning which practices are sexist, and thus need to be changed, and which may be retained on cultural and theological grounds.

Experiences and insights of the racially oppressed and those who have suffered under sexism provide hermeneutical tools for intercultural encounters and lead to a better understanding of the Christian faith. Those who have suffered bring special perspectives to what happens in the intercultural communications process, and are particularly aware of how power is misused in such circumstances.

The process within the ecumenical movement which led to the declaration of the biblical justification of apartheid as heresy provides one possible model for future agreements on moral issues which Christians face today. Since the question of apartheid did not arise in the early church, the Bible does not explicitly mention the subject, although portions of the Bible were used to support the policy.

However, the overwhelming majority of the churches were able to agree that those Christian churches which practised apartheid were excluding themselves from the Christian community until they changed both theology and praxis.

THE CONTINUING SEARCH FOR INTEGRATION

Throughout its history Christianity has shown an amazing capacity for integration. In the West the church integrated into itself Jewish, Hellenistic, Roman and Germanic elements. Elsewhere, older Christian traditions integrated Indian, Ethiopian, Syrian and Chaldean elements—to name but a few. Although this is a continuous process in the history of Christianity, it has become a controversial issue in recent centuries as newer churches in the Third World have sought to integrate religious and cultural elements from their traditional ways of life. Many traditions do not see culture and religion as two separate or even separable entities, and many languages do not have a specific word for "religion." Christians from different cultural backgrounds strive to live integrated lives, in which being Christian does not imply alienation from the cultural community into which one was born. Where culture and religion cannot be separated, this means that Christians strive to integrate their religio-cultural bonds and memories within their Christian identity.

Not everything is compatible with the gospel, as the previous section on racism and sexism has shown. The criteria for Christian authenticity propose a way to make such discriminations. The search for integrated Christian lives and communities must be carried out with diligence and vigilance, in openness to the Holy Spirit and in readiness to be corrected by the wider Christian community.

15

Report from the Ecumenical Conference on World Mission and Evangelization

Salvador, de Bahia, Brazil 1996

World Council of Churches*

As described in our introductory survey, "Faith and Culture in Perspective," the Conference Message and section reports from the 1996 Salvador de Bahia WCC-CWME Conference (24 November - 3 December, 1996) constitute the continuing legacy of that conference to the missiological discussion on faith, or gospel, and culture. Even though written in haste by conference scribes in the waning moments of the conference, these statements embody a remarkable treasure of missiological reflection. All future thinking on the subject must take account of, and will benefit by, careful study of these conference documents. A few paragraphs from the official version have been omitted to avoid repetition.

Conference Message

The conference on world mission and evangelism has met in Salvador, Bahia, Brazil, at a significant moment in history—the approach of the end of the century and of a new millennium.

Soon after the start of this century, the first comprehensive ecumenical mission conference took place in Edinburgh. It stated: "The work [of mission] has to be done now. It is urgent and must be pressed forward at once." The work of mission, however, did not turn out to be straightforward. Within four years of that conference the world was engulfed in war. Since then it has known massacres and mass deportations, another world war, the development of new forms of colonialism, life

---

* Reprinted from *Called to One Hope: The Gospel in Diverse Cultures*, ed. Christopher Duraisingh (Geneva: WCC Publications, 1998), pp. 20 - 25, 30 - 75.

196

under nuclear threat, the destruction of ecosystems by human greed, the growth and collapse of the Soviet bloc, violent and separatist ethnic struggles, rampant capitalism leading to an ever-greater gap between rich and poor.

We believe that it is still the church's primary calling to pursue the mission of God in God's world through the grace and goodness of Jesus Christ. Yet this mission, history-long, worldwide, cannot be seen today in narrow ways—it must be an every-member mission, from everywhere to everywhere, involving every aspect of life in a rapidly changing world of many cultures now interacting and overlapping.

In conference here in Salvador, we have sought to understand better the way in which the gospel challenges all human cultures and how culture can give us a clearer understanding of the gospel. It would be difficult to find a more appropriate venue for such a conference. Brazil has the second largest population of people of African origin of any nation. Salvador is a microcosm of the world's diversity of cultures and spiritualities. Yet this very place made us aware of the pain and fragmentation that comes from the racism and lack of respect for other religions that still exist in sectors of the Christian churches.

The theme of the conference was "Called to One Hope—The Gospel in Diverse Cultures."

The hope of the gospel is expressed in the gracious coming of God in Jesus of Nazareth. From the day of Pentecost this hope manifests itself as the fruit of faith and in the struggle of the community of faith. It reaches out to all people everywhere. This conference has been a foretaste and impulse of this hope.

In the conference we have experienced much which has given us such hope:
- the wide diversity of peoples and churches represented (in Edinburgh in 1910 the large majority of the participants were European or North American; in Salvador over 600 Christians of a wide spectrum of cultures from almost 100 nations participated in the life of the conference);
- the genuine attempt which has been made to listen and to share ways and wisdoms across cultures;
- the thrill of participating in the life of a community where the voices of young and old, women and men from Christian churches around the globe have all been speaking out;
- the willingness of the churches and mission agencies to admit past failures and to refuse to engage in stereotyping, and the determination to stay together and work together for the good of our common mission;
- the solidarity of standing at the dockside in Salvador where, for 300 years, the African slaves who were still alive after their capture and deportation were unloaded. By the "Stone of Tears" together we wept tears of repentance;
- the encouragement of participating in the rhythm of daily worship where the honouring and use of different sounds and languages did not result in a divisive and confusing "babel," but rather gave a hint of the unity and inspiration of a Pentecost;
- the privilege of sharing for a short time in the life of a continent and people with a rich cultural history and a diversity of religious spirituality, whose churches are responding to the challenges of social change and poverty through the embodiment of gospel hope.

It is our profound hope that this last great mission conference of the twentieth century has clearly illuminated that the gospel to be most fruitful needs to be both true to itself, and incarnated or rooted in the culture of a people. We have had a first-hand experience of seeing and hearing Christians from many diverse cultures expressing their struggles and hopes.

- We have heard the cries of pain from indigenous peoples who have faced the near extermination of their communities and cultures, and we have marvelled at their resilience and their determination to make connections between their indigenous spirituality and their Christian faith so that their identity is not divided.
- We have heard the longing of women around the world for a real partnership in church and society.
- We have listened to the voices of young Christians telling us that they do not wish to be objects of the church's mission but full partners in the work of mission, particularly in relating the faith to the energy and aspirations of youth culture today.
- We have learned from our Latin American hosts the importance of "doing" theology which seeks to create a "community called church," which is rooted in the life of the people amongst whom the church is set, and which shows itself, for example, in their response to the plight of the street children in their cities.
- We have heard the voices of Christians in the Pacific who seek mutuality with their Christian partners from the West, insisting that full partnership in mission is reciprocal, not paternalistic.
- We have heard the anger of African people, Afro-Caribbean people, Afro-Latino people and African people of North America at the horror of slavery, and we have heard how the faith, though presented to them in distorted forms, became the hope of liberation. We have admired their determination not to be trapped in a lament over history but to cooperate together in a strengthened partnership between African people and people of the African diaspora.
- We have been moved by the stories of disaster and disease which led one speaker from Africa to say, "Times are ripe for flirting with hopelessness," and we have been astonished at the strength and determination of African Christians, women in particular, to share the pain of their people and to combat despair and plant the seeds of both food and hope.
- We have benefited from hearing of the long-term experience of Asian Christians of living a life of Christian discipleship in multifaith societies, sometimes as vulnerable and threatened minority groups. We have also heard of a surge of grassroots missionary activity.
- We have been moved by the experiences of Christians in the Middle East living with the privilege and pain of life in a "holy land" torn apart by division and injustice, and their indignation at the way in which biblical texts are misinterpreted so that their culture is blemished and some are made to feel strangers in their own land.
- We have admired the commitment of those from the Orthodox and other local churches in the former Soviet Union and Eastern Europe now determined, in

the new atmosphere of religious freedom, to serve their people in such a way that the faith which sustained many through times of persecution might now be an equal blessing in times of new challenge. We have heard their protest at the ways in which rich foreign Christian groups are seeking to proselytize their people.
- We have recognized the caution of Christians in Germany about being too ready to see God's spirit in all human cultures, growing out of their painful memories of how the churches risked becoming captive to Nazi ideology in a previous generation.
- We have heard how the churches, against the background of the post-modern culture influencing much of Western Europe, are studying the phenomenon of secularism and engaging with those turning from traditional faith and seemingly seeking a private "pick-and-mix" spirituality.
- We have heard reports of the growing localism of North American churches which, while strengthening their commitment to mission and evangelism in their own context, may lead to an isolation and insulation from global realities.
- We have shared the concern of many at how the global free-market economy seems to exercise sovereign power over even strong governments, and how the mass media disseminate worldwide images and messages of every description which influence—and, some believe, undermine—community and faith.
- We have discussed how, perhaps as a reaction to these developments, new fundamentalisms are emerging in all world faiths, adding to the divisions in an already fractured world.
- We have heard how Christians in many places around the globe are engaging in serious dialogue with people of other faiths, telling the Christian story, listening attentively to the stories of others, and thus gaining a clearer and richer understanding of their own faith and helping to build a "community of communities" to the benefit of all.

In such ways we have recognized how the church engages in mission with cultures around the globe today. What then would we want to emphasize from this conference?

- The church must hold on to two realities: its distinctiveness from, and its commitment to, the culture in which it is set. In such a way the gospel becomes neither captive to a culture nor alienated from it, but each challenges and illuminates the other.
- Perhaps as never before, Christians in mission today need to have a clear understanding of what God has done in history through Jesus Christ. In this we have seen what God requires of individuals, communities and structures. The biblical witness is our starting point and reference for mission and gives us the sense of our own identity.
- We need constantly to seek the insight of the Holy Spirit in helping us better to discern where the gospel challenges, endorses or transforms a particular culture.
- The catholicity of a church is enhanced by the quality of the relationships it has with churches of other traditions and cultures. This has implications for

mission and evangelism and calls for respect and sensitivity for churches already located in the place concerned. Competitiveness is the surest way to undermine Christian mission. Equally, aggressive evangelism which does not respect the culture of a people is unlikely to reflect effectively the gracious love of God and the challenge of the gospel.
- Local congregations are called to be places of hope, providing spaces of safety and trust wherein different peoples can be embraced and affirmed, thus manifesting the inclusive love of God. For congregations in increasingly plural societies, inclusion of all cultural groups which make up the community, including those who are uprooted, marginalized and despised, is important. Strengthening congregations through a spirituality which enables them to face the vulnerability involved in this openness is critical.
- Small steps which involve risk and courage can break through barriers and create new relationships. Such steps are available to us all. They can be the "miracle" which changes a church or community's self-image and enables new God-given life to break forth.

Music at the conference has had a rhythm, a harmony, a beat. In a place with a deep African tradition it is natural that in our worship the beat of the drum has frequently been the vehicle to carry our souls to resonate with the beat of God's love for us and for all people. With hearts set on fire with the beat of mission and a prayer on our lips that many will share with us in being "Called to One Hope" and take and find "the Gospel in Diverse Cultures," we commend the fruits of the conference to Christians and churches everywhere. Our profound hope is that they too may be renewed in mission for the sharing of the knowledge of Christ, to the glory of the triune God.

Section I: Authentic Witness within Each Culture

A. DISCERNING THE SPIRIT AT WORK IN ALL CULTURES

THEOLOGICAL UNDERSTANDING OF CULTURES

Speaking of "culture" evokes many different words, terms and concepts: food, environmental influence, architecture, art, language, relationships, sexuality, humour, sports, education, communication, politics, economics, power structures, conflict management, traditions, values, rituals, religion, worship, spirituality—indeed all aspects of human effort. There is no way of being human without participating in culture, for it is through culture that identity is created. Culture is both a result of God's grace and an expression of human freedom and creativity. Culture is intrinsically neither good nor bad; it has the potential for both—and is thus ambiguous.

Some Christians emphasize that culture is an aspect of God's creation and others that cultures are of human creation. This difference of viewpoint clearly

allows for differing perceptions of gospel and culture issues. Common ground includes the following affirmations:
- Creation is the work of the triune God.
- Human beings are created in the image of God.
- Language, thought-forms and expressions are shaped by culture.
- God's word always reaches people through culture.
- The human response to God is always through culture.
- The gospel cannot be identified with particular cultures.
- Culture is not to be regarded as divine.
- No culture can claim to have grasped the fullness of God.
- As cultures increasingly interact with each other, it is possible for human beings to belong to more than one culture or to leave one culture and enter another.
- In the encounter between cultures a richer understanding of the divine mystery may unfold.
- As cultures change, new dimensions of God's presence and work may become known and expressed.

To celebrate God's presence in human cultures is to express the encounter between the human and the divine in all its richness and diversity.

The ambiguous nature of culture raises the question of discerning the work of the Spirit within culture. Most people would affirm that in many cultures the fruit of the Holy Spirit—"love, joy, peace, patience, kindness, generosity, faithfulness, gentleness and self-control" (Gal. 5:22-23)—as well as the pursuit of justice in human affairs, can be identified. Do these not testify to the presence of the Holy Spirit? All cultures, however, also exhibit evil: there are life-denying and oppressive elements in cultures which run counter to the fundamental values of human relationships. Sin is present in everything human, including culture. This does not mean that God is absent from these cultures; God is present in both judgment and grace in the midst of pain and suffering. The ultimate goal of God's activity in cultures is to bring about liberation, life and the knowledge of God for all (John 10:10; 17:3).

RELIGION, CULTURE AND GOSPEL

How do religion and culture relate to each other? Religion—a system of beliefs and practices—is part of culture. Culture is related to religion in many different ways: religion can be imprinted in or intertwined with culture; culture can grow out of a particular religion; religion can be a directing dimension of culture, alienated from culture, in conflict with culture, denied by culture, rejected by culture or concealed in culture.

The biblical testimony concerning the relation between religion and culture is diverse. In the Hebrew scriptures we find on the one hand the influence of elements from other ancient cultures and religions, such as wisdom literature from other parts of the Old Testament world, and on the other hand strong rejection of some elements of the religions and cultures of Israel's neighbours. In the prophetic tradition, Israel's worship itself is sometimes denounced for its emphasis on religious rituals coopted from its neighbours, to the neglect of justice (cf. Amos 5:21-24).

Many testify to having seen glimpses of God's presence and activity as well as having recognized the fruit of the Holy Spirit in people of other religious traditions, and can with confidence sing the ancient hymn, *Ubi caritas et amor Deus ibi est*, "Where there is charity and love, God is present." However, we can never say exactly how God is at work in any religious community.

If God's work in other religio-cultural traditions is affirmed, there are consequences for Christian mission. The followers of other religious traditions should be listened to as they express their relationship to God in worship and witness.

This, however, does not diminish the missionary vocation of the church. Christians are called to witness to God's revelation in Jesus Christ and their communion with God in Christ in the fellowship of the Spirit. We are also called to give testimony to liberation from oppression and death through the resurrection of Christ, who in self-giving love became powerless and was tortured and killed so that all may have life. We cannot keep this to ourselves; God's Spirit urges us to invite people everywhere to share in this life.

The triune God has not left creation without a witness. As the San Antonio conference stated: "We cannot point to any other way of salvation than Jesus Christ; at the same time we cannot set limits to the saving power of God" (San Antonio, p.32). Christians prayerfully and humbly ask: To what extent may other religions be acknowledged as being expressions of God's mercy and grace found in Christ? At what points do these expressions appear to run counter to God's fullness, life and love in Christ? Some do not doubt that people of other faiths experience decisive moments of deliverance, integration and communion which come to them as gift, not achievement, and that these experiences are akin to what Christians experience as salvation in Jesus Christ. Others question whether such experiences attest to the fruits of the Spirit, the presence and grace of God in them. Can a distinction be made between a spirit which is present in the whole of creation, including forms of culture and religion, and the Holy Spirit? Herein the Christian understanding of the very identity of God is at stake. The Christian faith affirms that God is one, and therefore the spirit present in the cultures and religions of humanity in mercy and judgment may be said to be none other than the Holy Spirit, that is, the Spirit of God who is eternally united to the Son and to the Father. Such convictions lead some to ask whether the triune God is redemptively present even where the gospel is not preached and Jesus Christ is not named as Saviour and Lord.

All creation comes to be through the Word (John 1), coheres in him and achieves its restoration and perfection in him (Col. 1:15-20). The gospel is the good news that the light that enlightens all took on our human condition in the person of Jesus Christ; and that in Jesus Christ is given the gift of God's very self, sharing the joy and misery of all humanity, freeing from all forms of domination and condemnation, and inaugurating the restoration of all creation.

The missionary task is both to proclaim the good news of Jesus Christ and to invite people to recognize and experience his presence and work among them and to respond to him. In this way some aspects of other religions may be seen by Christians as preparation for the proclamation of the gospel (Acts 17:16-34). However, at times the proclamation of the gospel may lead to open conflict with other religious traditions. It is of utmost importance to discern whether this conflict is the result of a genuine confrontation with the gospel message or of missionary insensitivity to other cultures. The fact that many people have experienced the gospel as "bad news"—not least when Western cultures are seen as examples of Christian ideals—must not be forgotten. On the other hand, there are numerous examples of communities and individuals, especially women and marginalized groups in many societies, who have heard the gospel as a call to conversion to Jesus Christ, and have experienced this as a conversion to greater freedom and a new hope.

B. DYNAMIC INTERACTION BETWEEN GOSPEL AND CULTURE

The incarnation of Jesus Christ, as testified to in the gospel according to John (1:1-14), is basic to an understanding of the dynamic interaction between gospel and cultures. In becoming human, Jesus affirms, fulfils, challenges and transforms cultures. It is the life of Jesus the incarnate, lived out in the realities of a particular context, that illuminates the very nature of God's way of salvation, the gospel. But within the mutual interaction between the gospel and cultures, the gospel functions as the new and inspiring principle, giving rise to the renewal of cultures through the transforming work of the Spirit.

GOSPEL ILLUMINATING AND TRANSFORMING CULTURES

In identifying the gospel's role in illuminating and transforming cultures, "transformation" is understood in various ways:
- Transformation means that the gospel becomes incarnate in the culture in which it is proclaimed, just as the Word became incarnate in human flesh (John 1:14).
- The gospel gives culture an orientation towards the glory of God. Such transformation opens up both those who witness to and those who receive the gospel to turn towards the mystery of God and the reality of others, drawing out what is best in them and in their cultures.
- Transformation means being freed from the oppression of particular aspects of culture; for example, Paul on the road to Damascus (Acts 9:1-19) is freed from deeply rooted religious prejudgments and undergoes conversion.
- Transformation means purification of certain elements of cultures in which the gospel is proclaimed.
- Transformation implies the empowerment of people to gain deeper insights into both the gospel and their own culture.
- Transformation further implies that a missionary entering a different culture to proclaim the gospel must begin a journey of conversion in knowing, living and loving that culture.

The transformation brought by the gospel may be described as a lamp "that gives light to all that is in the house" (Matt. 5:15). Such transformations are taking place in different parts of the world, bringing new meaning to religio-cultural activities such as marriage ceremonies, funeral services, liturgical rites and rituals related to health and healing.

There is diversity of opinion regarding the distinction between the gospel and the cultural expressions of "gospels". For some, the gospel can only be derived from the person of Jesus Christ; there is only one gospel. For others, the gospel is accessible only through cultural forms, and human understanding of the gospel differs from person to person; any human talk about the gospel is therefore an articulation of one of the "cultural gospels." This matter requires further consideration and exploration.

CULTURE ILLUMINATING AND INCARNATING THE GOSPEL

Biblical faith recognizes cultures other than the Hebraic, indicating that God can work through and within any culture. Yet there is only one gospel, manifested in many cultural expressions. Christian mission involves people gaining access to God's word in scripture in their own language and culture, and being empowered to interpret that scripture through the guidance of the Spirit.

The gospel may be made more accessible and given a deeper expression through human cultural activities. To affirm that cultures illuminate the gospel is to hold that culture, manifested in art and other forms of human creativity, enlightens and enhances our understanding of the gospel.

As Christians discern the gospel/culture dynamic, some cultural and cultic activities will be joyfully affirmed, others abandoned, others retained with changed meaning. God being active in judgment and in giving life, new dimensions of meaning will emerge so that each Christian community develops its particular worldview, lifestyle, cultic practice and ecclesial structures.

Not only can culture be used to express the meaning of the gospel but also, in a deeper sense, it can create values and give birth to new forms of human community.

PROBLEMS IN THE RELATIONSHIP BETWEEN GOSPEL AND CULTURE

The dynamic interactions between the gospel and cultures in human history have been both constructive and destructive. In many cases the gospel has illuminated and transformed particular cultures and has received illumination from and become embodied in them. But there are also cases in which the style of proclamation of the gospel has caused cultural alienation, because the culture has not been allowed to illuminate and give genuine expression to the gospel.

Because culture is constantly in flux and cultural expressions change from generation to generation, the interaction between the gospel and cultures must be a continuous process in every place.

Christians must be aware of the limitations of any culture, for there is always the danger of the gospel being domesticated and made captive to that culture. Similarly, there are situations where the gospel has been abused for political purposes or to exploit people.

AUTHENTIC INTERACTION BETWEEN GOSPEL AND CULTURES

Authenticity in witness has to do with the witness of persons of one culture to persons of another culture as well as the witness of a Christian community within its own cultural setting. In witness across cultures, those who witness must be faithful both to their own experience of Christ and to the cultural values and symbols of those to whom witness is given. The witness of a local church in its own community must be rooted in the culture of that community. The danger of inauthentic witness arises also when a church manifests loyalty to its cultural identity such that the gospel is made to serve the cultural interests of that church.

Different situations create different problems of identity. Some people live in places where numerous cultures interpenetrate and mix, and therefore their sense of cultural rootedness is confused (this "culture" is one that leaves people feeling rootless and in search of identity). Others come from a more clearly defined cultural background that gives a more secure identity.

All Christians have an identity and rootedness in Christ. Along with the need to understand the particularities of their different cultural locations, Christians need to affirm and strengthen the universal church, in which a common Christian identity is found.

True identity—the gift of the triune God—is strengthened as the scriptures lead Christians to a common faith in God, a common experience in the Spirit and a common hope in Christ, all expressed in diverse forms. The one hope portrayed in the scriptures includes both present liberation and the consummation of all things in Christ in glory.

C. VOICING THE GOSPEL: EVANGELISM TODAY

Christians today have much to share about evangelism that is either culturally sensitive or culturally insensitive. Culture-sensitive evangelism is facilitated by the task of pre-evangelism—a careful laying of the proper groundwork for discerning the appropriate time and place for proclaiming the gospel message.

A number of biblical texts offer helpful insights for the discussion on culturally sensitive evangelism. In Isaiah 61:1, for example, preaching and healing are brought together. The nurturing and selfless love of the evangelist is expressed in 1 Thessalonians 1:7-8: "We were gentle among you, like a nurse tenderly caring for her own children. So deeply do we care for you . . ." The motive of the evangelist is expressed in 2 Corinthians 5:14, "the love of Christ urges us on," and the humility of the evangelist in Philippians 2:5-8. The latter passage reminds us of the intimate relationship between "the messenger" and "the message" in evangelism as elsewhere. The events on the road to Emmaus (Luke 24:13-35) provide further insight into drawing alongside people in their journey. And in Mark 7:24-30, Jesus learns from a woman who remains in her own culture and religion; he does not ask her to change her religious loyalties—an example of living dialogue.

Greater discernment of the nature and values of a particular culture is important for Christians, especially in communities where there appears to be no separation between spirituality and culture. Some suggest that the integrity of the human person might be a more appropriate criterion for cultural discernment than the integrity of culture.

In the exploration of culture-sensitive evangelism, dialogue and cooperation in community development are seen as socially and culturally appropriate ways in which the gospel can be "made real." Dialogue does not, however, displace proclamation. As the San Antonio conference affirmed: "Witness does not preclude dialogue but invites it, and ... dialogue does not preclude witness but extends and deepens it. Dialogue has its own place and integrity and is neither opposed to nor incompatible with witness or proclamation. We do not water down our own commitment if we engage in dialogue" (San Antonio, p.32).

Some suggest that a way of making non-intrusive contact with communities of other cultures is that of "presence." An effort is first made to get to know and understand people in that community, and sincerely to listen to and learn from them. A general sharing of interests, questions, objectives and priorities might follow. At the right time people could be invited to participate in the story of the gospel. In some cases silent solidarity may be the most appropriate form of Christian witness.

Others insist that there is no substitute for preaching the word. While acknowledging that Christian presence within communities is important, they also see the need for witnessing to the signs of the dynamic movement of the Spirit and actively voicing the gospel. What sometimes deters people from proclamation includes feelings of guilt about past styles of evangelism.

In contexts where the dominant culture is hostile to the proclamation of the gospel message, some suggest the need to provide a "safe space" for spirituality to germinate, where the Jesus story can be revealed.

In this connection the nature of the relationship between words and works in authentic evangelism is to be considered: whether witness or unconditional loving service can alone constitute authentic evangelism, or whether they always belong together. As San Antonio affirmed: "The 'material gospel' and the 'spiritual gospel' have to be *one*, as was true of the ministry of Jesus ... There is no evangelism without solidarity; there is no Christian solidarity that does not involve sharing the message of God's coming reign" (San Antonio, p.26).

Honesty and openness are integral and vital to the process of evangelism. Of crucial importance is the integrity of all involved: the person offering the witness, the congregation or faith community to which the witness or messenger belongs, and the community to which witness is being offered, the social and cultural integrity of which must be carefully respected.

In relation to the authenticity and integrity of the missionary messenger, it is important that he or she act in a spirit and manner appropriate to the gospel, in a Christ-like way. For some, integrity is synonymous with faithfulness to the language and meaning of the scriptures and therefore has to do with the content of the gospel message. For others, integrity means a more general faithfulness to Jesus Christ.

Often missionaries present differing interpretations of the gospel. To the extent that this represents a faithful endeavour to address particular communities in ways appropriate to their differing (sub)cultures and understanding, this diversity may be healthy.

Some, however, find such differing interpretations problematic and contrary to the ideals of common witness. When Christians apply what has been learned about cultural sensitivity in the mission of the church to relationships between sister churches and among different parts of the same church, this diversity can be enriching and can promote unity.

Other problems in voicing the gospel may also be identified—for example, the manner of issuing of "the invitation" often used in popular/mass evangelism, which for some has misleading theological implications. In such situations it must be clear that it is Christ who extends the invitation and calls for a response.

CONCLUSION

Each culture has its own hopes. All such hopes are expressed in particular cultural perspectives. Any witness to God's offer of the eschatological hope in Christ must relate to the present hopes of the culture in which the witness is given. The gospel proclaims the victory of life over death through the risen Christ who has defeated death; our hope is to participate in "the power of his resurrection" (Phil. 3:10). The hope which underlies Christian mission is to help all people to come to know Christ and find salvation in him. Today hope has a face and a name and is alive. Christ is our hope.

Section II: Gospel and Identity in Community

INTRODUCTION

The gospel addresses all aspects of human life, including the structural dimensions of culture. In understanding the relationship between the gospel and cultures, the focus has often been on the symbols and values of particular cultures. In an exploration of the structural elements of culture in relation to particular groups within a society, it is necessary to hold together two reference points: identity (which may be defined in many ways, for example in terms of race, gender, ethnicity, age) and community.

Power has often been misused to crush the identities of marginalized and excluded persons and groups. The gospel—the good news of the saving love of God for all people made known in Jesus Christ—has also been misused by dominant groups to deny or distort the identities of people and to perpetuate marginalization. Many of these marginalized people, however, have found in the gospel empowerment for their struggle against life-denying forces.

Increasingly, tensions arise between different ethnic groups in a multicultural and multi-ethnic context. These ethnic tensions are often exacerbated by religion. The Christian faith has sometimes been misinterpreted and misused to reinforce the identity of one ethnic group over that of another, thereby leading to the fragmentation of community. But the gospel clearly promises community across ethnic and other boundaries. The imagery of "the body" in the New Testament undergirds such an understanding of community.

A further element of the structural dimensions of culture is globalization. Economic globalization promotes a single economic community focused on the accumulation of wealth—creating increasing poverty and unemployment and leading to the further marginalization of the poor and the exclusion of many. Economic globalization seeks to impose a single consumer identity throughout the whole world through corporate control, the media and technology. This process leads to a loss of self-identity. This form of homogenizing economic community which enriches the few and excludes many is contrary to the values of the gospel.

The conference theme speaks of the one hope to which Christians in their diverse cultures are called. This is a hope both for the restoration of creation and its liberation from bondage to the abuse to which it has been subjected (Rom. 8:19-23), and for the gathering up of all things in Christ (Eph. 1:10). In the early church in Jerusalem (Acts 2:42-47), people from diverse backgrounds experienced a foretaste of the hope which is to come within the new community, the church. There are today situations in which solutions seem impossible and hope is dim. In such cases Christians are called to a missionary presence, sharing in the suffering and thereby witnessing to the cross and to Christ's conquering of death.

It is the power of the Spirit which enables mission. This mission proclaims God's intention that all—with their languages and their cultural and spiritual heritages—should be affirmed as people of worth. Christian mission also has to do with identifying and even suffering with those whose identities have been denied. The liberating message of the gospel is not only that *the identity of each* is affirmed but also that all are taken beyond their own identity into *the one new community of the Spirit* (Acts 4:32-35).

Greater clarity is needed in describing this new community of the Spirit. Is it identical to the visible church as seen in the Acts of the Apostles? Or is it a wider community in the world, whose hallmark is love?

A. GOSPEL AND CRUSHED IDENTITIES

Marginalization through economic, political, social, cultural and religious forces is a reality in all societies. People are marginalized because of, for example, their age, gender, class, caste, race or ethnicity, and experience mutilation of their identities.

Groups which have been excluded and oppressed include the following:
- indigenous peoples;
- Africans in the diaspora;
- women;
- children (especially street children), youth, the elderly;
- persons who are casualties of economic, social and political wars (immigrants/migrants, refugees, those who make their living from the garbage heaps of big cities, prostitutes, single and teenage mothers, drug-users, alcoholics, child labourers);
- poor, illiterate, unemployed or underemployed people, and those with skills inadequate for the high-tech demands of the current global market;
- persons living with HIV/AIDS;
- persons who are physically or mentally differently abled;
- persons with sexual orientations other than that of the majority in their society, and their advocates;
- religious minorities.

Many who suffer oppression are running out of hope because they continue to be exploited, excluded or ignored, and have internalized negative images of themselves projected by dominant groups within the culture. However, some of those who are denied full self-expression in society nonetheless live the Christian virtues of faith, hope and love. They find hope in the living Christ. Their struggle against oppression lies in their faith and hope that God loves them, sees their suffering and cares for them. They seek respect for their identity, to be understood and taken seriously. They do not see faith and hope as passive waiting for the future. Rather they believe that faith and hope give them power and creativity in their struggle for justice and fullness of life, both of which are central to the witness and mission of the church. As Christians they believe that all this *will* happen, because of power from God and from each other as they join in solidarity.

INDIGENOUS PEOPLES

Indigenous peoples in all parts of the world have suffered the decimation of their population by colonization and the loss of their culture and spirituality, which emphasize interconnectedness, solidarity and reciprocity with the whole of creation. These peoples, once so closely related to the land, today have only limited access to land and other resources, as well as to vital representation and decision-making within societal and church structures. The gospel communicated to these peoples was distorted insofar as its interpretation emphasized elements such as separation of the body and soul, and individualism rather than community.

We call on the churches to respect indigenous identities and to work towards the full participation of indigenous peoples in all aspects of church life. We affirm the following recommendations of the (November 1996) indigenous spirituality consultation, which called on the World Council of Churches and its member churches, ecumenical bodies and other churches to:

- be in solidarity with indigenous peoples, Afro-Latinos and Afro-Caribbeans irrespective of faiths and traditions and to walk with us in respect;
- work in partnership with indigenous peoples, Afro-Latinos and Afro-Caribbeans to re-examine their history of absolutism, verticalism and intolerance and to reconstruct the spiritualities and theologies of the church, eliminating all expressions of Christianity that practise aggression against indigenous spiritualities;
- promote the meaningful participation of indigenous peoples, Afro-Latinos and Afro-Caribbeans within all church structures and decision-making levels, allowing for full and equal partnership among indigenous and non-indigenous members;
- promote the development of curricula and the teaching by indigenous people of their own spiritualities and theologies in church-related educational institutions;
- empower indigenous peoples, Afro-Latinos and Afro-Caribbeans and accompany them in advocating indigenous social justice issues for self-determination and land rights.

We affirm that many of the above recommendations apply to other marginalized groups as well.

YOUTH

Young people (especially young women) searching for their identity and role in the church and society have often felt ignored and patronized by older people, who sometimes refuse to enter into dialogue on matters of faith and other issues relevant to youth.

We call on the churches to commit themselves to full ministry with young people, to teach them and learn from them, to trust them and accept them as active partners in the church and its mission, rather than treating them as objects of mission.

Many young Christians live out their faith in alienating cities and fragmented cultures and struggle with the fracture between generations. Only as churches become fully rooted in their societies will they be able to address the issues that particularly affect youth today. Increasing numbers of young people in this post-modern era are afraid of the future, unemployed, manipulated by the media and market forces, bewildered by the competing/conflicting Christian cultures and unable to reconcile the gospel of Jesus Christ with the traditional practices of the churches as they experience them. In this context we call on the churches to bear witness to the resurrection hope.

Young people are distressed by the past sins and present failings of Christian community and Christian mission. They call for a church which not only knows how to use words but which loves the living Word, and so includes and loves young people. Indigenous young people especially are often torn between their cultural identity and their Christian calling.

We call upon the churches to act concretely insofar as they are able, to support (financially and otherwise) the training and education of young people to equip them for the demands placed upon them.

WOMEN

Men and women in the churches are encouraged to recognize each other's worth and identity and to work in partnership. We affirm the work of the Ecumenical Decade of the Churches in Solidarity with Women, which has raised awareness of structures and practices in church and society that have prevented the full participation of women. The churches need to denounce violence against women and children and to be aware that most acts of violence take place in the home.

The churches are called to commit themselves to developing women leaders who will take responsibility and exercise leadership within the church. They are also encouraged to help create space where women's voices can be heard, both as women and within the community of men and women. For reconciliation to take place the pain that women have borne for generations must be shared and heard. Where possible, collaborative relations should be established with secular agencies which are working with and for women.

As churches seek to relate to marginalized people and to enable their empowerment, they are called to:
- encourage such people to see themselves as sons and daughters of God rather than as victims;

- enable Christians to affirm all people in their community as "beloved of God";
- welcome into the life of the church community people living with HIV/AIDS, providing support for them and their families and friends especially in times of sorrow and grief;
- act in solidarity with groups excluded from their economies because of policies of the World Bank, International Monetary Fund, etc.;
- establish ministries among peoples devastated by inter-ethnic strife;
- develop styles of leadership that foster community.

It is also important to place emphasis on programmes that enable Christians, especially marginalized groups, to reread the Bible from the perspective of their own cultural context. Such programmes may include:
- enabling other members of the church to hear the Bible interpreted from the perspective of oppressed people;
- helping Christians to understand that certain biblical texts have been used to justify oppressive practices, and to deal with them in such ways that the Bible becomes a force for liberation and life.

In relation to the above, we commend again to the churches for study and action the sections of the WCC document "Mission and Evangelism—An Ecumenical Affirmation" (1982) which deal with doing mission "in Christ's way."

B. GOSPEL, ETHNICITY AND IDENTITY POLITICS

Migrations and other movements of people throughout history and up to our time have made homogenous societies a rarity. Nearly every society today is becoming increasingly multicultural, multireligious, multi-ethnic and multilingual. This has led in many cases to a renewed and intensified claiming of ethnic identities, with a rise in mutual suspicion, tension and hostility. Often this manifests itself in efforts by people belonging to one ethnic group to dominate another politically . . . Ethnicity refers to a collective group awareness shaped by factors like ancestry, homeland, language, culture and religion. . .

Most often, perhaps, ethnicity becomes divisive and conflictual when a group feels its identity and survival threatened by social, economic and political forces. The sociological make-up, demographic realities and geographical location of a group may evoke memories of old historical conflicts and bring about new ones. Distorted images of those who are ethnically different, portraying the order as dangerous and even demonic, exacerbate such conflicts. Religious symbols and myths reinforce the divisiveness of ethnicity (Salvador preparatory papers, p.31).

The church is called to proclaim the gospel in such a way that people of different ethnicities are invited to respond in faith and are invited to receive the gift of the Holy Spirit, who incorporates them into the body of Christ. Each is given a new identity as a daughter or son of God. Each is bound by love to the other as parts of one body. Yet each part has its own identity. If one part hurts, the whole body feels pain. The whole body shares Christ's openness and vulnerability.

Identities thus ought not to be constituted defensively, in competition with or in fear of others, but rather must be understood as being complementary and of intrinsic value, for all people are children of God. Christians are called to see the face of God in others, as all are called to be part of the one body.

The gospel reconciles and unites people of all identities into a new community in which the primary and ultimate identity is identity in Jesus Christ (Gal. 3:28).

ETHNICITY AND IDENTITY POLITICS

Identity politics exists when elements constituting the identity of one segment of a society are used as leverage for political power and socio-economic advantage over against other segments. Identity politics is problematic because this way of using identity is based on exclusivity. Identity politics leads people to understand identity as static and impermeable rather than fluid and open to change. This is particularly the case when, for example, ethnicity is used as a highly politicized concept by one ethnic group to organize itself and to perpetuate its own interests at the expense of other ethnic groups.

Ethnicity is a valuable gift of God. The varieties of ethnic belonging and identity—when they remain open to and respectful of others—are to be affirmed and valued.

Some churches, however, have supported identity politics, legitimizing community-destroying concepts of identity which have led to violence and war. Churches identified with a particular ethnic group should not allow this to reinforce the controlling, dominating and destructive effects of identity politics. Rather, the churches are called to raise their voices on behalf of minority identities—specifically, vulnerable groups of marginalized people, including women, youth and children. We condemn utterly the use of systematic rape as an instrument of war and of identity politics.

The mission of the church in relation to ethnicity is to enable every person to experience love and acceptance as a child of God. This will be helped by:
- creating space in worship, pastoral care, education and other areas of church life for experiences and encounters to enable people to see the face of God in "the other";
- enabling personal encounter and intercultural learning processes among people of different ethnic belongings;
- providing authentic information about "the other," particularly in situations of tension and conflict;
- enabling processes of non-violent resolution of conflict;
- advocating and allocating resources for peace research and training for mediation in areas of conflict.

God wills fullness of life for all people. The church's understanding and actions related to ethnic identity must therefore be measured by criteria of justice, freedom, participation, non-violence and self-reliance. As in the body of Christ special honour is given to the weaker parts, justice for the poor, neglected and marginalized and protection of the human rights of people of all ethnicities are a precondition and sign of the community for which the church yearns.

NATION-STATE, NATIONALISM AND ETHNICITY

The boundaries of modern nation-states have been defined through war, conquest, colonization and treaties. For many countries in Latin America, Africa and Asia these boundaries were drawn by colonial powers, often with support from the churches, in a way that separated tribes, ethnic groups and even families. As a result these national identities are often artificial; and attempts to maintain them have sometimes involved the dominance of a single ethnic or religious group or the creation of a homogenized "national" culture which denies the rights of other groups . . . Many minority peoples have had their sense of "nation" violated by the influx of a new majority (Salvador preparatory papers, pp.34-35).

While the identity and integrity of some nation-states is threatened by divisive internal forces, the major threat in other cases comes from international or global forces. Since the process of globalization seems unavoidable, the churches should work to ensure the preservation of ethnic values which enrich life in community. The positive values of ethnicity and sovereignty of peoples and nations in the face of the forces of globalization are to be affirmed.

Actions which the churches and ecumenical bodies could take in this respect include:
- Churches in which there are ethnic minorities and/or indigenous peoples should be encouraged to include study of ethnicity and ethnic values in their programmes of theological formation, and to include people from such minorities in decision-making structures and delegated representations.
- The human rights desks of the churches and councils of churches should be encouraged to develop strategies of advocacy for indigenous groups who have lost their lands to economic exploitation.
- The churches should become familiar with separatist movements and challenge or support them as appropriate through international networking and advocacy for the rule of justice and peace.
- The WCC should study political situations involving ethnicity with the aim of strengthening the peace-making and human rights efforts of the churches, giving special attention to the resolution of violent conflicts.
- The WCC should support international agencies in mediating boundary disputes through dialogues and referenda involving regional and local government representatives, leaders of the ethnic groups concerned and the general public.

UPROOTED PEOPLES

The movement of people for political and economic reasons has been a continuing phenomenon for centuries. Wars, natural and environmental disasters and long-term political and economic upheavals continue to create millions of refugees, migrants and asylum-seekers . . . Many people whose religious and cultural background is different from the majority in the country in which they now live represent the second and third generation in their adopted countries. But the response to their presence has been increased xenophobia, hatred and violence, along with ever more restrictive laws to control immigration as governments throughout the North close their borders. These people of different cultures experience many kinds of oppression and exploitation (Salvador preparatory papers, p.36).

The church's involvement with uprooted people has largely focused on social services and assistance. While affirming the importance of this role, the churches should also exercise a prophetic role, analyzing the causes of uprootedness and engaging in advocacy.

In view of the large numbers who are uprooted by war, interethnic violence, persecution and natural disasters, the churches are called:
- to exercise constant vigilance to enable uprooted peoples to cross national frontiers for the sake of survival;
- to listen to, learn from and be changed by uprooted people, their stories and experiences, praying for and with them, and welcoming them into the community;
- to stand with and aid those who have been deprived of their basic human rights due to lack or denial of legal documentation;
- to bring together representatives of immigrant groups and governments to work for the improvement of the lives of uprooted people;
- to make special efforts on behalf of immigrant youth, who often find themselves straddling two cultures and having to take on parental responsibility for younger siblings.

Even those deemed by the authorities to be in a country illegally are children of God. The basis for rule of government must be justice for all, protecting the welfare of the poor and ensuring that the basic needs of all are covered. "The alien who resides with you shall be to you as the citizen among you; you shall love the alien as yourself" (Lev. 19:34).

QUESTIONS AND TENSIONS

Diversity of denominational and theological backgrounds leads to a variety of responses to questions such as the following:
- What constitutes Christian identity? What are the marks? What are the criteria for membership in the body of Christ?
- Are all people called to be part of the body of Christ? Are there ways other than through Jesus to answer God's call?
- What does being members of the one body imply for relations between churches of different ethnic backgrounds?

C. GOSPEL, GLOBALIZATION AND LOCAL COMMUNITIES

People everywhere are increasingly faced with the impact of globalization. The churches need to discern those elements of this process which are liberative and those which are destructive. On an economic level globalization is likened to invasion and colonization, controlled mostly by policies of bodies like the International Monetary Fund, World Bank and World Trade Organization. At the base of globalization is the liberalization of the economy at both the national and international levels—more or less voluntarily in the North, and forced by structural adjustment programmes imposed on the nations of the South, particularly those with crippling external debt. Globalization is accompanied by intensified competition which privileges the powerful and further marginalizes and excludes the weak, who are blamed for the circumstances resulting from this exploitation.

Not only is globalization an economic matter but it furthers the racial divide, creating global "apartheid." The policy-makers of the transnational corporations and international financial institutions are largely from North America, Europe and Northeast Asia. Those who suffer the most violent and devastating impact of globalization policies are the peoples and nations of the South, and the South in the North. The market enriches a few and makes many poor. Large numbers of people are excluded.

Greater economic polarity is the result, with increasing violence, political instability, migration and displacement. Economic migration often leads to xenophobic backlash, manifested in tougher immigration policies and the sanctioned oppression of all who can be placed in the role of "the other" by virtue of race/ethnicity/indigenous status, age, gender or sexual orientation. These dislocations in national economies lead to the break-up of families, as breadwinners (female and male) receiving bare subsistence or below-poverty-level wages are forced to relocate for survival. Recognizing the negative impact of the policies and conditions of the international financial institutions does not release from responsibility those in the South who are the beneficiaries of these decisions. By their silence and acceptance of these privileges, they become co-conspirators in the sin of exploitative globalization.

A further aspect of globalization has to do with the degradation of the environment, which calls for urgent strategizing and action. Increasingly people are recognizing that they live in a world in which "what goes around comes around." Globalization has led to a situation in which one country's pollutants create death in other countries. Communities everywhere are facing the effects of, for example, the excessive use of fossil fuels and problems related to the production of nuclear energy. Attention must thus be given to the development of alternative renewable fuel resources. The dearth of firewood in many countries of the South, partly as a result of deforestation, has put stress on women who have to search farther and farther afield for fuel for cooking and to provide warmth. Deforestation also affects the course of rivers and the availability of water. This in turn affects community life, contributing to the rural-urban exodus, particularly of young people.

Information technology is the most powerful instrument of the process of globalization. Information and messages communicated through the media—satellite television, advertising, films and computer technology (including the World Wide Web and electronic mail)—shape the identity of the world community as a whole and influence the identity of local communities and cultures. The media globalization effort and its message are driven by those who control the world market.

That message suggests that there is redemption through consumption, that the ability to consume means success, and that "being connected" means "being community"—in contradiction to the gospel's understanding of a community of live connectedness as being God's hope for God's people. More importantly the media often objectify and commodify women and stereotype racial/ethnic groups and gays and lesbians, debasing and degrading all. They tend to give youth a false image of being invincible, portraying technology as a source of wisdom.

The Internet and other communication systems hold the potential of enabling communication and solidarity among oppressed peoples. We call upon the churches to work towards a new communication order which challenges unjust power structures and allows the voices of the people to be heard.

We call upon the churches to examine the meaning of the gospel and its values vis-à-vis the destructive forces of globalization and the market. The Christian claims concerning the sovereignty of God stand in opposition to the totalitarian pretensions of the market economy. Christians must declare their opposition on theological grounds to any idolization or absolutization of the market. The messianic claims of the market and the consumerist life-style are in sharp conflict with the Christian confession that Jesus Christ is Lord. The churches should not be intimidated by globalization and cultural imperialism, but rather should confront the "centres of power" with the power of the gospel.

The churches need to reaffirm that God's purpose includes liberating all people from all forms of exploitation and exclusion so that they can live and share their lives in freedom and justice. We call upon the churches to support communities and groups which are resisting the exploitative and exclusionary dimensions of globalization.

We call upon the churches to work towards alternative models of community development, economic systems and fair trade practices, and to strengthen bodies such as the Ecumenical Church Loan Fund and the Ecumenical Development Cooperative Society.

We call upon the churches to be ever mindful of the biblical calling to care for the creation. Christian stewardship demands a just sharing of the earth's resources.

We call upon the churches to examine ways of counteracting the globally conveyed cultural images which have a homogenizing effect on homes, communities and churches the world over. The churches should work towards a more equitable balance of power in communication, with genuine two-way cultural sharing, in which the weaker parties are neither exploited nor their identity distorted. Moreover, the churches must do all they can to counteract negative images of oppressed people, for such people carry within them the image of God.

We call upon the churches to affirm the value of face-to-face contact. They should avoid being seduced into using the methods of the market in the church and in evangelism. The nature of the church's participation in the communication process within the global culture and economy should be carefully considered.

We call upon the WCC to re-examine its policy of providing translation/interpretation into only European languages, in order to make its work accessible to people who do not know these languages and to enable them to participate more fully in ecumenical gatherings. We are reminded that the churches at times have themselves been involved in imposing a single culture on other parts of the world, for instance during the colonial mission period, thus participating in the process of cultural imperialism.

CONCLUSION

The churches need to be empowered for culture-sensitive evangelism which takes seriously people's history and cultures. Thus will the gospel be proclaimed through people's own cultural symbols, myths and rituals, stories and festivals.

When Christians are prepared to cross cultural frontiers in openness to the Spirit, the mission of God in Christ advances as they meet each other in giving and receiving, teaching and being taught, understanding and being understood.

Section III: Local Congregations in Pluralist Societies

INTRODUCTION

After long years of encounter between a visiting pastor and a prisoner, the latter decided to accept Jesus Christ as Lord and Saviour. When the man was eventually able to leave his cell and recover freedom, the pastor was worried: would the congregation accept the former prisoner and include him fully in its life? The same kind of question had already been raised by Paul in his letter to Philemon and the church meeting in his house: would Onesimus feel that the liberating power of the gospel he had discovered in prison with Paul was real when he came back to the place from whence he had fled?

These examples show how essential is the role of each local congregation in God's mission. Like the early church in Acts, it has the privilege to live in joy the presence of the risen Christ and is called to embody as community the priorities set by Jesus in his own life. For many people, acceptance or refusal to become members of a church is linked to positive or negative experiences in or with a local congregation, which can be either a stumbling-block or an agent of transformation. It must be added, however, that Christian networks, solidarity groups, student and youth movements, urban rural mission-related groups, women's movements and others often play as important a role in the front lines of mission as do local congregations. The personal witness of Christians in family, workplace and society is also irreplaceable.

Exploration of the conference theme includes a consideration of the role of the local congregation in inculturating the gospel, making the gospel meaningful in its own context and expressing the inclusive nature of God's mission in the world to reconcile and unite all creation and humanity with God.

A. INCULTURATING FAITH IN LIFE

The conference theme speaks of a common hope, implying that our common hope is in Jesus Christ. We work together towards a renewed understanding of our common mission. As witnesses to the good news, we understand that our worship plays a crucial role in the building of strong spiritual community.

We begin with the humble statement that the scriptures are a divine source of good news. We encourage a wider dissemination of the Bible in many languages, placing in people's hands and hearts the tools for understanding and growing in faith. The moment scripture reaches its audience it is contextual. From the language in which it is read to the methods of interpretation employed and the kinds of authority attributed to it, scripture offers rich variety to a diverse humanity. From our distinct cultures and with a commitment to making the Bible accessible, we would promote its reading in an intercultural way. In our rich diversity, we may also find a richer understanding of the sacred texts.

In the church's liturgical life, culture and gospel interact and transform, illumine and challenge each other, shaping people for mission. People come to worship God using the eyes and ears of their culture, and through these same eyes and ears they may glimpse God's smile and hear the echo of God's voice. Along with the scriptures and worship, the sacraments mediate the real presence of the Holy Spirit in our worshipping communities—a presence which is also experienced in funerals and other rites, on pilgrimage, etc.

Symbols speak to the heart and to the mind. They are windows to heaven and help us relate to the divine. When we speak of symbols we recognize two rough overlapping categories: cultural symbols and cross-cultural symbols. We share a variety of symbols and images throughout Christianity, and at the same time cultural specificity dictates how these and other symbols will be incorporated into the environment of worship. Cultural history, values and aesthetics will influence the incorporation of these elements into meaningful worship—for example, the arrangement and ornamentation of worship space.

In exploring worship and cultures, there are two perspectives which are both complementary and contradictory. On the one hand, it is essential that Christian communities be (re)educated to receive anew the ancient and universal symbols. Too often Christians are unable to understand the fullness of the rich tradition with which they have been gifted. Many worshippers are unaware of the full meaning of the symbols which adorn their sacred spaces, and do not reflect on the significance of, for example, the hymns; thus they are not fully prepared to meet God in the traditional symbols and rituals. For many, learning to read icons and understanding liturgical forms and rituals can be greatly enriching and empowering. The churches must take seriously the task of education—particularly of children and youth (much of this has been taken on by laywomen)—so that liturgical symbols and theological concepts might become more accessible and better understood.

On the other hand, churches which have emerged from a colonial history have much work to do in reclaiming the symbols of their own cultures and relating them to their present experience of the sacred. For centuries, Christian societies conquered territories and used violence against local peoples, destroying their life and culture and taking their land. Too often what was holy for many communities—music, gesture, language—was put away from the churches. This calls churches today to repentance for a history in which the indigenous experience of encounter with the divine has been suppressed and rejected. Any missiology which encourages encounter with another culture, tradition or local church without showing respect for the relationship to the divine which is already at work there, must be critiqued. Even within a specifically Christian context, if the gospel is to penetrate and take root in the society it must be grounded in the people's own sense of holiness. The churches are therefore called to participate in the dismantling of all unjust structures which depreciate and dehumanize people.

With regard to the task of liturgical renewal, many Christians struggle to maintain a creative tension (particularly in worship) between the preservation of traditions and their meaning, and the renewal of liturgy relevant to the context, including freedom for spontaneity and expression of emotions. Those who have contributed to and are engaged in the task of liturgical renewal are to be commended, and need the prayers of all that their work will remain Spirit-filled.

In many congregations there exist power structures which diminish the place and influence of women, youth, so-called lower classes, ethnic and immigrant groups. Among those who are least respected are children and differently abled people. Even when potentially important decision-making positions are held by women, young people or members of minority groups, what they say is often not really taken into consideration because of the inferior status given to their input. This also affects the powerful oppressor, for example, men in male-dominated systems, who by their attitudes and actions dehumanize themselves.

It is essential for the church's renewal that steps be taken towards the empowerment of youth. Youth need to be engaged in mission, in liturgical renewal and in decision-making processes, thus sharing in the task of discerning the movement of the Spirit. The proposal to ensure 25 percent representation of youth in church bodies and related activities must be borne in mind. Their place within decision-making bodies at local and other levels must also be guaranteed, even if this requires structural changes and amendments to rules. What are the ways in which space can be provided for young people in the churches at all levels so that they feel fully part of Spirit-filled communities? Many elements of youth cultures should be recognized as valid cultural expressions. To encourage young people to remain in their countries and cultivate strong links with their church, people and culture, it may be helpful for the churches to participate in programmes creating employment for youth.

The inculturation of the gospel also involves . . . enabling the empowerment of oppressed people both within and beyond the church, such as women and the Dalits in India. Dominant groups such as men who hold power in a local congregation may need to question their styles of leadership and change their ways of relating, in order that renewal of the common life and healing of relationships may be made possible. The role played by church leadership in the discernment of the Holy Spirit should be carefully examined. How can the congregational leadership become stepping-stones rather than stumbling-blocks in the process of renewal in the power of the Holy Spirit?

The Holy Spirit can touch anyone in any culture and context. Yet the fact that so many Christians have left their church communities because they have not been able to see the Spirit at work there is troubling. How can the church both prepare people for meeting God and also remove the stumbling-blocks which any culture—but specifically dominant and colonial cultures—has placed as obstacles to the movement of the Spirit?

Important missiological work into the next century will include giving more attention to the discerning of the presence and work of the Holy Spirit. Through this the church may become more self-critical in relation to its use of symbols, its practices and its presence in the world. A set of criteria for discerning the presence of the Holy Spirit is found in 1 John 4. They include the fact that the Spirit bears witness to Jesus Christ as Lord, that the Holy Spirit must be discerned *in community*, and that Spirit-inspired actions build up community, bearing fruits of love, unity, justice and peace.

B. BECOMING SIGNS OF GOD'S INCLUSIVE LOVE

The challenge to transform the life of the local congregation faces individual Christians as they function in this primary unit of faith expression. The challenge of facing the inconsistency between the verbal expression of faith and its practice in each person's own experience is often uncomfortable. However, provoking a healthy and challenging discomfort in this respect in the life of local churches everywhere is desirable.

The local congregation is meant to be a community of fellowship flowing from the all-embracing love of the God it serves. In the African "economy of affection," receiving the other is to the benefit of all: you are because I am—I am because you are. Each is enriched by receiving and affirming the other. The stranger may be the one bearing the gifts, even the very gift of the Holy Spirit.

For the church to become inclusive, it must recognize that its hopes are not the only hopes expressed in the world. In a world filled with hopelessness, people everywhere desire hope. Jesus Christ embodies hope for all the world. What is the content of this hope in the concrete realities in which local congregations live?

- It is the hope in the mystery (surprise) of resurrection, the renewal of life in which strength can be found for all needs.
- It is the hope that each human being will recognize his or her worth before God and will strive for the healing and wholeness of each person and of the community.
- It is the hope that God's reign of righteousness, justice and peace will be experienced on earth as human beings undergo a fundamental transformation wrought through God's grace and become Christlike.
- It is the hope, founded in Christ's triumph over evil, that the principalities and powers will not triumph but that the will of God shall prevail.
- It is the hope of Christ's coming in fullness and of the final unity of all things in God, who is "all in all" (1 Cor. 15:28).

Christians have a specific calling, but the hope God offers is for all. This truth provides the missionary imperative for the church in the 21st century. The church is called to be the vehicle through which this hope is communicated to the world.

Evangelism is the joyful communication of hope, the proclamation and sharing of a life of hope; people both inside and outside the church need to hear this gospel of hope. Evangelism is a reaching in and a reaching out, proclaiming the gospel in words and actions. Through the witness of congregations and of individual Christians, the gospel can penetrate society and transform culture—even secularized culture—acting as a liberating force in contexts of hopelessness or of struggle for dignity and justice.

Though local congregations are called to be people of promise, witnessing to a common hope for all humanity, in reality they often express fear of the unknown and uneasiness with those who are racially, ethnically or culturally different. Some of these fears are born of ignorance as well as people's need to preserve their own identity. Churches, like many other social organizations, desire homogeneity and often find groups that are different "threatening." Such situations arise as communities become increasingly multi-cultural and the needs of migrant groups, for example, confront them, or when the community has to relate to persons with a sexual orientation other than that of the majority. The church must be willing to confront cultural arrogance or racism, especially within its own body. Christians can learn from the encounter of Peter and Cornelius in Acts 10 how those who are "different" can be God's instruments as well.

Trust is not possible where fear reigns. Some churches long for sufficient trust to be able to embrace the unknown or the different. This trust is the gift of the Holy Spirit, who has the power to transform and unite.

Individuals and groups need to feel that they are fully respected as the persons they are and that their identity is affirmed—particularly when they are different from the majority in a local situation. When it is evident that congregations have merely "accommodated" or "made provision for" those among them who are different, the latter are likely still to feel unaccepted. Therefore care should be exercised by the majority to demonstrate true acceptance and an inclusivity which witnesses to Christ's all-embracing love.

In this the church is challenged as to whether its raison d'etre is more its mission of sharing and living the gospel, which includes serving the needs of humanity, or rather the preservation of its own identity. In what ways are these—the call to share the gospel and serve humanity and the desire to preserve the church's identity—in tension or in symbiotic relationship with each other? What are the values by which the church lives? What standards must be upheld at all cost, including the cost of self-giving love?

Before the church—and the local congregation—can become a household of joyful cooperation in accomplishing its task within the mission of God, walls will have to be dismantled. One way to start doing this is by entering into authentic contact with those who have been excluded. In many places the young people may already have indicated their frustration by refusing to be part of the worshipping community. By taking the youth seriously, engaging in authentic dialogue with them and learning from their openness to those "outside," local congregations may break down some of the walls.

Other ways have been suggested:
- Where distinct communities exist along racial or ethnic lines within a local congregation, encouraging them to celebrate together the multicultural richness of the church as a privilege and as a gift of God.
- Encouraging different language groups in a congregation, though they may worship in separate parts of a church building or at different times, to come together for social interchange.
- Developing various forms of church membership to accommodate people from different backgrounds.
- Making provision for language training for clergy (appropriate to the context), including time spent in other cultural milieus.
- When change in a congregation is called for, ensuring adequate discussion among all sectors concerning what is essential and what may be negotiable.
- Promoting intercultural Bible-reading among Christians from different backgrounds, in order for them to be enriched mutually in their understanding of the gospel of Jesus Christ—thus demonstrating how other cultures throw new light upon the scriptures.

Living with people from many different cultures is an emerging ministry which recalls the life of the early church, and is a foretaste of the "household of God" towards which we all move.

Churches giving common witness in an ecumenical spirit of mutual respect and accountability is yet another sign of God's inclusive love. As the WCC document "Mission and Evangelism—An Ecumenical Affirmation" (1982) states: "Witness that dares to be common is a powerful sign of unity coming directly and visibly from Christ and a glimpse of his kingdom" (para. 24). Congregations are called to cooperate locally in mission and not to compete. It is imperative for churches and local congregations involved in cross-cultural witness in another context to cooperate with churches in that context, recognizing that all are part of one ecumenical family. Such cooperation has become more and more urgent in recent years, as the free-market ethos increasingly influences the mission practice of Christian communities and individuals.

C. WITNESSING IN RELIGIOUSLY PLURAL SOCIETIES

Local congregations everywhere are called to give account of the hope of a restored human community in Christ, especially in situations of increasing religious plurality. Exploring facets of this call and ways of equipping Christians for this ministry is thus vital.

Issues confronting human communities open up opportunities for people of different faiths to enter into dialogue. In central India, for example, people came together to rebuild after an earthquake, in spite of the then-prevalent communal tensions between Hindus and Muslims following the destruction of the Babri mosque by Hindu militants. In contexts such as so-called post-modern societies, all religions are faced with the challenge posed by a culture which has rendered neutral the question of truth, understanding pluralism in itself as *the* truth. In such cultures, religion is relegated to the private sphere. We affirm that the search for justice and peace and the search for truth are at the core of human life and community relations. Dialogue is thus essential where people struggle to remain human.

Before entering into dialogue with other religious communities, with individuals searching for meaningful religious experience or with those of no faith, a local congregation should be clear about its own identity in Christ, for dialogue implies that Christians bear witness to their experience of the good news of Jesus Christ.

But mission must be "in Christ's way" (San Antonio, 1989). People were called by Jesus to *follow* him; but not all were called to *respond* in the same way. There were many types of relationships with Jesus, depending upon one's commitment, humility, faith, etc. In mission there is place both for announcing the name of Jesus Christ and for dialogical relations with people of other faiths.

To dialogue is to witness to the love of God revealed in Christ. This requires mutual respect and openness to learn from others. It is wrong for Christians to pass judgment on partners in dialogue—just as they cannot impose conversion, which is the work of the Holy Spirit. Furthermore, witness has to do more with the reign of God than with affiliation to particular denominations.

Dialogue is about reconciliation where there is alienation, about building up a community of communities. The motivations for dialogue should be clear. These motivations may vary among Christians, and the emphases may differ from one context to another. Dialogue may be seen as a search for truth on both sides. Some Christians enter into dialogue with the desire to call others to discipleship practised within the Christian community. Others see dialogue as an opportunity to foster among the partners discipleship in a larger sense, referring to the dynamics of God's mission and its priorities. In contexts of conflict, the primary significance of dialogue may be to bring or maintain peace between religious communities. In such contexts, dialogue can be seen as a foretaste of the ultimate hope for the unity and reconciliation of all things in God (cf. Eph. 1:9-10).

The increasingly multireligious nature of many societies raises major theological questions which are reflected also in the reactions of people in local congregations. The presence of God in societies, cultures and religions independent of the presence of a church is one such issue. Aboriginal people in Australia, for example, witness powerfully to such experience. Early Christian theologians such as Justin Martyr spoke of "the seeds of the Word" among the cultures of the world. Many today recognize that Christ transcends time and space and reveals himself to those whom he chooses. In turn, people respond to Christ in their own cultural ways. This makes it possible for Christians to become open to the truth revealed in other cultures and traditions. The journey of Christians thus takes place in a process of both continuity and change, integrating the revealed truth that Christians encounter on their pilgrimage. But in so doing, a Christian community should never lose the centre of its faith: Jesus Christ, crucified and risen. To tell this story is the specific privilege of the churches within God's overall mission.

It is important to reaffirm the statement of the San Antonio world mission conference that "we cannot point to any other way of salvation than Jesus Christ; at the same time we cannot set limits to the saving power of God." With San Antonio, we affirm that "these convictions and the ministry of witness stand in tension with what we have affirmed about God being present in and at work in people of other faiths; we appreciate this tension, and do not attempt to resolve it" (San Antonio, pp.32,33).

On the journey of dialogue, Christians—as well as their partners from other religions—may be surprised, for Christ may encounter them where they would never have expected him (cf. Matt. 25: 31-46). This raises the question: to what extent is it possible to discern the presence of the Holy Spirit among people of other religious convictions? It is recognized that values such as humility and openness to God and to others and commitments to solidarity and the way of non-violence are found also—and sometimes more so—among people of other faiths. Galatians 5:22-23, which speaks of the fruit of the Spirit, can guide the minds, hearts and intuitions of members of local congregations as they search for marks of the Spirit in the world. The capacity for such discernment is itself a gift of the Holy Spirit.

A number of factors may prevent the local congregation from entering into dialogue with neighbours of other faiths:
- Though there may be plurality in their community, many people in local congregations prefer the comfort of their own particular cultural group.
- People in local congregations often feel embarrassed meeting strangers or facing people from unfamiliar cultures, partly because they have not been exposed to diversity.
- Some people are not at all interested in dialogue and seldom think about the meaning of being a church and about the church as a "family of families."
- Church leadership is often unprepared and ill-equipped to motivate the members for dialogue.
- Christians often have difficulty engaging in dialogue when they are a minority in their particular society or when they are or feel threatened by other religious communities and/or fundamentalist groups.
- Dialogue may be difficult in contexts where a church supports or identifies itself with the dominant culture influencing all sectors of social and economic life, where people of other faiths are a minority.
- People of faith often hesitate to enter into dialogue in situations of conflict or where religious freedom is denied.

Nonetheless there are many examples and expressions of dialogue, such as the following:
- A congregation in Indonesia is encouraged to have a positive attitude to marriage between people of different faiths.
- A congregation in Sweden lets Muslim neighbours who come to various church activities use its parish hall for their meetings and prayers.
- Muslims in Bulgaria are helping Christians to build churches and schools.
- The inner-city religious council in the UK is helping members of the different religious groups to come together to discuss and advise government on matters of common interest.
- Programmes such as the Programme for Christian-Muslim Relations in Africa (Procmura) help the churches enable their members to relate constructively to Islam.

- Christians in, for example, the Caribbean have lived from birth in religiously plural societies. Members of the same family or community may belong to different faiths and hold differing religious convictions. Yet they live as a single family or in a harmonious neighbourhood without conflict, even participating in each other's religious ceremonies, celebrations and worship. In fact, individuals' ideas of God may be drawn from more than one religious tradition.

The following practical steps are suggested to encourage dialogue in the local neighbourhood:
- training members of local congregations to be sensitive to the religious practices of people of other faiths. Christians in Lebanon, for example, were keen to help Shiite refugees fleeing from the Israeli bombs and brought them food—which the Muslims refused, since they were not sure that it had been prepared according to Islamic custom. Some of the Christians felt terribly frustrated because they did not understand the nature of the problem. Awareness programmes concerning customs and beliefs are needed: how to meet people of other faiths, how to behave in ways that will not shock, how to build bridges rather than walls. Experience shows that initiating such training requires specialists who can in turn train multipliers;
- initiating dialogue among leaders of religious groups;
- teaching about other religions in schools and theological seminaries;
- holding conferences and seminars where people have the opportunity of hearing leaders of other religions;
- publishing or publicizing for local congregational use educational materials (in print and other media) on interfaith relationships;
- recognizing the gifts of young people to encounter others in an open-minded way, and giving space to the abilities particularly of women to reach out with sensitivity to others—thus using these gifts of God positively to break barriers to dialogical relationships.

Genuine sharing can take place only when partners in dialogue encounter each other in a spirit of humility, honesty and mutual respect, ready to take risks in becoming exposed to one another and sharing one another's view of life, its meaning and purpose.

Section IV: One Gospel—Diverse Expressions

INTRODUCTION

The "call to one hope" comes to churches living and witnessing to the gospel in a variety of ways, each in relation to its local culture. Through the Holy Spirit churches are led to recognize such marvellous diversity as a gift for their mutual enrichment and to discern within it the unity that binds them together, reflecting the triune God whose inner life is a fellowship of three persons. As churches share life with one another across cultures and engage in mission together, God is glorified and God's love in Christ made known.

A. SHARING DIVERSE EXPRESSIONS OF THE ONE GOSPEL ACROSS CULTURES

CONTEXTUALITY AND CATHOLICITY

Any authentic understanding of the gospel is both contextual and catholic. The gospel is contextual in that it is inevitably embodied in a particular culture; it is catholic in that it expresses the apostolic faith handed down from generation to generation within the communion of churches in all places and all ages.

The gospel or good news of the reign of God announced by Jesus Christ is addressed to all human beings irrespective of race, gender, class, religion or culture. It is the Holy Spirit who helps the church to make known this gospel of life to all nations. It is by the power of the same Spirit that Christians are called to one hope in Christ. In sharing this hope with all humanity the church recognizes the work of the Holy Spirit, who inspires and guides and who perfects the creation.

All human cultures in their diversity are part of God's creation. Cultures are formed as a result of the task and responsibility given by God to all humankind to cultivate and take care of God's gifts (Gen. 1:28-30; 2:15). All human beings understand reality in terms of their own particular cultural perspectives constituted by their collective memory, experience, creativity, interpersonal relationships, religious beliefs and practices and physical environment, and expressed in their own particular language.

The gospel of Jesus Christ encountering any given culture becomes incarnate in and illuminated by that culture, but also transforms and transcends that culture. A fuller understanding of the catholicity and contextuality of the gospel must take into account the complexity of diverse cultural groupings, their historical and theological traditions, their interactions and particular perspectives, while at the same time centring on the simplicity and transparency of the gospel of love that invites all human beings to recognize that they are children of God, called to community with God and with each other.

The local churches in early Christian history expressed their faith through their own cultural media. In their different liturgical traditions, for example, they expressed the one faith in diverse linguistic, musical and symbolic ways. These churches manifested the catholicity of the faith through their diverse cultural resources and identities and through their communion with one another.

Identity and context on the one hand and communion and catholicity on the other are not opposed to each other, but are complementary. Cultural contextuality in the Christian sense does not mean isolated and self-contained expression of the gospel but affirmation of the gifts of each culture for the proclamation of the gospel in communion with other contexts. Catholicity does not mean a universality that sweeps away particular identities, but is the expression of the fullness of truth that can be experienced in each particular context. The Greek *kata-kolon* (from which "catholic" is derived) means "according to the whole" and so indicates the holistic quality of truth rather than any geographic or quantitative dimension. Catholicity requires that different contexts be in communion with each other and respect and challenge each other in the freedom of the Spirit. Together, contextuality and catholicity become signs of authenticity for the local as well as the global reality of the church.

New Testament narratives illustrate that the gospel refuses to be monopolized by one culture—for example, Jesus' encounter with the Syrophoenician woman (Mark 7:24-30) and the understanding of the gospel across language barriers at Pentecost (Acts 2). The ministry of Jesus Christ and the giving of the Holy Spirit at Pentecost are evidence of how God has claimed all persons and situations as the context for God's healing, justice and love.

"SEEDS OF THE WORD"

The gospel is the word of God communicated to all humanity in the incarnate Christ, testified to in the biblical scripture and proclaimed by the church; it is not limited to an interpretation of particular biblical texts. Gospel values are present in all cultures in the form of life, justice, freedom, reciprocity and holistic relations with creation. Therefore the gospel is not the property of any particular culture. The spirituality of different people must be respected as an expression of their integral faith. As such, particular language, interpretative devices, symbol systems or forms of Christian worship in one culture are not binding in other cultures. However, in mutual respect and in a transparent act of communion and love, these may be shared among cultures without coercion, enriching the expression of the gospel.

An early Christian understanding of the "seeds of the Word" in all human cultures is derived from the way the fourth gospel used the Greek concept "logos" to communicate the mystery of Christ to the Greek-speaking world. This was a significant landmark in the passage of the gospel from its Jewish matrix to the Hellenistic world. In the history of the church this concept reminded Christians that no cultural situation in itself can be labelled as closed to the presence of Christ. Within all cultures are found insights and wisdom that can be understood as expressions of the word. The diverse forms in which such expressions might be found are to be fully respected. Christians individually and in community continue to explore how the gospel can best be expressed in their own cultural forms; these attempts deserve the respect and support of other Christians. They will at the same time want to test the appropriateness of their findings in the mutual relationship of catholicity with others.

Criteria for testing the appropriateness of such contextual expressions of the gospel in mutual relationship with other churches include:
- faithfulness to God's self-disclosure in the totality of the scriptures;
- commitment to a life-style and action in harmony with the reign of God;
- openness to the wisdom of the communion of saints across space and time;
- relevance to the context.

USE OF POWER

The secular power of the church in its human institutional dimension is undeniable. Money, material possessions, state connections, history, etc., affect the way churches relate to each other and with cultures. Only when the power of the church is used in the service of the gospel is the apostolic authority *(exousia)* granted to the church by Christ manifested in the world.

The apostolic power of the gospel is expressed by the church in word and sacrament for healing, forgiveness and reconciliation and against death and destruction. The nature of the gospel's power is self-emptying, expressed fully through the cross and resurrection of Christ (Phil. 2:6-8). Churches should take the example of Christ in the exercise of their secular power (Matt. 20:25-28).

It is recognized that imbalances in temporal or secular power exist and can impede even the best-intentioned encounters among churches and with cultures. A dominant force has the potential to intimidate, coerce or end interaction with a less powerful counterpart. The dominant force may be unaware of the impact of its words or actions on the other.

The authority to teach belongs to the apostolic commission given to the disciples by Christ (Matt. 28:19-20). In faithful witness to Christ, Christians exercise this authority in interpreting the scriptures and transmitting the life-giving gospel to all people. A conciliar exercise of the teaching authority as exemplified in the ecumenical councils of the early church is desirable at all levels of the present life of the church. Since this authority is located in the whole body of Christ, any personal or structural expression of faith should be judged by the whole body using appropriate structures of dialogue and participation.

The mechanism for settling disputes varies from church to church. Resolving differences among churches is complicated by the various polities and ecclesiologies that have evolved in the churches. Deciding what is the proper interpretation of a biblical text or an ethical issue depends on the conciliar dialogue among the churches against the backdrop of the spiritual and theological heritage of the whole church.

SYNCRETISM

Dynamic interactions between the gospel and cultures inevitably raise the question of syncretism. From one perspective, syncretism is merely a mixture of elements from different sources. In that respect, any cultural expression of the gospel is syncretic. Theologically, syncretism has tended to mean a blending of elements of different origin or which are in conflict, hence a perceived failure to maintain a faithful correspondence to the gospel. Clarity and care are needed in the use of this term in Christian relationships, since its application is closely linked to the reality of power imbalances among the churches.

Accusations of syncretism have been made by both larger and smaller churches. Powerful historic churches have sometimes accused small and newly emerging Christian communities of syncretism. Accusations have also come from minority churches, as in the case of the Confessing Church in Germany during the Nazi period taking a radically critical position against the mainstream church, which had mixed nationalistic political ideology with Christian faith. It is important that syncretism be judged apart from the relative "power" of the accusing body.

Authentic witness to the gospel is threatened when Christians, knowingly or not, align their faith with life-denying and exclusivist ideological, political and socio-economic schemes, or when their actions betray Jesus Christ crucified and risen—the ultimate source of and standard for human faith and hope. The criteria to discern syncretism must be centred on Christ and grounded in a Christian witness characterized by life-affirming, inclusive, liberating and community-building attitudes. These criteria are to be applied sensitively within particular local contexts.

Some practices and customs which were once negated and rejected as "pagan" and "superstitious" are now recognized as authentic elements of people's spirituality. The use of certain musical instruments and forms of traditional worship are cases in point. The profound need of many peoples to include the living presence of their ancestors in an organic and holistic vision of reality is not seriously considered in some Christian churches. Other Christian traditions, however, provide for this need through commemorative feasts, prayers, liturgical celebrations or visual arts. It is the task of the church to give theological meaning to this profound need through the incarnate Lord, crucified and risen from the dead, who gives the promise of eternal life.

In rediscovering the catholicity of the church in each cultural context it is the incarnation, life, death and resurrection of Jesus Christ that together constitute the known standard for such discernment. Destructive and death-dealing elements in every culture are judged in the light of that standard.

INTERCULTURAL COMMUNICATION

Grappling with the complexity of cultural diversity and the simplicity of the gospel of love raises the question of mediating the meaning of the gospel across cultures. Many elements can prevent the genuine communication of the good news from culture to culture, including fear of other cultures, arrogance about one's own culture, prejudices against others, and stories and jokes about others.

The assumed cultural "superiority" of some cultures has sometimes made "bad news" out of the good news. The Bible interpreted through certain cultural norms in some so-called Christian societies has been used to suppress and marginalize indigenous peoples, women and youth and to perpetuate racism, slavery and other evils.

The need for community at a personal level as well as at the level of social cultural groupings is a gospel imperative that binds cultures in the Spirit, who leads all into sharing and fellowship, speaking and listening, challenging and supporting each other (John 17). Christians need each other to discern the one gospel of Jesus Christ in their diverse cultures. Each can help the other in the struggle to live out the gospel in any particular culture. Mutual respect and receptiveness to one another's gifts are essential for genuine communication. True communication of the gospel does not create a false hierarchy between persons. The encounter becomes a special moment of grace, revealing new possibilities of communion free from self-serving interests. Intercultural communication of the gospel is not a one-time event but a continuous dialogue of love and mutual exchange of the life-giving message. In this ongoing dialogue the power of language, gesture, art, image and symbol should be fully explored and utilized.

B. TOWARDS RESPONSIBLE RELATIONSHIPS IN MISSION

The theme "Called to One Hope—The Gospel in Diverse Cultures" reflects the recognition that this one hope is expressed in different ways and within different cultural contexts. This compels the church to face the challenges of responsible relationships and methodologies in mission. These challenges are even more pronounced with the end of the cold war, when the dominant forces of the world seem to be imposing on all cultures values driven by a free-market economy. In today's world a critical appraisal of the form and practice of mission is crucial so that competitive and divisive mission methods may be avoided. In the light of this danger, the San Antonio declaration that "to be called to unity in mission involves becoming a community that transcends in its life the barriers and brokenness in the world, and living as a sign of at-one-ment under the cross" (San Antonio, p.28) rings with renewed urgency.

Being united in mission is therefore an imperative as churches respond to the call to one hope and live and witness to the one gospel in its multiple facets.

MISSION AND UNITY

Past mission conferences and WCC assemblies have yielded a number of ecumenical missiological insights, many of which continue to be relevant to the work of mission today. Since at least the Whitby world mission conference (1947), partnership in mission has been understood as an essential way of following Christ's call; and a number of documents have been produced on "common witness." The WCC document "Mission and Evangelism—An Ecumenical Affirmation" (1982) states:

> Common witness should be the natural consequence of [the churches'] unity with Christ in his mission . . . In solidarity, churches are helping each other in their respective witness before the world. In the same solidarity, they should share their spiritual and material resources to announce together and clearly their common hope and common calling (para. 23).

While many of the convictions and commitments made in recent years have been put into action, much remains to be done. Nevertheless, churches and mission agencies agree that:
- "Mission is *the mission of God* whose 'love has been poured into our hearts through the Holy Spirit' (Rom. 5:5), inviting the community to become God's co-workers (cf. 1 Cor. 3:9) in God's continuing act of re-creating and uniting the whole of creation" (Salvador preparatory papers, p.76). The *missio Dei* takes place in multiple directions in the whole world and results in the transformation of human communities.
- A holistic understanding of mission as including both evangelism and service leads the church to faithfulness to God's continuing act in Christ. Indeed mission challenges "the whole church to take the whole gospel to the whole world" ("The Lausanne Covenant," 1974, para. 6). Such mission is engaged in by and for persons of all races and social strata, women and men, young and old, lay and ordained, poor and rich, and persons with different abilities.

Mission and unity are inseparably linked; mission in unity remains a goal to which the church aspires. Visible signs of commitment to the goal of unity include collaboration, cooperation and networking among churches and mission agencies in the same area, across cultural and denominational boundaries, and across national and regional boundaries.

Traditionally, some parts of the church have understood mission as an activity outside their own borders, while others have understood mission as primarily focused on their own contexts. In recent years it has been said that "the primary responsibility for mission rests with the local church." Some suggest rewording this to read: "The primary responsibility for mission, where there is a local church, is with that church in its own place." Local congregations are thus called to be missionary congregations.

Since the task of evangelism is primarily the responsibility of the local church in each place, any international mission effort must recognize and respect this. Sister churches can however assist each other's local mission. Where churches are not actively engaged in evangelism efforts, there may be need to challenge each other, in affirming ways, towards authentic proclamation and living out of the gospel.

MUTUALITY IN MISSION

Churches need each other both locally and globally. This need has been expressed in a variety of ways in mission history.

In recent years the structures of various mission agencies—such as the Communauté évangélique d'Action apostolique (CEVAA), the Council for World Mission and the Vereinigte Evangelische Mission (UEM)—have been transformed to reflect more adequately mutuality in mission and increased commitment to South-to-South relationships. Many other models undoubtedly exist.

No matter what the structures, churches, mission agencies and local congregations should be called to the practice of a common discipline of mutual cooperation in mission, taking into consideration various experiences and new models. In the search for such a discipline, a number of key insights and core values have been identified in recent ecumenical discussions. They include:
- mutual challenge and encouragement;
- the creation of "safe spaces" in which honest speaking and real listening occur;
- the sharing of resources in ways that promote genuine interdependence;
- shared decision-making in the context of mutual respect for each other's priorities;
- patience and appreciation for the dynamic nature of relationships;
- openness and a continuing search for greater solidarity;
- transparency and mutual accountability.

Some forms of global partnership have been a hindrance to local ecumenical partnerships. Bilateral denominational mission relationships have sometimes distracted churches from fostering local ecumenical relationships and ignored the local ecumenical instruments already in place. Churches everywhere should value, strengthen and utilize ecumenical mission relationships at all levels. Ecumenical institutions should also be challenged to place mission and evangelism among their priorities.

The WCC and its member churches and affiliated bodies should intensify dialogue with non-member churches, agencies and associations, formally and informally and at all levels, in order to share visions and practices for mutual challenge and encouragement in mission—for the challenge to mutuality in mission in response to the call to "one hope" applies to all churches everywhere. Through conscious effort to share experiences and explore common issues in mission in a prayerful spirit, the churches may be helped to avoid repeating mistakes of past unilateral and colonial patterns of mission.

TOWARDS COMMON WITNESS

The (draft) WCC document "Gathering into Unity: Affirming Mission in Fidelity to the Gospel" (1996) is a commendable framework for addressing issues of common witness and proselytism. Among the affirmations in that document which undergird authentic common witness are the following:

> Participating in God's mission is an imperative for all Christians and all churches, not a specialized calling for individuals or groups. It is also an inner compulsion, based on the profound demands of Christ's love, to invite others to share in the fullness of life Jesus came to bring (cf. John 10:10) . . .
> The ground for our common witness is that:
> - we proclaim and worship one God and Creator;
> - we confess the same Jesus Christ as Lord and Saviour;
> - we are moved by the one Holy Spirit who empowers us;
> - there is one gospel which we proclaim and to which we witness;
> - there is one mission of God in which we share as God's co-workers (1 Cor. 3:9; 3 John 8).
>
> As Paul says: "There is one body and one Spirit, just as you were called to the one hope of your calling, one Lord, one faith, one baptism, one God and Father of all, who is above all and through all and in all" (Eph. 4:4-6) ("Gathering into Unity," paras. 6,18).

The new contexts in which the churches are called to common witness today expose increased obstacles to such witness. One major obstacle is proselytism. The (draft) document asserts:

> Different churches understand proselytism in different ways. Here it is taken to mean the encouragement of Christians who are considered members of one church to change their denominational allegiance through ways and means that "contradict the spirit of Christian love, violate the freedom of the human person and diminish trust in the Christian witness of the church" (Orthodox consultation on mission and proselytism, Moscow, 1995).

Proselytism—which may be open or subtle—is always a wounding of koinonia at the centre of the life Christians are called to live amidst their differences (Phil. 2:2-5; Rom. 15:2-7). It discredits the work of the Holy Spirit in each person and church, and must always be distinguished from conversion in Christ that is biblical, free and genuine.

Proselytism is a destabilizing factor, especially for mainline churches and even, in some countries, for society. The WCC New Delhi assembly described it as "a corruption of Christian witness" . . . [It also] emphasized that the difference between authentic witness and proselytism is a matter of "purpose, motive and spirit as well as of means" . . .

There are a variety of manifestations of proselytism. One form, of which many churches complain, is the offer of interchurch aid in human, material and other forms (for example, kilos of rice for conversion, clothing for baptism, language classes as a bridge to the future) as inducement to join another church. Yet such assistance could have been a sign of Christian love and solidarity and an expression of common Christian witness . . .

The churches need to assess their own internal life to see whether some of the reasons people change church allegiance may lie with the churches themselves ("Gathering into Unity," paras. 32-34,36,43).

We decry the practice of those who carry out their endeavours in mission and evangelism in ways which destroy the unity of the body of Christ, human dignity and the very lives and cultures of those being "evangelized;" we call on them to confess their participation in and to renounce proselytism. We also decry expressions of Christian triumphalism in religiously plural contexts.

At the same time, however, we rejoice in the religious liberty now available in many parts of the world, especially within Eastern Europe. This freedom opens up new opportunity to work for the renewal of the church, the rebuilding of the body of Christ and the spiritual re-enlightenment of believers. It also provides opportunity for the world church to support and strengthen the historic churches in Eastern Europe as they seek new guidelines for mission and renewal of ministry.

Local churches in other contexts around the world are faced with other crises. Some have to deal with socio-political conflicts and large numbers of displaced persons, while others (in minority situations) have to cope with persecution from fundamentalist systems. These may also be opportunities for the world church to support, strengthen and engage in common witness.

It is important for all who feel called to mission and evangelism to engage in such with sensitivity and concern for the churches already in that place. Discipline for mutuality in mission should always be respected.

Specific actions that could be taken include:
- that the central committee of the WCC be requested to commend to the churches for study and action the "Gathering into Unity" document following its adoption;
- that a dialogue be initiated among those involved in mission within as well as outside ecumenical circles to address proselytism and others issues related to mutuality in mission.

CONCLUSION

Called to one hope in Christ, we commit ourselves to take seriously our common call to mission and to work towards mission in unity. We actively seek a new era of "mission in Christ's way" at the dawn of the third millennium, enriched by one another's gifts and bound together in the Holy Spirit, to the glory of the triune God.

Index

"accommodation," 43
Accra International African Seminar 1965, 147-48, 150, 152
acculturation, 169
Acts, Book of, 1-2, 21-22, 37-38, 44, 50-51, 139, 186, 217, 221
"adaptation," 2, 43, 92, 155
Ad Gentes, decree, 92, 101, 170
Africa: Christianity in, 19, 24-27, 46-47, 54-65, 138, 140-41, 144, 146-56; indigenous culture in, 54-65, 76, 135, 137, 148-53
African Independent Churches, 24-25, 49, 59, 149, 152-53, 155
African synod, 58-60, 64-65
African Traditional Religion—A Definition (Idowu), 151-52
AIDS, 134, 139, 208, 211
alienation: of African Church, 56-60; from own culture, 33; missionary, 8, 12
American culture, 104-16
Analects, Confucian, 77-79
ancestor veneration, 10, 64, 118
anima naturaliter Christiana, 169-70
annunciation, women's interpretation of, 85-86
anthropocentrism vs. theocentrism, 31
anthropology, 7, 44, 46, 48, 141
apartheid, Bible used in support of, 194-95
Arabic language, 147
Aram (Keshishian) I, 29-40
Armenian Apostolic Church, 29, 32-33
Asia, Christianity in, 76-103, 117-32
Asian Colloquium on Ministries 1977, 118-19
assimilation, 172-73

assumption, 171
authority, church vs. state, 107-10
Ayandele, E. A., 156

Baëta, Christian, 147-48, 150
Bahia (See, Salvador de Bahia CWME Conference)
Bangkok CWME Conference 1973, 8
Baptism, 181-84
Basic Christian Communities, 48, 54, 64-65, 91, 99-102, 141-42
Bediako, Kwame, 146-56
Bellah, Robert N., 104-16
Bible, the: interpretation of, 76-87, 107-8; reading, 140-42; translation of, 2, 7, 60, 79-80, 151, 154-56, 187, 218; used to support racism, 194-95; women in, 84
"Bible Christianity," 59
"Bible women," 80
Bimwenyi, Oscar, 57
Bishops' Conference of the Philippines 1900, 124-25
bishops' conferences, regional, 4-5, 8-13, 91-103, 117-19, 123-25
Blomjous, Joseph, 56
Borsch, Frederick, 115-16
Buddhism, 4, 43, 77-79, 102

California, University of, 109
"Called to One Hope: The Gospel in Diverse Cultures" (WCC), 10-12, 29-30, 134-44
Cámara, Helder, 136
Cameroon Mass, 63
Canberra WCC Assembly 1991, 10, 31, 33-34, 39, 40n. 1, 139

235

Candomblé, 139
canon law, 61-63
Carey, William, 79
Cartigny Statement on Worship and Culture, 178-80
catechesis, 70-71, 100
catholicity: 118; vs. contextuality, 185, 189-95, 226-27
Chalcedonian Definition of the Faith, 24
Chicago school economists, 110-11
children, plight of, 38-39, 208
China, Christianity in, 50-51, 79-81, 86-87
Christianity: capacity for integration, 195; as critique of culture, 72-75; fundamentalist, 59, 163, 224; history of, 17-27, 118, 148-53; inauthentic, 104-16; shift to Third World, 3-4, 23-24, 122-23, 147-53, 195; "split-level," 48; traditional values in light of, 128-32; as universalizing, 22-23
"Christianity and African Culture: The African Contribution to Theology" (Mulago), 150
Christianity in Tropical Africa (Baëta), 147-48, 150
Christian Message in a Non-Christian World, The (Kraemer), 34
Christian Worship: Unity in Cultural Diversity (LWF), 179, 180-81
church buildings, 177-78
"Church in the Modern World, The," constitution, 6, 97
Circle of Concerned African Women Theologians, 145n. 6
civilization, 162-63
Clement of Alexandria, 27, 169, 170
cold war, 108-10
colonialism, 33, 57, 122, 124-25, 141, 148, 213
Commission on World Mission and Evangelism of the WCC (CWME), 4-5, 8-13
communication, intercultural, 69-75, 185, 190-93, 229-30
Communist world, collapse of, 115
community, 207-17
Confessing Church, 228
Confucianism, 77-79, 118
Congregation for the Propagation of the Faith, 118

conscientization, 125
contextualization, 5, 32-34, 42-51, 177-84, 226-27
Coptic rite, 63
covenant vs. contract, 105-8
cultural embeddedness, 69-75
culture: evangelization in, 55-65; fundamental aspects of, 5-7; as historical process, 91, 95-97; liberative vs. oppressive aspects, 140-44; "of life," 36-37, 40; polycentric, 54, 56, 61-65; right to, 69, 73; situations in, 68-75; as source of tension, 30-34; views of, 160-66

dance, 10, 86
Dao de jing, 77-79
"Decree on the Church's Missionary Activity," 6
de Mesa, José M., 117-32
denominational extension, 48-50
De Principiis (Origen), 24
Dewey, Joanna, 81-82
dialogue, 34-35, 86-87, 92, 98-99, 134, 140, 223-25
Drego, Pearl, 85-86

early church: christological controversies in, 71; Council of Jerusalem, 21-22, 44, 51-52, 118; Jewish vs. gentile culture in, 1-3, 18-22, 26-27, 32, 44, 50-51, 148, 195; local churches in, 226; writers on other cultures, 169-73
Eastern Orthodox Churches, 10, 33-34, 198-99
ecclesiastical hegemony, 49-51
ecosystem, human, 159, 164-73
Ecumenical Decade of the Churches in Solidarity with Women, 210
ecumenical movement: on culture, 29-40; hermeneutic of, 39; and marginalized, 143-44; rise of, 4-13
Edinburgh CWME conference 1910, 10, 196-97
encounter: crosscultural, 45-47; of gospel and culture, 92-95, 196-92
Ethiopia, Christianity in, 63, 149, 195
ethnicity, 30, 34, 207-17
Eucharist, the, 181
eurocentrism, 3-4, 51, 57-60
Eusebius of Caesarea, 169, 170

INDEX 237

Evangelii Nuntiandi, Apostolic Exhortation (Paul VI), 6, 61, 92, 95, 166, 167, 170
Evangelii Praecones, encyclical (Pius XII), 170
"Evangelization in the Modern World" synod 1974, 118
Exodus, Book of, 84-85

Federation of Asian Bishops' Conferences, 91-103, 117-19, 123
formation programs, 102
Francis Xavier, S.J., 3
freedom, Christian vs. Lockean, 105-16
Freud, Sigmund, 163
Friedman, Milton, 110-11
fundamentalism, 59, 163, 224

"Gathering into Unity: Affirming Mission in Fidelity to the Gospel" (WCC), 232-33
Gaudium et Spes, constitution, 69, 92, 120, 122-23, 160, 162, 170-71
Genesis, Book of, 194
Geneva WCC meeting 1995, 29-40
ginhawa, 128
globalization: and homogenization of culture, 54-60; of injustice, 137-38; of market economy, 11-13, 57-58, 207-9, 215; and mission, 38-40, 142-44; of monoculture, 30-31; of pluralism, 30, 34-35; and technology, 9, 11, 215-16
Gnostics, 27
God: and hope, 220-22; as preceding missionaries, 153-54; in religions, 202-3, 223-24
Good News, gospel as, 98, 186-88, 192, 202
Good Society, The (Bellah et al.), 104-5, 111
gospel and culture, approaches to: action model, 70-72; catholicity vs. contextuality, 185-95; contextualization, 42-51; covenant vs. social contract, 104-16; ecumenical, 4-13, 196-234; eurocentric, 3-4, 12; human ecosystem, 159-73; incarnation, 29-40; indigenizing principle vs. pilgrim principle, 17-27, 45; mutual respect and critical interaction, 120-32; one hope, 134-44; orality, 76-87; polycentric, 54-65; self-realization of local churches, 91-103; situations as determining balance, 68-75; through but not in culture, 29, 33-34; translatability, 146-56; Word-oriented, 7-8
gratitude as element in culture, 165-66
Gulf War, 108-10
Gutenberg, Johannes, 82
Gutiérrez, Gustavo, 23-24

healing, 37-39
Hellenistic culture in early church, 2, 18-22, 26-27, 148, 195
hermeneutics: as challenge of contextualization, 51; cross-cultural, 62, 71, 185-95; cultural, 140-44; ecumenical, 39; oral, 76-87
Hinduism, 4, 77-78, 102, 118, 222
Holy Spirit, 6, 10, 12, 190-92, 199, 201, 220, 225-26
hope, inclusive nature of, 134-44, 220-22, 230
human rights, 103
Hussein, Saddam, 108

identity: Christian, 195; and community, 207-17; personal, 8; politics of, 11, 211-14; spaces for, 165; theology affirming, 72, 125-27
ideologies, hidden, 31
Idowu, Bolaji, 25-27, 150-52
incarnation, 5, 29-40, 51, 146, 147, 159, 166, 168-69, 182, 187
inculturation: vs. articulation, 172-73; defined, 5; early experiments in, 3; judging validity of, 68, 73-75; origin of term, 43, 52n. 2, 57; vs. syncretism, 55-56; theology as, 117-32
India, Christianity in, 50-51, 79-80, 86
indigenization, 2, 31-34, 146, 150-53, 156
indigenizing principle, 17, 21-27, 44
indigenous peoples, 209
individualism, 105-16
industrialization, 98-99
in-reach, 39-40
insertion, 171
Instrumentum Laboris (African synod), 58-60, 64-65
integrity of gospel, 68, 74-75, 191-92
International African Institute, 147
International Theological Commission, 55
Irenaeus of Lyons, 169-71
Irish monks, 18-20

Islam, 4, 34, 78, 147, 222, 224, 225
Israel, history of, 25-27

Jenkins, Paul, 150, 156
Jerusalem, Council of, 21-22, 44, 51-52, 118
Jesus Christ: born in specific culture, 182; church as body of, 105-7; in cultural contexts, 9; and freedom, 105; God in, 202-3; as judging culture, 35-37, 40, 182; and inclusive cultural attitudes, 2; as witness to hope, 136; vs. written book, 31
Jewish culture in early church, 1-3, 18-22, 26-27, 32, 37
John XXIII, 56
John Paul II, 6-7, 55, 59, 60, 69, 92, 96, 100
Justin Martyr, 27, 169, 170, 223

Kanyoro, Musimbi R. A., 134-44
Kelber, Werner H., 77, 81
kerygma, oral, 81-84, 186
koinonia, 39-40, 61
Korea, Christianity in, 10, 48
Kraemer, Hendrik, 7, 34
Kyung, Chung Hyun, 139

Latin America, Christianity in, 159-73
Lausanne Covenant, 7-8, 230
Lausanne International Congress on World Evangelization, 7-8
Leviticus, Book of, 25
literacy, 79-84
liturgy: local vs. transcultural elements, 180-84, 218-20; Roman, regions within, 63-65, 100
local churches, 54-65, 91-103, 118-23, 155-56, 217-234
Locke, John, 104-10
logos, 27
Lumen Gentium, 92, 168, 170-71
Lutheran World Federation, 142-43, 177-84
Luykx, Boniface, 63

Mao Tse-tung, 50
marginalized, the, 97-99, 143-44, 207-17
Mark, gospel of, 81-82, 84
market economy: as globalized, 11-13, 57-58; as totalitarian, 110-15
Marxism, 24, 105, 161-62
Massy, William, 112-13

Matthew, Gospel of, 81-82, 84
Mbiti, John S., 25-27, 148, 150, 152-53
Medellín Conference, 160
Melanesia, Christianity in, 44, 47
Melbourne CWME meeting 1980, 9
metanoia, 38, 68, 74-75
Missio Dei, 155-56, 167, 230
Missiology, 7
mission: and globalization, 38-40; at home, 39-40; in next century, 141-44; organizations in, 4-13, 49-51, 231-32; practice of contextualization in, 42-51; in religiously plural societies, 222-25; and unity, 230-34; Western male dominance in, 142-43
"Mission and Evangelism—An Ecumenical Affirmation" (WCC), 211, 222, 230
modernity, 164
Moltmann, Jürgen, 135
Mulago, Vincent, 150

Nairobi LWF consultation 1996, 177-84
Nairobi WCC Assembly 1975, 8-9
nationalism, 125, 163, 186, 213
Nazi period, churches in, 228
new evangelization, 54, 60-65, 169-73
Nicea, Council of, 18-21
Nigeria, Christianity in, 151
Nitze, Paul, 109
Nobili, Roberto de, 3, 56, 92, 118
North America, contextualization in, 44
North vs. South, 143-44, 188

Octogesima Adveniens (Paul VI), 99-100
offense of the Gospel, 45-47
Ong, Walter J., 82-83
Oral and the Written Gospel, The (Kelber), 77, 81
oral culture, 64, 76-87
Orientalium Ecclesiarum, decree, 63
otherness of indigenous culture, 159-61

Paul, Saint: on church as body of Christ, 105-7; conversions by, 21-22; and culture, 25, 27; mission to gentiles, 2
Paul VI, 6, 55, 60, 61, 63, 69, 95, 99
Pentecost, 32, 186, 197, 227
Pentecostalism, 59
Peter, Saint, 2, 221
Petrine ministry, 61-62

INDEX

Philippines, Christianity in, 117-32
pilgrim principle, 17-27, 104
Pius XII, 56, 170
pluralism: cultural: 2-5; global, 30, 34-35; local congregations and, 217-34; religious, 4, 222-25
polycentric evangelization model, 54, 56, 61-65
pop culture, 164
Popenoe, David, 111-12
poverty, 11-13, 36-37, 97-99, 159-60, 166-67, 173, 207-9
Practical Anthropology, 7
"Predicament of the Church in Africa, The" (Idowu), 150-51
preferential option for the poor, 166-67
preparatio evangelica, 170
Primal Vision, The (Taylor), 46-47
privatization of religion, 106-16, 222-23
production as element in culture, 165-66
progress, 162-63
propositional thinking, 70-71
proselytism, 232-33
Protestant evangelicalism, 7-8, 79
Puebla conference, 164-65, 171, 174n. 20
Pui-lan, Kwok, 76-87
Puritans, 3

Qur'an, the, 78-79

racism, 36, 73, 163, 193-95, 197
Rahner, Karl, 170
Reading the Bible as Asian Women (Chung/Jenkin/Matsuda), 84-85
reconstruction, cultural, 72
Redemptoris Missio, encyclical letter (John Paul II), 6-7, 60
re-evangelization of the west, 12
regions: cultural, 61-62; liturgical, 63-65
religions, God's work in, 201-3
religious life, 101-2
resistance, cultural, 72-73, 165-66
Resurrection, 130
Ricci, Matteo, 3, 56, 92, 118
risk, necessary, 68, 74-75
Roman rite, regions within, 63-65, 168

Sacrosanctum Concilium, constitution, 63
Salvador de Bahia CWME Conference 1996, 9-12, 134-44, 196-234

salvation, 37-38, 128-29
San Agustin, Gaspar de, 124
San Antonio WCC Conference 1989, 10, 35, 206, 223-24
Sanneh, Lamin, 154-56
schism, fear of, 60
Schreiter, Robert J., 68-75
Scripture: in light of local practice, 25, 27; oral vs. written, 76-87
Second Vatican Council (*See*, Vatican II)
secularism, 30, 31, 58, 59, 144
secular power of the church, 227-28
semina verbi, 170-71
sexism, 36, 193-95
Shorter, Aylward, 54-65
situations: as determining faith/culture balance, 68-75; vs. tradition, 126-32
slave trade, 10, 166-67
social contract, 104-16
social reality, culture in, 162
Society of African Culture, 57
solidarity, cultural, 73
South African Black Theology, 24
South-to-South relationships, 231
Stanford Institute for Higher Education Research, 113-14
Stauffer, S. Anita, 177-80
Suess, Paulo, 159-73
superstructure, culture as, 161-62
Swidler, Ann, 111
syncretism, 11, 35, 48, 55-56, 70, 139, 152-53, 191-92, 228-29
synods, role in cultural polycentrism, 62

Taylor, John V., 46-47
technocracy, 57-58
Tertullian, 27, 169-70
Thailand, Christianity in, 43
theology: and action, 24-25; and African religions, 148-53; in Asian context, 117-32; inculturation of, 101; local, 23-27, 118-23; neo-scholastic, 119, 122, 128; on other cultures, 169-73
Theology of Hope (Moltmann), 135
theory vs. practice of contextualization, 42-51
Tiananmen Square massacre, 86
totalitarianism in U.S. culture, 108-15
Towards an Indigenous Church (Idowu), 151

traditional values in light of Christianity, 128-32
transcendence of gospel, 68, 74-75
translation: of Bible, 2, 7, 60, 79-80, 151, 154-56, 187, 218; of faith, 2-3, 146-56; of liturgy, 63-65
truth: cultural criteria for, 40-41; in oral vs. literate traditions, 83-84
Tutu, Desmond, 144

United States, Christianity in, 104-16
"unity in diversity," 6, 38, 61
Universal Catechism, 70-71
urbanization, 58, 144

values vs. anti-values, 161
Vancouver WCC Assembly 1983, 9-10, 40n. 1
Vatican II: authors cited, 169-73; on canon law, 62; on catholicity, 118; on culture, 6, 55, 57, 58, 69, 73, 126; on liturgy, 63
Venn, Henry, 25
vernacular languages, 79, 147, 151
vestments, 151
violence, 36-37, 39

Walls, Andrew F., 2, 17-27, 29, 45, 146
Weber, Max, 162
Wellborn, F. B., 148
Wesley, Charles, 44, 45
Wesley, John, 44, 45
Western culture, dominance of, 12, 30-31, 33, 51, 54, 57-60, 80, 122, 150-56, 188-89

Whitby world mission conference 1947, 230
Whiteman, Darrell L., 42-51
wholeness of church, 38-40
Whose Keeper? (Wolfe), 110-11
Wire, Antoinette, 82
witness, 11-13, 136, 222-25
Wolfe, Alan, 110-11
women: Bahia on, 210-11; Bible interpretation by, 76-87, 140-42; in Church leadership, 64, 219; empowerment of, 11, 198, 208; interests of, 56; literacy of, 79-81; rights of, 105; subjugation of, 73; trafficking in, 138
Word, the, 7-8, 77, 156, 170-71, 190-91, 202, 227
World Council of Churches: Commission on Faith and Order, 184n. 2; Commission on World Mission and Evangelism (CWME), 4-5, 8-13, 134-44, 196-234; gospel and culture study process, 29-30, 134, 185-95; "Programme to Overcome Violence," 37
worship, 177-84, 218-20
Worship and Culture in Dialogue (LWF), 178-79

Yoruba religion, 26
youth, 11, 56, 198, 210, 219
Y.W.C.A., the, 76, 80, 87

Zaire Mass, 63
Zen tradition, 79
Zimbabwe Liturgy for Second Burial, 63-64

Of Related Interest

Two earlier volumes in the New Directions Series

Volume 1, Basic Statements, 1974-1991
James A. Scherer and Stephen B. Bevans, editors
ISBN 0-88344-792-4

"The language and style of presentation are very clear and precise. It constitutes useful handbook for all scholars and students . . . a good guide for missionaries. . . . The book reveals and helps us to understand the missionary outlook and attitude of the entire church in the modern period."
— *Sr. Namita, S.I.C.*

Volume 2, Theological Foundations
ISBN 0-8344-953-6

"The voices of these articles are diverse, women and men, Protestant and Catholic, clergy and lay, first and third world. . . . Scholars, teachers and serious students of missiology will find this a valuable and convenient resource for their research and study."
— *Peter Gilmour, Institute of Pastoral Studies Loyola University*

Please support your local bookstore, or call 1-800-258-5838.
For a free catalogue, please write us at
Orbis Books, Box 308
Maryknoll NY 10545-0308
or visit our website at www.orbisbooks.com

Thank you for reading *New Directions 3.*
We hope you enjoyed it.

Of Related Interest

The New Catholicity
Theology between the Global and the Local
Robert J. Schreiter, C.PP.S.
ISBN 1-57075-120-X

The most important single resource in print on how the local theology movement has given new shape to a classic notion — "Catholicity." An amazing synthesis of social, scientific, theological, and common sense insights into one of the deepest traits of Christianity in our time.

"For those of us who are seeking a theological path that avoids both a homogenizing globalism and a relativizing localism, Schreiter is a wise and reliable guide. May his brand of catholicity flourish."
— *Richard Mouw, Fuller Theological Seminary*

Changing Frontiers of Mission
Wilbert R. Shenk
ISBN 1-57075-259-1

A master of mission thought meditates on the issues that face the Christian tradition in both the West and globally. There is no one like Shenk in singling out the neuralgic issues.

Please support your local bookstore, or call 1-800-258-5838.
For a free catalogue, please write us at

Orbis Books, Box 308
Maryknoll NY 10545-0308

or visit our website at www.orbisbooks.com

Thank you for reading *New Directions 3*.
We hope you enjoyed it.